TABLE OF CONTENTS

NOTES FOR A MAGAZINE

In the days, weeks and months following the November 2016 election, two notable things happened for me as the editor and publisher of *Sinister Wisdom*. First, support for the journal and its work grew exponentially. More women subscribed to the journal and supported it financially. Fear of the Trump presidency reminded many of us of the importance of lesbian institutions like *Sinister Wisdom*. While the journal is hardly flush financially, it has money to pay the printer and the mail house as well as create a few extras to delight our readers and supporters. (Be sure to check out the 2018 Lesbian Badge enclosed with this issue!) The journal still is an institution that relies on my volunteer time and energy to keep it afloat—along with increasingly time and volunteer energy from young women as interns and volunteers. *Sinister Wisdom* is hardly an endowed institution like the Poetry Foundation, but through the renewed generosity of lesbians, we continue our work.

The second thing that happened is that lesbians around me and *Sinister Wisdom* started talking about the importance of resistance and regime change in 2018. The idea of a Dump Trump issue emerged from those conversations. Members of the *Sinister Wisdom* board of directors with key volunteers produced the issue you have in your hands in the realization of that vision of lesbian participation in resistance and regime change.

Lesbian political writing has always been important to me. Essays by Audre Lorde, Adrienne Rich, Minnie Bruce Pratt, Mab Segrest, Joan Nestle, Julia Penelope, Anita Cornwell, and dozens of others shaped my thinking as a young reader and writer and my political sensibilities. Journals like *Sinister Wisdom* are where I found many of these important and influential essays. This issue continues that tradition by shining a light on lesbian political writing, work that is so important in this moment of political resistance.

When you receive this issue, *Sinister Wisdom* will be conducting our fall fundraising campaign. I hope you will contribute to support the work of *Sinister Wisdom*, if you can. You most likely have already seen a promotion for the fundraiser – and the 2019 calendar that *Sinister Wisdom* intern Sara Gregory produced.

I will be honest, when Sara came to me with the idea of a calendar, I wanted to say no. In addition to the regular editorial work of four issues of *Sinister Wisdom*, I had taken on the challenging of editing *The Complete Works of Pat Parker* and then editing the letters between Parker and Lorde. I was tired and wanted just a simple year at *Sinister Wisdom* with nothing extra. *Sinister Wisdom*, however, is not about what I want but what lesbians need. Sara saw the need for more lesbian herstory and for a way to mark the days of 2019. The calendar project took flight. I hope you will purchase one or a few to share with friends. It is beautiful. I am so proud to have it out in the world.

The 2019 calendar demonstrates my greatest hope for *Sinister Wisdom*: that she be a vehicle for lesbian imagination and innovation. If there is a lesbian art and culture project that you want to do, reach out. I always welcome guest editors. I'm itching for someone to initiate a podcast about *Sinister Wisdom* and for a group to coordinate an audio recording of material from each issue. There is so much that lesbians need at this particular moment. Let's imagine new lesbian projects; let's do them together.

In sisterhood,

Julie R. Enszer
Fall 2018

MELANIE KAYE/KANTROWITZ
POET, ESSAYIST, ACTIVIST, TEACHER, COMRADE.
1945 – JULY 9, 2018

Courtesy of Leslie Cagan

Editor of *Sinister Wisdom* 1984 – 1987
Sinister Wisdom 25 – *Sinister Wisdom* 32

About Melanie, her long-time partner Leslie Cagan said, "Her moral compass was always set in the right direction, and she always had the courage to speak out, to take action, and to bring others along with her."

Courtesy of Leslie Cagan

ANGELA BOWEN
CLASSICAL DANCER AND TEACHER, BLACK
LESBIAN FEMINIST ACTIVIST, AND PROFESSOR
FEBRUARY 6, 1936- JULY 12, 2018

Courtesy of Women Make Movies, www.wmm.com

About Angela, her long time partner Jennifer Abod said, "Angela Bowen has confronted racism, sexism, and homophobia for over six decades, transforming her own life, and the lives of those around her."

NOTES FOR A SPECIAL ISSUE

After forty-one years of publishing, Sinister Wisdom is still renowned for its commitment to lesbian visibility and supporting work that keeps the word "lesbian" in bold relief. What better way to sustain our prominence than to produce an issue marking the Trump Era in lesbian history? Or marking the lesbian history of the Trump Era? ("Call for Submissions," 2017)

For this special issue of *Sinister Wisdom 110: Legacies of Resistance: Dump Trump*, we are featuring serious, satirical, and humorous writing in varied genres and forms, e.g., email correspondence, essay, poetry, short fiction, blog entries, novel excerpt, and interview—all reflecting lesbian ideas, notions, and actions of/for what it will take to unseat the Trump regime. Novelist Breena Clarke, Cheryl Clarke's sister, called it "A helluva of a backlash" against those brief eight years we had the experience of Barack Hussein Obama, the first African American president. We should work to make Donald Trump the "one-term" president the Republicans threatened to make Obama, maybe even a half term, though we shudder to think who and what would follow.

Joan Nestle grapples with these times in her meditation, "Lesbian Polemics: Without Apology":

Eighteen years ago, I had to select the books I would need in my new hemisphere, the passionate thinking, the visions of possibilities, words of friends and comrades, honed by movements, their weight my history. Now they sing out again, bulwarks of meaning in this stricken time. It was the vote of Black American women that dealt one of the first major defeats to Trump's agenda. From the so-called margins, dismissed power gathers, the hurts so deep, the knowledges always alive. I knew this as a bar fem in the 1950s, a knowledge more precious than marriage vows. Every part of our histories touched by exile because we threatened hegemonic power, because we had uncontrollable bodies, because our kiss or touch or bend of body was considered obscene, I call again into being.

As does Joan Nestle, "Legacies of Resistance" also calls us (all) "into being" and into action. The writers herein are calling our "uncontrollable bodies" *on* into the fray. Language is corrupted, concepts of the heterosexual "national family" are extolled, the "brute force" narrative dominates, difference is pathologized, and art and education are being defunded and censored. How do we still sustain literature as radical resistance? In keeping with *Sinister Wisdom*'s tradition of literary radicalism and legacies of resistance, we accepted manuscripts that address issues of electoral politics, popular culture, the exercise of privilege in current feminist/ LGBTQ/left political organizing, fascism historically and in our midst, lesbian traditions of resisting repression, scapegoating of trans people, the price of gender nonconformity in the Trump era, racial profiling, "grab them by the pussy," and ideas of exile.

Teresa Hommel offers generous insights on the post-election responsibilities of the electorate and the challenges to democracy, in her article "Democracy or Trump." Fiction is as necessary as ever, and Blanche McCrary Boyd and Laura S. Marshall both give us fanciful and timely portrayals of the current President and Vice President in "One for Mike Pence" and "Tiny Hands." Continuing with our fiction penchant, H. Ní Aódagaín's emotive "Inauguration Day" provides a sobering reflection on the intersection of personal and political despair. Joan Nestle, quoted above, gives us writing as lyrical in "exile" and expatriation as it was when she called us all to lesbian activism from her Upper West Side Manhattan apartment almost twenty years ago. Pamela I. Sneed presents three-pointed monologues: "*The Parable of the Sower,*" a riff on the prescience of Octavia Butler's iconic novel, "Uprising," and "Post Election," which all mourn the outcome of the 2016 election. Denise Conca offers the experimental "this time," a poignant piece on the changes of landscape and neighborhood in San Francisco. Jewelle L. Gomez in "Roseanne Barr vs. Roseanne Connor," does not lose her critic's comic sense as she despairs of the two Roseannes' support for the current regime. In tandem with Gomez we reprinted two blog posts, "Oprah for President" and "What Happened at the Lorraine Motel," by historian Claire B. Potter, aka "The Tenured Radical," which examine again the intersections of popular culture and history in American life. Amy Karp's "The Awful Years," a sequence of poems, plumbs the personal loneliness and regret in the wake of the 2016 election, and Cheryl Clarke's "History," the closing poem in the issue, a nostalgic reverie of history and memory. In "two words," Alexis De Veaux, veteran black feminist writer, refuses to waste her intellectual energy on the current version of patriarchy, along with "Women's History Month Bitchfest" by BITCHES BOOKS AND BRUNCH, a Queens (NY) book club, who deride Facebook's policy about profanity, especially after the revelation of Russian hacking.

Writing and art are forms of cultural citizenship in a white supremacist capitalist hetero-patriarchy. The lesbian/queer voices of dissent we include speak truth to power, write our own herstories/theirstories, and address these aforementioned themes from our own locations at this historical moment and those that are imminent. The writing of Fran Winant, another veteran lesbian feminist, explores genealogies of fascist repression and highlights nonlinear patterns of totalitarianism across time and space. She also creates a witchy world where magic and woo offer feminist sites of healing, transforming, connecting, and organizing. Alexis Clements examines barriers and walls, noting the ways in which the natural environment slips through the urban cracks, much like militancy can be organic in pushing against xenophobia and Islamophobia. In "Invertebrates," Jean Lee focuses on structural inequality in impoverished classes, mainly those that target communities of color, and juxtaposes it with youthful love and desire as a way to critique marginalization and invisibility. Anne-christine d'Adesky provides an incisive critique of the vestiges of slavery and racism under the Trump regime. She excoriates the KKK and neo-Nazism, and she archives activism on the streets from Ferguson to Charlottesville. Sarah Schulman's and Morgan M. Page's interview questions gender binaries and the consequences of undoing gender; they, moreover, focus on queer suicide and remembering trans lives in order to bridge conversations in our communities.

In addition, Russian poet Oksana Vasyakina writes about the female body, evoking the spirit of the Amazon, the "fury" of our ancestry, and that our bodies can be a locus of both personal empowerment and political rage. Likewise, in "Remember," Grete Miller reminds us of the importance of memory, poetry, and testimony—beautifully captured, in her words, "my camera. my weapon"—as an ongoing activist project. Red Washburn explores self-care as activism in national and individual states of gendered trauma. Lastly, revolution is multi-layered from pain management to critical consciousness, as Katia Perea notes in her discussion of detoxing, reforesting, and calling out (and in) during this time when our "local misogynist became president."

Some pieces in this issue consider beliefs, values, and conceptions of the world and the self as individuals choose how to move through the current reality. Kate Conroy and Marty Correa's "FACE" explores the shock of re-entering the world after this last election through a piece combining prose, poetry and photography. Freesia McKee's "Fresh Pineapple" muses on an individual's engagement with the world while under the specter of an uncertain future. In 'The World Has Been Revised,' Stevie Jones contemplates changes – both internal and in the world. E.F. Schraeder's "Breakfast with Tiffanies" raises questions of self-image, memory, and choices. And Meagan Lyle's "Let's Raise the Bar" considers questions of how to work effectively for change in a way that best reflects one's personal and political values.

This issue also includes the work of a number of photographers. There are three portfolios: images of the activist group Revolting Lesbians at their various actions curated by Anne Maguire; an art portfolio by Adriana de Luiza and Ife da Sylvia, sharing a section of their multi-media, multi-locales work entitled *Cracks in Civilized Landscapes*; and a portfolio by Morgan Gwenwald, "Still Marching After All These Years," reflecting on over forty years of lesbian activism and the impact of Trump. Other photographers whose work has helped enliven this issue are Saskia Scheffer, Ivy Kwan, Donna Aceto, Camila Medina Braz, Kate Holten, and Eric McGregor. We also are delighted to have cover artwork, "Inferno City," from Pamela I. Sneed.

All these contributors emphasize the ways in which struggle is a lifelong vision and commitment to realizing a better world, even if we argue that the Trump era represents a particularly urgent call to action. And to echo Morgan Gwenwald, lesbians have been doing this work a long time. As always, we include a range of lesbians/queer voices of all races, ethnicities, ages, abilities, religions, and gender identities. We explore what Trump politics has meant to us as lesbians/queers, document its chronology, reflect on historical resistance, and commemorate the power of lesbian/queer art and activism against a hostile state. And finally this issue is an issue against forgetting that, lesbian resistance is, as Joan Nestle says, older than the Trump era and will last longer. As a testament to lesbian resistance to patriarchal and heterosexual culture (writ large), we honor all the readers and editors who have sustained *Sinister Wisdom* for forty-one years, particularly current editor Julie R. Enszer, who has kept our tradition of radical lesbian literature going into the twenty-first century. We give this issue to the resistance that will dump this oligarchy onto the trash heap of tawdry robber barons.

Cheryl Clarke, Morgan Gwenwald, Stevie Jones, Red Washburn,
Guest Editors
Fall 2018

LESBIAN POLEMICS, WITHOUT APOLOGY
Joan Nestle

I lived in the first century of world wars. Most mornings
I would be more or less insane.

– Muriel Rukeyser

I sit surrounded by print-outs of Masha Gessen's writings from the *New York Review of Books*, *The New Yorker*, and anywhere else I can find her words. All are crucial communiqués for my lesbian survival in this time: her migration history, from Russia and back again and back again; her queer history; her years of thinking about how autocrats degrade their societies in their lust for unquestioned power; her brave acceptance of living with shifting identities, shifting national outlines, as her body itself shifts to protect its very being; her investigative courage to dis-order national emotional expectations, to pull out of us deeper understandings of the judged, or of the forgotten histories of ethnic cleansing where the unwanted poets are sent away to impossible regions.

This is how I write, pulling in to me the voices that let me reach for meaning, in a time when there is a national push for a willed, cruel ignorance. I thought it would be easy to write about the Trump disaster that is America today, but it is not. The sheer depth of the madness, the killing totality of the wanted destruction of critical thinking, of cultural complexities, of historic insights, of empathic maps of connection, smother my belief in language. Have not we all been raging in the same way, in a mixture of disbelief and grief, as Black and Brown bodies fall, as all we thought we had won spills like sand through wrinkled fingers. The sheer cruelty of Trump's national desires, his words as accepted political utterance, bring crashing down the edifice of public hope.

"Thank you, my friends. Thank you. Thank you. We have lost, and this is the last day of my political career, so I will say what must be said. We are standing on the edge of an abyss. Our political system, our society, our country itself are in greater danger than at any time in the last century and a half. The president-elect has made his intentions clear and it would be immoral to pretend otherwise. We must band together now to defend the laws, the institutions, and the ideals on which our country are based."

These are words Gessen wishes Hillary Clinton had said the night Trump came to power, instead of the usual extending of the neutral all-is-forgiven hand. This is not the time for neutrality but for fierce calling out. Trump had made clear what he stood for all through the campaign, well on his way to normalizing migrant hatred and abuse of women. He was never just another candidate and never just a clown. This is how it happens. All the way here in Melbourne, Australia, I hear the boots on the march, and Fascists of all types are throwing away their pretense of civility. Individual rights of expression, particularly of dissent, are being curtailed; journalists die at the highest rate ever. Gay Pride events in Eastern Europe, becoming one of the few public places where anti-nationalists can raise their voices, are attacked by hooligan mobs. Trump calls for the vetting of personal e-mails before one is given a visa to visit the land of the free, hides his taxes, little by little rises above democratic processes. He boasts he can shoot a man in Times Square and get away with it, as he enters the White House.

Perhaps we thought Reagan was the worst, with his trickle-down economic cruelty and union-busting exuberance, all done in a haze of vague incompetency; before then Nixon with his lust for deception and racial slurs, both in my lesbian feminist time, but it all began so much earlier, this lesbian sense of national crises, of the power of a president to hold us up or betray us to the bone. The death of Franklin Roosevelt, 1945: dirges ringing out the windows of our Gun Hill Bronx street, housewives moaning their loss. Thus, at age five, I heard my first national sound, all the way from Washington, DC. By the time of Joseph

McCarthy, I was a full-fledged deviant, a commie pinko kike queer. The rhythms of national hatred stay with us as much as the lilting melodies of the jukebox songs that we fished to in the 1950s red-lit lesbian bars. "Go back to where you came from." A land with a conscience that sometimes was America.

Then the Obamas: so hopeful they frightened the ruling corporate classes, so open to the complex histories of our times, forthright enough to publicly recognize America's often brutal interventions in the world. For eight years America was one of many struggling polities, trying to do better, not an armed-to-the-teeth exceptional State, but one that knew within its own borders economic suffering abounded, exclusions were rife, and prison, the American Black man's other homeland. After the George Bush years, my lesbian self took a deep breath, the rainbow coalition arching over the white monuments of Washington. The Obamas, steeped in the history of Chicago grassroots organizing, brought another kind of polemic to us, marked by a thoughtfulness made steely by their assessment of this nation and what it would take from its first Black family. Flaws, yes, but a national decency prevailed. Or so it seemed, but brooding in the corners, America's virulent strain of racism gathered strength, encouraged by Trump's minions in ways we are still discovering. How did this world of hope where queers of all colors stood in streets weeping with joy at Obama's victories, where a multicultural America changed who we saw and heard in public life, who sat at tables of decision making, transforming the histories in the room, how so quickly did the face of power become so white again, so *FOX News* again? Now a rich White man sits once again in a room of rich White men, launching missiles and calling Central American would-be migrants human refuse. Expected solidarities break: right-wing gay pro-Trump groups grow, white women rush to adore the President, some leading American Jewish groups pledge their support to Trump, calling him Israel's best friend, ignoring the cruelty he visits upon other histories of exile.

"There's a man goin' round taking names." (African American spiritual)

The layering of history: losses so deep they threaten the sinews of our political bodies, almost explode our communal hearts. But our devastations are countered by our persistent subversions. On my desk is *Conditions: One*, April 1977, in which Adrienne Rich, in an interview with *Conditions* founding editor Elly Bulkin, speaks of her fall from grace with the American literary establishment: "Yet reviewers, critics, tended to say 'Here she [Rich] was, this skilled craftsman, this fine poet, but then she went off the rails and became political and polemical . . .'" For the lesbian body, polemics was a song of desire against the pathologizing professions, a chant of resistances too many to name, histories of deviance embracing the life-giving insights of feminism, not in the name of sovereignties but enacted visions of gender freedom, of coalitions demanding new formations. Lesbians are polemical, we have had to be, calling attention to the histories that were absent or ruptured, to the fragmented lines, to missing rhythms, to a touch so dear all was risked.

From my treasure horde of lesbian polemics is *Home Girls: A Black Feminist Anthology*, edited by Barbara Smith in 1983, in which members of the Combahee River Collective gave us these words from its eminent "Statement":

> Above all else, our politics initially sprang from the shared belief that Black women are inherently valuable, that our liberation is a necessity not as an adjunct to somebody else's but because of our need as human persons for autonomy . . . it is apparent that no other ostensibly progressive movement has ever considered our specific oppression as a priority or worked seriously for ending of the oppression. (Smith, ed., 1983)

Eighteen years ago, I had to select the books I would need in my new hemisphere, the passionate thinking, the visions of possibilities, words of friends and comrades, honed by movements, their weight my history. Now they sing out again, bulwarks of meaning in this stricken time. It was the vote of Black American women that dealt one of the first major defeats to Trump's agenda. From the so-called margins, dismissed power gathers, the hurts so deep, the knowledges always alive. I knew this as a bar fem in the 1950s, a knowledge more precious than marriage vows. Every part of our histories touched by exile because we threatened hegemonic power, because we had uncontrollable bodies, because our kiss or touch or bend of body was considered obscene, I call again into being. Countries will use their so-called respect for us as proof of how civilized they are, while they destroy the future of an occupied people. Our queerness is too queer for such a bargain, our lesbian feminisms too inclusive for such narrow definitions. I call into action all our historic *refusals*—lesbian, feminist, anti-nationalist, anti-White supremacist—to politely accommodate the brutal use of national power. My desk here overflows with the writings of my generation, my comrades, who I have kept close all these years, all during this time of endless wars. You know them; many of their words have lived on the pages of this journal. Analytical, passionate, poetic, short lines, long lines, safeties risked for the larger thing. New generations find their ways. Naked feminists dance on top of the ballot boxes in Italy, making Berlusconi hide his face in shame, a naked woman's body not controlled by him and others like him. The Pussy Riot women, their backs raw with the cracks of Cossack's whips, their faces peering out from between cell bars, their suffering exiled to the far reaches of Russia's vast lands, but we know, we remember, we will use their polemic dance of defiance. We struggle both for the life of a facts-based reality and the right to dream of and create new worlds of human value.

Now, now, on the streets and in small rooms where actions are planned, in the stillness of night when we look beyond ourselves, as Muriel Rukeyser wrote in her 1963 poem,

In the day I would be reminded of those men and women
Brave setting up signals across vast distances
considering a nameless way of living, of almost unimagined values.
As the lights darkened, as the lights of night brightened
We would try to imagine them, try to find each other.
To construct peace, to make love . . . to reach the limits of
ourselves and go beyond.

A profound polemics never to be shamed for its insistences. I am never just a Jew anymore, I am an "anti-Occupation Jew." I am not just a lesbian anymore, I am an "anti-Trump lesbian." Once "lesbian" was a modifier, now it needs to be modified while our resistance to the growing power of oligarchs must never be. This resistance must be constant, driven as much by the promise of our past knowledges as by our wise despairs. Sappho, a throwaway moment in lesbian history so often, refused even the poetic meters of the warmongering classes. Refusing to sing of "arms and the Man," of the heavily soldiered ships in the harbors, she created lines where women's bodies embraced, strong in their declaration of desire and wise in their comfort with ironic refusals. Oh how persistent her fragmented voice, her condemned voice, her banned voice, has proved. Lesbian polemics, the imaginative body speaking to the unjust State, the deviant turned "refusnik," calling out the doggerel of Trump nationalisms.

Trump is the beat of marching boots, trump, trump, of fat wallets landing on polished corporate tables, thump, thump, of hatreds spilling over into national permissions to take Black lives, of guns and more guns, of bombs and bigger bombs, trump, trump, trump, sold to all comers. Towering real estate and militarized capitalism—is there any other kind?—filling up and spilling over into Trump family pockets. Of police in Gaza or Texas coming in the middle of the night to imprison, to deport, to evict, to murder. Extreme nationalisms, armoured borders, claimed or wanted sovereignties, barbed-wire-topped walls, orchestrated fear turned solid with glass shards and snarling dogs, walls, walls, trump,

trump. Political corruptions, nepotism gone wild, gerrymandering a people off the map. The fault lines of America, the playground of the NRA. We know, we see, we take action, holding dear to the texts of thought and beauty that do honour to life.

Let these words be my signal flashing out across the seas, to all of you who are working to create caring sense, in these times, to all of you old like me, whose bodies shake or falter but still you stand against the domesticated violence of guns, march against killing racism, visit the refugee detention centers, refusing to allow the unwanted to remain unseen. To all of you, young and clear seeing, not intimidated by vested power, asking the right questions, developing your own polemics of passionate contestation, I see your light, I live for it.

In the pages of this journal, so old some express surprise it still exists, so young it sings new lesbian ways of dreaming, let our resistance to the Trump autocracy, and all the killing realities connected to it, leap into life, the pages here like the wide streets where a people march to say "No More," a solidarity made of up of our complex differences, moving together beyond the Wall.

Notes:

1. Rukeyser, Muriel. *The Collected Poems of Muriel Rukeyser* (New York: McGraw-Hill, 1978).

2. Gessen, M. "Autocracy: Rules for Survival," *NYR Daily* (November 2016), http://www.nybooks.com/daily/2016/11/10/trump-election-autocracy-rules-for-survival/. See also the following by Gessen: "Donald Trump's Political Prisoners," *The New Yorker*, October 12, 2016; "How Donald Trump Degrades Us All," *The New Yorker*, January 14, 2018; "To Be, or Not to Be," *The New York Review of Books*, February 8, 2018; "Trump Marks A World Without AIDS Day Without Gays," *The New Yorker*, December 2, 2017; "Why Autocrats Fear LGBT Rights," *NYR Daily* (July 2017).

3. African American spiritual as sung by Paul Robeson in 1955, +man+going+round+taking+names+by+Paul+Robeson.

4. Bulkin, Elly (ed.) "An Interview with Adrienne Rich," *Conditions: One*, vol.1 no.1, 1977.

5. Smith, B. (ed.) *Home Girls: A Black Feminist Anthology.* "Combahee River Collective Statement" (Kitchen Table Women of Color Press, 1983) 274.

Joan Nestle, in Australia, working on *Lesbian Polemics, Without Apology*

REVOLTING LESBIANS:
NOTES FROM AN ACTIVIST, 2017–2018

Anne Maguire

Revolting Lesbians is a direct action group devoted to following the money, exposing the right-wing agenda, and fighting for justice. Our first meeting took place at Maxine Wolfe's home in Brooklyn on Saturday, November 11, 2017. It was a potluck dinner attended by Jo Macellaro, Maxine Wolfe, Marie Honan, Chanelle Elaine, Terry Ferreira, Lori Herbison, Jean Carlomusto, Roberta Degnore, Anne Maguire and Jillian. My first email reference to a group called Revolting Lesbians was dated September 2017 – Jo Macellaro came up with the name of this fictional group as a means to blow off steam during ridiculous moments at Rise and Resist meetings – so we would comment on the proceedings, along with a few other lesbians, as Revolting Lesbians. After a while Jo and I began to consider starting a real lesbian group so we started to put feelers out, along with Maxine who was also in Rise and Resist at the time. There had been a group in the Bay Area in the late 1980s with the same name – they worked on women political prisoner issues. By our first meeting I had already designed two logos – the one with the labrys was dumped for the one with the lightning bolt. At that meeting we decided that we definitely wanted to work on issues with a goal in mind. We were not adverse to spending a lot of time on research, discussion around tactics and strategy, and taking time to figure out a plan of action or to design a campaign. It took many meetings, lots of research and discussion, before we decided that following the money would be a central focus for us. From there we made a strategic decision to focus on the secretive, right-wing mega donor, Rebekah Mercer, and began our campaign to remove her from the board of trustees at the American Museum of Natural History. As of April, 2018, we have been joined in our work by Amanda Lugg and Elizabeth Maxwell.

For more information, check out our Facebook page or visit our website:
facebook.com/RevoltingDykesNYC/
http://revoltinglesbians.org/

This portfolio of photos and captions traces the growth of Revolting Lesbians and resistance actions in New York City. Photos are arranged in chronological order. A special thanks to all the photographers who let us use their images and made certain these actions were preserved.

Rise and Resist: No Ban, No Wall, No Raids action
at Trump Tower, April 2017. Photo by Erik McGregor (l to r, Jo
Macellaro, Richard Prins, Jenny Heinz)

Twenty-five protesters wearing "No Ban", "No Wall", or "No Raids" T-shirts were arrested in Trump Tower after three banners were successfully dropped in the hotel's lobby. This was the first major invasion of Trump territory and the first large civil disobedience action in Trump Tower since his election. The action gave me great hope for Rise and Resist – it was a smart and timely demonstration – excellent civil disobedience training, a great message, lots of pre-planning, wonderful banners and a great plan to execute their drop, a wonderful support team, great media coverage, and a bit of luck. Through this action I had the good fortune to meet Jo Macellaro, Ivy Arce, Laurie Cotter, Maryellen Novak, and Lorenzo De Los Angeles for the first time.

Rise and Resist: First of three **The Emperor Has No Clothes**
actions, September 19, 2017. Photo by Katie Holten

Playing with the Hans Christian Andersen fairytale, *The Emperor's New Clothes*, the participants wore body suits, orange wigs, and red ties and cycled as naked Trumps to midtown on CitiBikes. The action took place during Trump's first speech at the United Nations. We walked around Times Square and then took the subway back downtown to the LGBT center on W13th Street. This was a very popular street action which got a great response from passers-by.

The second Emperor action was at a Trump fundraiser for the RNC at Le Cirque Restaurant on September 26, 2017. Despite working with some great people, by the third Emperor action, a watered-down version in the Halloween Parade on October 31, I had left Rise and Resist. The relentless haranguing from within R&R (accusing the Emperor satire of body-shaming), combined with tiresome paternalism, arrogance, and casual misogyny, made it impossible to continue working in this group. In addition, creating a longer-term, more sustained campaign was more appealing than constantly reacting to the horror of the Trump administration.

SOS Direct Action: Resistance Carolers at Cambridge Analytica, December 17, 2017.
Photo by Ivy Kwan http://www.sos-action.org

SOS Direct Action was Jo Macellaro, Marilyn Oliva, Anne Maguire, Jake Rowland, and Bill Monaghan. We formed outside of Rise and Resist around the same time that Jo and I were also getting Revolting Lesbians off the ground. The Rebekah Mercer theme was already present – the carol action was held outside the offices of Cambridge Analytica and Reclaim New York, both organizations very much tied to Mercer's dark money and later Cambridge Analytica would come under greater scrutiny due to its use of Facebook data in presidential election shenanigans. Verse one of our carol, to the tune of *Silent Night*, went:

> Violent Right
> Out of sight
> Koch Money
> Is not free
> Rebekah Mercer is going too far
> Breitbart News, Cambridge Analytica
> Democracy they scorn
> Democracy they scorn

KALADAA CROWELL   SHANTA MYERS   BRANDI MELLS   KERRICE LEWIS

SAY HER NAME

Revolting Lesbians: **Say Her Name** protest at the Women's March, NYC, January 20, 2018. Poster designed by Jo Macellaro

Even though Revolting Lesbians was set to launch at Sunday's January 21st action against Rebekah Mercer, our first action was at the New York Women's March. Four lesbians were murdered at the end of December 2017. They were all Black lesbians and little attention was being paid to the brutal slayings, and the murder of three of their children. We made lots of posters and put the word out. We said their names:

"Say Her Name: Brandi Mells. Shanta Myers. Kerrice Lewis. Kaladaa Crowell."

Shanta Myers, 36, and her girlfriend Brandi Mells, 22, were murdered along with Shanta's daughter Shanise, 5, and son Jeremiah, 11, in Troy, NY, on December 21, 2017

Kerrice Lewis, 23, murdered in Washington, DC, on December 28, 2017

Kaladaa Crowell, 36, murdered with her daughter, 11-year-old Kyra Inglett, in West Palm Beach, FL, on December 28, 2017

Revolting Lesbians: **Revolt Against Rebekah Mercer at the American Museum of Natural History**, January 21, 2018.
Saskia Scheffer

This action was the public launch of Revolting Lesbians' campaign to remove Rebekah Mercer from the Board of Trustees at the AMNH. Prior to the street action, on January 15, we sent a letter to every trustee and board member at the AMNH – not one member responded. Here are two paragraphs from the letter:

> We are writing to you because, as a Trustee of the American Museum of Natural History (AMNH), you are charged with the responsibility of ensuring the museum continues its mission – "to discover, interpret, and disseminate – through scientific research and education – knowledge about human cultures, the natural world, and the universe." Fulfilling this mission requires that all aspects of how the museum is run be above reproach. For this reason, we believe it is past time for one of your colleagues

on the board, Rebekah Mercer, to either resign or be removed. ...

Regardless of the independence of AMNH's scientific research, Rebekah Mercer's position as a trustee creates suspicion about that independence, and brings the integrity of the museum into question. It also offers Mercer legitimacy outside of her alt-right domain. She is a powerful right-wing activist, and a racist, who uses her fortune as a destructive force to thwart fundamental democratic principles. *For these reasons, Rebekah Mercer must resign, or you must act to remove her from the board.*

Digo O Nome Dela: Marielle Franco protest held outside
the Brazilian consulate, NYC, March 20, 2018.
Poster by Jake Rowland

Following the assassination of a Brazilian city councillor
of African heritage, who worked on behalf of the poor and
disenfranchised favela residents of Rio de Janeiro, Revolting
Lesbians joined a protest outside of the Brazilian consulate
in New York on March 20, 2018. Franco fought against police
violence, gender violence, and for reproductive rights. In 2017 she
presented a bill with the Rio de Janeiro Lesbian Front, to create a
day of lesbian visibility, which was defeated by a 19–17 vote.

Revolting Lesbians: Jo Macellaro in the **March for Our Lives**,
March 24, 2018. Photo by Camila Medina Braz

Revolting Lesbians joined the **March for Our Lives** protest which was organized by students in response to another mass-shooting, this time at Marjory Stoneman Douglas High School in Parkland, Florida.

We made and carried black-and-white placards with bullet holes that stated: "Butches Not Bullets", "Femmes Not Firearms", "Lesbians for Gun Control", "Another Lesbian for Gun Control", and "Ban Assault Weapons." *Business Insider* chose "Butches Not Bullets" as its most creative poster.

Revolting Lesbians: Friday 13th Horror Show Action at the American Museum of Natural History. Friday, April 13, 2018.
Photo above by Donna Aceto, photo below by Ivy Kwan

Taking advantage of the superstitions around the day, and date, Revolting Lesbians created a Mercer Horror Show at the American Museum of Natural History on Friday, April 13. Nine of us dressed as creepy Rebekah Mercers, wearing hooded capes and masks, droning and hissing, as we death-marched through the museum. The visual we wanted was Rebekah Mercer being escorted out of the museum, by museum security, because she should not be on the board of trustees – the action worked. Part of our agenda is to expose and reveal who Rebekah Mercer is, where the Mercer Family Foundation money fits in the underworld of dark money and politics. To that end each creepy Mercer wore a bloody sign as part of the costume, like "I'm Rebekah Mercer and I fund and direct Cambridge Analytica." Others included references to Breitbart, Reclaim New York, Emerdata, and the Heritage Foundation, etc. As we were escorted out we chanted "Mercer Money is killing our planet, Kick her off the Board, God damn it!"

We were joined in this action by Marilyn Oliva, Kellen Gold, Bill Monaghan, Natalie James, Ivy Kwan, and Charlotte.

WIND OF FURY - SONGS OF FURY

Oksana Vasyakina
Translated by Jonathan Brooks Platt

The sling of my rifle presses on the base of my neck and
in the hollow of my shoulder-blades...
— Monique Wittig, "Virgil, No!"

I'll stitch the wounds on your body with my hair
                    and kiss them until they heal
My black-browed companion rises
        my black-browed companion opens her eyes
And I see them like butterflies
                        moving fast in the dark
                            and flashing
She smiles baring sharp teeth in her strong mouth
We walk across the red dust
I can't see where your body ends
                I can't see where your small hard fingers end
You say that beyond the horizon there might be something for us
                        and for other women like us
Slowly we move as fires flicker behind us and warm our backs
There are no nights they're finished
        where thousands of hands dropped in desolate factories
There are no nights they're finished
        where all the lovers fed on one another
There are no nights they're finished
        where dragonflies and lightening bugs are transfixed by
                            the blaze
No nights
    they've dissolved in the blaze
Now there is only red dust
The wind doesn't whip it up

The wind is finished
                    where becalmed seas have drunk their fill of oil
The wind is finished
                    where I breathed a confession of love in your ear
And you lifted your head
To meet my eyes
And we saw the blaze

***

I don't see any women on the dark squares
        at night their transparent silhouettes wander in
                            mushroom-shaped treetops
        in empty metro cars I squeeze a key into my tense and
                            sweaty palm
                        and I emerge from the underground passage
                            into the world of men
I see them in their clothes styled to look like military uniforms
        above swim brackish eyes
        they slip along my body
        they give me a signal:
                            you're just a woman
        you were born to disappear/you were born to dissolve into a
cloud of ashen fingers trembling with lust/you were taught to get
wet at the mere sight of their
        terrible smiles/to sigh from their gaze that cuts your body/to
choke on it
        I walk along narrow streets through the whisper of catcalls hey you
        Across the squares I walk like I'm naked
        Through dark parks I walk
                            trying to distinguish the shadows of trees
from the shadows of men
        After a tender meeting with my beloved I'm walking

And I carry the warmth of her kisses in my belly
After a tender meeting with my beloved I'm walking
                        And I remember every hair on her
body
After a tender meeting with my beloved I'm walking

            I'm walking
            I see the look
            That she gives me each time we part
            This looks says
kill anyone who dares to touch you

                    ***

My mother has become an Amazon
                    she sat upon a boulder
                        and in one stroke cut off her left breast
To make it easier to hold the bow
To leave nothing for the feeding of babies
her right breast became heavy wood long ago

Mama woke up one day
And decided – what mama was
Is no more
        she got on a train and went west and then south a ways

        she rode and thought: I am an Amazon
        the ivory gears of steel factories rustle beneath me
        my evil past lies beneath me
        my children who were never born lie beneath me
Enough   now I will be happy
Now I will be warlike and beautiful
Now I will pierce the bellies of men

My fingernails sharpened like knives
anyone who doubts I have become an Amazon will learn the truth
I'll spit in his face

And mama sat on a stone
The stone as if covered in frost
                        shards of mica glistening in the sunlight
Mama felt a chill
And inside herself she repeated: now I will be an Amazon
And she drew a sharp black knife across the base of her breast
                                Blood filled her eyes

The pain hardened in her body

She understood that rejecting her breast was not enough
She had to become a lesbian
And she will if she has time
If she has the strength to rise from the cold stone
And walk across the desert
To meet her sisters

***

I had a lot of blood in me
                        It has all gone black with fury
I have no enemies
                They've drunk their fill of my fury
The one who dared to touch
                My white body
                        My tender white body
                                My white body
star-strewn with birthmarks
The one who dared to touch me
                        My fury will sing in your throat

I will walk with heavy steps my iron steps   across your fingers
that dared to touch me   and sow crowds of gnawing worms in
your eyes and all your parts still defecating and slowly moving   I
will hack them off and feed them to a dog   and the dog gone mad
from your foul meat   will run across the steppe run along the
roads stumbling from madness   in its eyes madness and a chasm
and from the wasting of its own flesh the dog will drop dead

That's how the life of your filthy dick will end
    Everything else that's left of you
I will leave upon the earth under the wind

Unburied
            And women will come
                        To urinate on your body
                                To spit upon your breast
                                        To comfort themselves
And defile you

                        ***

Their faces are made of earth and sawdust
        their faces tinted yellow in the light of factory lamps
                all of them looking as a thousand-headed woman
                        all of them waving with the hand of
thousands
Their alarm makes the leaves of heavy trees tremble
their stomachs absorb potatoes and meat by the ton
they are looking at us with one full face

And if a tear should fall from their eyes
                        we'll all choke on the salt
                                salt will eat through our skin
And if a woman loses but   one   organ   of her   body

another will say – take my breast take my fingers
there are so many of us   that   there is enough
sweat and flesh   for everyone
And no one will notice

and not one of them will say
and not one will dare call   you   damaged

* * *

they sleep under the earth
       like large tired beasts
moles and shrewmice feed off their sweat and dead skin
I hear them breathing under the dry barren soil
sometimes in the steppe you see hollows in the sand
   between bushes of thorns
     the passage of oxygen to their dozing nostrils
sometimes you can come and listen
    to their singing as one a single song in their sleep
    it has no words only a drawn-out sound
υ υ υ υ υ υ υ υ υ υ υ υ υ υ υ υ υ υ υ υ υ υ υ hυ υ υ υ υ υ υ υ υ υ υ υ υ
υ υ у у у у у у у у у у у у у у
they are sleeping
    they are waiting for the dry cratered earth
      inflamed from their strides
to touch the sky

and they will walk
  their hair long with time sweeping the roads
    collecting thorns dry grass and roots in their braids
and they will walk
  drinking up lakes when they stop to rest
and they will walk

          tucking the hem of their skirts into their belts
     each will walk
                    inhaling the air
                         with a breast without breasts
     and exhaling
                         the slate-gray spirit of fury and destruction
     and they will walk
                         leaving traces
     all these women – disfigured by violence. murdered. imprisoned
by feelings of guilt. humiliated. broken.
     they are lying in the earth
     they are walking across the earth – to the kindergarten to
collect their children – the fruit of domestic violence.
     into a shop for bread and milk – to feed their rapist
     they sit on swollen penises with a whisper: and you said you
didn't want to, look how wet you are

     they moan from the pain cutting through their vaginas

                         they are all lying in the earth
     they can walk this earth
     they can sleep
     they can drink tea in the kitchen
     swallow sticky sperm
                    they are all under the earth
     in the dark

     and there is no language
     to describe the fury
     it sleeps like a tired animal
     in their hearts

     many throw up their hands – how can we punish our rapist. we
can't touch that. the ones who raped us. or are raping now. the
ones who will rape again.

who are they
we can't stop it
we can't respond with violence
we can't do anything at all
we look on petrified
and wait

when N. was in the fifth grade   during   the   breaks   the
boys from her class and the parallel one waited in ambush for
the girls in the dark hallway   the girls were afraid to walk there
alone this dark intestinal hallway can be found in every school
the boys (and in the fifth class that's 10- and 11-year-olds) waited
for their female classmates in threes   they'd   push   them   up
against the wall pull down their skirts and stick their hands in their
pants   the noise of the break drowned out the girls' screams   the
scream dissolved   when the girls told their teacher about
it   she smiled and said   they like you   that's all
those insensitive to violence explain it as attraction or deny its
existence   when the girls didn't find the protection of an
adult woman   several of them hid in the corners of the hallway
it was called using live bait   one of them was the bait
she walked back and forth along the hallway during the half-
hour break   until the little rapists arrived   they   came
and surrounded her   pushed her up against the wall and then
the other girls came out of the dark corners and doorways   they
went up behind the backs of the little rapists   and beat them
beat them   as hard as they could   they emptied little juice-
boxes on their heads   spat in their faces   the little rapists
cried and told their parents   there was an investigation the   little
rapists cried – it's not fair

there are no words in their song
                              only drawn-out sounds

some of them have no breasts no teeth
many of them remember the faces of their rapists
                                    and all that was done to them
but as if not to them
                        but with some other bodies
                        other bodies someone else's vagina
                        someone else's hair
                        someone else's eyes
their glassed over eyes watched
and couldn't cry but only blink and see

they couldn't make a sound but howled howled howled
about the loss of their body
the loss of their will
the loss of self under the earth
they howled
        and their howl didn't hit the walls didn't rebound to their ears
it dissolved in the rootless gray   earth
the earth dissolved their bodies
the earth eased their pain
the earth sang the petrified to sleep
the armless the eyeless
just as long as it doesn't hurt so much

A. tells me   that when the murder of a woman is discovered
they only try the perpetrator for murder   it's like a sale
the second thing is free and you can choose any second thing
with the same price or less   all the rapists who kill women
are given   a few years of freedom on top of their sentence
for murder   A. adds this means   that almost all women
who were murdered   were raped first   and   only   then
killed

    the wedding gold

has fallen from their fingers
now darkness is our home
now subterranean darkness is our home
now hideous, subterranean darkness is our home

my mother told me   he only beat me once   yes, just one time
compared to that rapist who lived with her after the divorce
one time is just a fart   this fart dissolved in the air   w h e n
she said   I have forgiven all of them   and you will learn
to forgive   I will never forgive

I lie in the darkness under the earth
              I lie and beneath me I sense
                        other women sleeping in the
darkness
      their hearts beat in their ribcages like whispers
interspersed
with a song of hatred and pain
I feel under the earth
I feel above me
                winds are blowing full of fury
they sing the song of fury
and call us to rise and walk
      to avenge ourselves

our womanly tribe

he only beat me once   when he found out I cheated on
him   the linoleum was covered in blood   and the wallpaper and
the molding   good thing the wallpaper is pink imitation marble
I thought at the time   the blood won't show   and then   when
my eyes filled with blue spots   when I spat the shards of my front
teeth onto the linoleum he threw me against the radiator   i t

was summer so it wasn't hot   he raped me for several hours
and then   when it was already getting light   he brought me a
bucket and a rag   and told me to clean up the mess   I couldn't
stand up for a long time   everything hurt   no tears thoughI
heard the birds singing outside my window in the dawn and   him
snoring on the other side of the wall   he was sleepingI got up
and mopped the floors

    We are covered in a crust
                  of blood and sperm
    she stretched out her skin
    she lowered us into the earth

    new breasts will grow
    new lips will grow
    new hair will grow
    black breasts black teeth
    black hair will grow
    new black with fury

    awash in blood up to the vagina
    it will harden into a black scab
    an invincible armor
    it will grow into our meat
    and there will shine upon it
    like clean steel on a black ground
    long sharp spikes

    we'll tuck our skirts into our belts
    so we don't soil them in the blood of our enemies
    so everyone we meet will see
    how our legs have gone red
    up to the vagina our legs are red

with the blood of rapists
they won't be able to hide from the blood
the wind will lead us in their tracks
the wind of fury
the wind of vengeance
the wind lifting us
sweeping the earth
the wind of fury
the wind of vengeance

***

motionless at the bottom of the plain
they gaze into the distance
women waiting for a new world

their hands will grow full with care
the moist muteness between their legs will shudder into life

when at last just one returns
from a walk in the heat
from the smoggy city
from the war
from idle strolls along paths hard from the heavy tread of men

when they return

they will see that our eyes are dry we've learned to see thin
bent shadows among the quiet trees
our eyes see the plain settling under years of movement
and the horizon rises above our heads
they will see and will cover our eyes with their hands   and
our strained inflamed eyes will rest and grow moist

our eyes have already seen it all
we saw the light it ended before our eyes and then lit up again
they'll cover our bodies with heavy bellies
they'll warm our skin with their hot love
they'll help deliver the heavy burden of expecting a new world
with them we'll give birth to a new glorious entrancing world
of precious beings
precious people whose steps leave only light and pure water
    upon the earth
grown still for a moment

the wind

brings the smell of fire
brings flakes of ash
sometimes it smells of burning skin
the wind
moves our forelocks
caresses the hairs on our calves

it sings – no one will come
no one will ever return from the war
no one will return from the walk
no one will return home

you must fall upon the ground
yielding to a gust of wind
give up the pain of waiting to the earth
to grow and sprout anew
to grow up and walk
to become convinced

that there never have been any men

***

we smell of body and earth
we drag a trail of blood behind us

blood on the grass it means we're alive

and nature is alive and it carries us upon its body

it takes a great strength to bear our weight

we move out wide and on

this means they'll hear our howl   they'll hear it and be terrified
that's not the wind in the trees brushing through rough hollows
that's not an animal moaning caught in a trap
                                     it's us breathing
it's our pores secreting the poison steam of pain
and everything changes when we pass

the green grass under our feet is filled with blood
charmed beasts set off after us
and become indistinguishable from one another
their bodies weave together into one cruel black body
with a multitude of paws and heads
a multitude of sharp nipples

they follow us and with each day their bodies grow more firmly
        into ours

we walk with our exhausted body close to the earth
with myriad glands drained of milk
with the plucked petals of lips
and we gather up everything that crosses our path

no one will touch us now
those who reached their hands toward us have stuck to our
    body and move with us
those who looked at us with lust have dissolved in our black
    blood
and choked on our black anguish
and without noticing have themselves become our body
those who saw us out of the corner of their eye sleep without
rest   he sees before him he catches
the scent of our terrible body   our heavy body

only the earth can bear our body
when it is covered with us   and swallows us   and explodes

***

And if I am not these bright-red

        Desperate poppies
Above the graveyard earth
    collapsed under the earth

        Then who

      Their procession
With tender petals like the fingernails of infants
    They touch the air on the wind

      And if I'm not them then who

Above the paternal grave fluttering like the flame of flowers
           Black flies land on my face
           The sticky steppe sucks in my gaze

Who am I
If not these bright-red poppies
                    No not crimson
                    Bright-red
             Translucent in the sunlight
They cast the shadow of threads upon the dry earth
                    The blood has faded
The blood will grow up through the earth

TWO WORDS

Alexis De Veaux

Show quoted text
To: luminousleather
From: bdpoet
Subject: Dump Trump

Alexis: is there something you have already written that would be appropriate for our "Dump Trump" issue of *Sinister Wisdom?* Best,
Cheryl

Show quoted text
To: bdpoet
From: luminousleather
Subject: two words

Cheryl,
Thanks for thinking of me and reaching out on this. I don't write about Trump. I protest against him. I speak against him. I only have two words to say in regards to him, ever: FUCK TRUMP.
Take care,
Alexis

Photograph by Saskia Scheffer

The Future is Non-Binary

TO USE MY VOICE IN CRESCENDO

Amy Karp

I trained myself to look away   I trained myself to ground
my weight in   become so still that when it all shattered
I'd remain intact   hunkering within myself as if this made
anything withstandable

I found myself fragmented further   I found the pieces growing
even sharper   I found my curves being dismissed and
denigrated   as if to read always in excess

to stand within myself I had to stretch beyond what I'd
inherited   I had to find wealths of hubris I'd never imagined
I had to try to keep myself safe in their clothes their language

there is no place for me   whole in America   there is
nowhere that wishes for me to stretch into myself   to   take
up as much space as I can muster to use my voice in crescendo

once when evaluated by a senior colleague he told me I should
bang the board for emphasis   forgetting the body that I
inhabit   the weight of my body shaking as if my breasts
were invisible   as if they had not taught me who I was
way back when

STARES OF THE STATE

Amy Karp

When the stamped paper arrived in the mail we'd already
disintegrated   we'd been followed from the courthouse
holding hands like traumatized children   *is that your sister*
is that your sister at our backs for blocks   the black dress I'd
worn to my father's funeral clinging to my skin in the suffocating
September sun

your hand squeezing could not protect us nor could the waters
we spilled for years after   caught between love and the
state   the way you'd go to sleep feet from me instead of
the inches that had webbed the years between us   as if the
heart could withstand it if the will could

I always knew it would break me   stepping before the judge
I felt the last snap   the way there is never any way back to
where I've you've been

the ways the heart can freeze in suspension the way the spirit
can waver under the stares of the state   the way they
could ask us anything and we the needing could not refuse
the way the energy of the officials will never seep out of my
skin the months before and the muscles clenched with
everything that was stolen from us by borders states straights

some things will never be reclaimed some   indignities   can
never be corrected   some bullets are meant to kill the very
subjects which they claim to save

the world it seems does not know how to sing a different
tune does not know how to turn directions   does not know
how to alchemize hate

THE VIOLENCES ACCUMULATE

Amy Karp

when we sit with each other and pretend we do not have
symbolic value   the violence of the erasure   the ways
the details get lost in blurred lines   polite conversation

when we sit with each other and pretend the violences
accumulate the hold of the hands that perpetrated get stronger
tighter   the wounds of the words begin to puncture
the threads holding it all together begin to untether

breaking apart until there are turned backs unanswered calls
a silence so heavy with the truth of our castes   where we
live and how it fits us

LATER

Amy Karp

none of it sits well with me anymore I have lost the stomach
for endless swallowing   I have lost so much of myself treading
I have never known when enough was enough

I knew when we were standing there I'd lost again   I felt the
unhinging of my own proclivities   I felt the self of my self
sinking   I placed the box and then I sat in it

sitting has never proven difficult   it is the crawling out I
struggle with   as if proclaiming my own survival was too
extravagant

I have envied the ease of white men the   way   they   choose
themselves first   the way they can walk down the street
inside themselves

hours before the club was gunned down   hours before queers
were told who they are and why   there was a white man
walking toward us   veering menacing   something pointed
out from his hand

later we will tell each other we had both thought he was
going to kill us   that our hands joined together in our
breaking sorrow incited   you wondered how you'd defend us I
wondered how I'd bear to watch us die

on a hill in Sonoma county I grow disgusted at the pastoral
virtue given to weddings   I turn in revolt at the opulent
display   my mother perplexed   angered   and all I can get
out is   hours before we thought we were going to die and
then the club was on fire   queers were scattering everywhere
and suddenly America cares

WE WALK NAKED

Amy Karp

(A Secular Prayer for Surviving the Trump Years)
It is only when we sleep, in the confusing morass of consciousness, are we as naked as when we were born.

Awake, we swim in the illusion of being covered, blockading the centers of the chest with blades and metals, armored this way, as if to escape the inevitable fragility of unanchored life.

I found a blazing example of your existence the other day and I wanted to run to tell you of this discovery. Until I remembered the earth that has claimed you.

There is a steadiness in reaching toward the ground, a reassuring beat from its core thousands of miles beneath breathing and erupting.

In death, I must think of the physical world. I must pound myself painfully against these walls, the showers of waters reminding me with heat, that I remain here, alive.

DONALD TRUMP AND THE GLORIFICATION OF RAPE CULTURE

Lorrie Sprecher

Democracy died the day Trump was elected president. It was an epiphany for me. Why had I believed it was impossible for him to become president of the United States? He was the logical culmination of the American ethos, the ultimate symbol of capitalist rape culture: a billionaire who grabbed women's pussies without permission. In fact, he was American rape culture's greatest achievement.

Every day Francine and I watched the horror unfold as the orange clown made his inappropriate cabinet selections, appointing white supremacists, climate change deniers, Wall Street billionaires, and people with no relevant experience whatsoever to high positions in his government. It was as if dinosaurs or something else extinct had taken over the United States. Everyone we knew was in deep, profound despair.

"Do you know what it's going to look like when all of Trump's people descend on Washington, DC?" I asked.

"Um—a white power rally?" Francine suggested.

"Like a clown car exploded."

Fifty-three percent of American white women had voted for a rapist.

"Seriously," Francine said, "who let the white people vote?"

Every weekday leading up to Trump's inauguration, Francine came over after work, and we watched the latest atrocities on the BBC and PBS news broadcasts. Could it be a coincidence that we had elected someone accused of raping a thirteen-year-old girl for president and in Turkey, government ministers proposed a bill to pardon rapists of children as long as they marry their victims?

There was a severe spike in hate crimes post-election, many carried out specifically in Donald Trump's name, while Trump refused to disavow the endorsement of neo-Nazis, white supremacists, and the KKK. In the ten days since the election, the Southern Poverty Law Center counted eight hundred and sixty-seven cases of harassment and intimidation against immigrants, African Americans, Muslims, Jews, and LGBT people. There were no such things as hate crimes against women, apparently, and how would anyone ever count them all?

He endorsed the Philippine president's campaign of extrajudicial murders and refused to take daily intelligence briefings that were supposed to prepare him for his transition to president because, "You know, I'm, like, a smart person. I don't have to be told the same thing in the same words every single day for the next eight years. I don't need that. But I do say, if something should change, let us know." He discounted all reports about Russian hacking and compared the American intelligence community to Nazi Germany. On the news, crying Syrian nurses ripped babies out of incubators while Russia bombed Aleppo, and Donald Trump talked about creating a national registry of Muslims. He owned stock in the company that was building a pipeline, which could poison the Standing Rock Sioux tribe's drinking water in North Dakota, and cops used rubber bullets, tear gas, and water cannons against Native American protesters.

It had been the longest week in American history.

BLACK HISTORY MONTH
WITH DONALD TRUMP

Lorrie Sprecher

"I don't want to go to a racist country," said the Syrian refugee about America on the news.

On February second, Trump met with African Americans in the White House to commemorate Black History Month. Francine and I listened to his speech with open-mouthed awe.

"Well, this is Black History Month," he began, "so this is our little breakfast, our little get-together."

"Wasn't it clever of black people to fit all of their history into only one month?" I said.

"During this month, we honor the tremendous history of the African Americans throughout our country," Trump said. "Throughout the world, if you really think about it, right? And their story is one of unimaginable sacrifice, hard work, and faith in America."

We watched Trump's lips move in disbelief.

"Is he talking about slavery?" Francine asked. "He makes it sound like slaves came to America on purpose because they had faith in our wonderful country."

"Firstly," I said, "I was unaware that African *Americans* existed all over the world. Black people from Africa and France are also African Americans?"

"Last month we celebrated the life of Reverend Martin Luther King Jr., whose incredible example is unique in American history."

"Unique?" Francine practically squeaked.

"I am very proud now that we have a museum, National Mall, where people can learn about Reverend King, so many other things, Frederick Doug—Douglass is an example of someone who's done an amazing job that is being recognized more and more, I notice."

"*What?*" I yelped.

"Oh my God, he thinks Frederick Douglass is still alive and works at one of his bankrupt casinos," Francine said.

"Except that he doesn't like to promote or rent to black people, as various lawsuits against him attest."

"I like how every group's a monolith," Francine said, as the orange toxin turned back to his favorite subject, his own self-aggrandizement. She imitated him. "*I have a great relationship with the blacks. I've always had a great relationship with the blacks.*"

"*I love the Muslims,*" I mocked him. "*I think they're great people. I'm just going to ban them.*"

"I'm doing good for the Muslims," Trump had told CNN. "Many Muslim friends of mine are in agreement with me. They say, 'Donald, you brought something up to the fore that is so brilliant and so fantastic.'"

"Fantastic people," Francine said. "Like the Pakistanis. And, as he tweeted on Cinco de Mayo, '*The best taco bowls are made in Trump Tower Grill. I love Hispanics!*'"

"Those rapists, drug dealers, and murderers," I said, because that's how Trump characterized Mexicans, "don't know the first thing about Mexican food."

"What about the Jews?" Francine asked. "He's good with Jews."

Trump had addressed the Republican Jewish Coalition by saying, "I'm a negotiator like you folks. Is there anyone who doesn't re-negotiate deals in this room? Perhaps more than any room I've spoken to."

"He's the least racist person that you have ever met," I said, repeating something Trump had actually claimed.

Later, when a reporter asked what the hell the president could possibly have meant about Frederick Douglass, Sean Spicer clarified Trump's remarks.

"I think he wants to highlight the contributions that he has made, and I think through a lot of the actions and statements that he is going to make, I think the contributions of Frederick Douglass will become more and more."

This came after Spicer's statement about Trump, "I mean, just the other day, he sat down with Martin Luther King Jr." He actually meant Trump had met with Martin Luther King III and didn't realize those were two different people.

Frederick Douglass has been dead since 1895. Martin Luther King Jr. was assassinated in 1968.

OPRAH'S CIVIC RELIGION CAN'T HEAL OUR DIVIDED NATION

Claire Bond Potter

I turned off #GoldenGlobes2018 about 45 minutes into the show as Hollywood worked awkwardly to grapple with months of revelations about sexual harassment. I was impressed by what I was hearing from the awards stand from people like Frances McDormand. But I was also offended by host Seth Meyers' repeated jabs at Kevin Spacey, the only gay man other than the elderly George Takei to have been accused of systemic sexual harassment during Hollywood's #MeToo tsunami. Go ahead: Call me a "feminazi," tell me I am humorless, politically correct—I don't care. Only a room of straight people, or people nervously pretending to be straight, would have thought such jokes were not homophobic.

But what else can you expect from a group of people, from an industry, that promotes fictional violence against women? An industry full of men that have marketed women's bodies for a century and who are now rebranding themselves as cutting-edge feminists? It isn't that I don't appreciate the effort—but when was the last time you saw Hollywood solve a social problem?

Thus, it did not surprise me to wake up and find that the other work of the evening had been to draft Oprah, who had won the Golden Globe for lifetime achievement that night, as the 2020 presidential candidate who can heal our wounded and divided nation.[1]

Oprah is, of course, no less qualified than a great many other people who have run for the highest office (especially the individual currently occupying it), and she is a great deal more qualified than some. She is in many ways an inspirational figure,

---

1   Read "Oprah Winfrey's Rousing Golden Globes Speech," January 10, 2018, *CNN.com*.

a modern version of Russell Conwell, the early twentieth-century speechifier, Baptist minister and founder of Temple University in Philadelphia, who promised his audiences that there were "acres of diamonds" before them, just waiting to be gathered.

But one of my goals for whatever political life comes after Donald Trump would be for both political parties to stop selling the presidency to the highest bidder. Even the idea of an Oprah candidacy is a desperate move on the part of Democrats. It is not only a capitulation to the enthusiasm for political novices that brought us Donald Trump, but also—more importantly— it is another sign that liberals are just as susceptible to savior complexes as right-wing populists—and left-wing populists.[2]

It's not that I don't like Oprah. In fact, I admire her enormously. Her vast, middlebrow empire has relentlessly promoted African American art, literature and performance, creating work and visibility for severely underemployed, and often overlooked, culture workers. She is smart, generous, kind, a terrific businesswoman, and in many ways, very principled. She seems to have both a boyfriend (last year an Oprah watcher noted that, "There are at least two roles we know she doesn't plan to try: president of the United States, and wife"); and a girlfriend (as Gayle King told a reporter last year for the umpteenth time, "If we were gay we would tell you." Of course, they would.)[3]

Oprah has also managed to articulate the paradoxes of black womanhood better than almost any other cultural figure: in fact, you might argue that, culturally, she paved the way for the reception of Michelle Obama as a beloved First Lady. Although I

---

2 Frank Bruni, "Is Oprah the un-Trump or the un-Clinton?" *The New York Times* (January 10, 2018).

3 Caven Sieczkowski, "Sorry America, Oprah Will Never Run for President," *HuffPost*, June 16, 2017; Jamie Feldman, "Here's Why Oprah and Stedman Have Never Gotten Married," *HuffPost*, August 15, 2017; and Natalie Finn, "Gayle King and Oprah Winfrey's Fierce Bond: How Their Friendship Has Outlasted Every Rumor, Spat and Scandal," *E! News*, November 21, 2017.

find Oprah's public dieting deeply disturbing, she is living many women's body image issues out loud, which I can't help but admire. I would even propose that, aside from how lucrative it is to promote commercial dieting products, she intends these public displays of body dysphoria to be provocative. Because of this, Oprah has probably done as much as any other public figure to urge women—and women of color in particular—to attend to their physical and spiritual well-being.

But back to the presidency: my problem with the idea of President Oprah is that politics is not a hobby, it's not a cultural intervention, and it's not a branding device. It's not an activity you turn to when you are bored with all the ways you know how to make money and influence people, and it isn't a lifestyle change. Politics is a *profession*, and if the dysfunction of the past year should have taught us anything it's that people who don't know anything about politics can get elected, but they have a significant chance of screwing up once they get there (are you listening to me, Cynthia Nixon?) Along with others, I am skeptical that, even if Donald Trump were better educated, more intellectually curious, and better able to pay attention, that he would be a crashing success, even as a conservative lawmaker.

Journalist Joe McGinniss predicted this wave of celebrities entering politics way back in 1968. In his first book, *The Selling of the President*, McGinniss declared the Richard Nixon–Hubert Humphrey campaign to be a turning point: television, he declared, had finally come of age in electoral politics. While it is true that candidates had been using TV advertising, political consultants, polling, and data modeling for some time, 1968 was the first national contest in which both campaigns openly hired advertising agencies to sell their nominees like, as McGinnis put it, toothpaste. Political values had receded from the stage, he wrote, and both parties had given up strategies based on organizing the electorate around the meat and potatoes issues on which they disagreed.

The result, McGinnis argued, were political candidates that were as empty as the television characters they were now expected to be. "The television celebrity is a vessel," he wrote. "An inoffensive container in which someone else's knowledge, insight, compassion or wit can be presented....On television it matters less that [the candidate] does not have ideas. His personality is what the viewers want to share."[4] Not surprisingly, one of Nixon's media strategists was a young Roger Ailes, later the visionary CEO of Fox News.

Democrats, many of whom seem to be able to be able to hold in their heads both an extensive critique of the Hillary Clinton candidacy and astonishment that Clinton did not win, seem to be desperate for a quick fix to the Trump presidency. The calls to impeach Trump that began almost as soon as he was elected are one reason why many conservatives flock to defend a president who many, not so secretly, find indefensible. This desperation also leads to flights of fancy that people who will be even further past retirement age than Trump is now could be president (Joe Biden? really?); that younger versions of other successful candidates could be president (finding someone like Joe Biden—but younger!); or that Oprah would be as popular a candidate as Trump—but smarter, nicer, younger and kinder.[5] As McGinnis predicted fifty years ago, to these prognosticators, the substance doesn't matter, as long as the package is compelling.

Yet would Trump voters, many of whom seem to be able to like Oprah and dislike people of color more generally, be fooled by this sleight of hand? Satirist Andy Borowitz is skeptical. He has already imagined how Trump would campaign against Oprah, minus the charming nickname he would undoubtedly come up with for her:

4 Joe McGinnis, The Selling of the President 1968 (New York: Penguin Books, 1969), p. 22.

5 Ed Kilgore, "Here's a 2020 Strategy: Stay Home Joe!" The Daily Intelligencer, March 10, 2018.

"If she were President," Borowitz quipped after the Golden Globes, "You better believe that she would make every single American join her book club."[6]

It's also worth noting that the penchant for promoting rich people as presidential candidates did not begin with Trump. Like many billionaires—Michael Bloomberg, Carly Fiorina, Mark Cuban, Ross Perot (who really did run)—Oprah's candidacy has been predicted as a possibility since September 2006, when she loaned her platform to a young Senator from Illinois on *Larry King Live*. Barack Obama's candidacy began to take off and was boosted again when she endorsed him in May 2007. While it's well known that Oprah lost audience when dismayed Hillary Clinton backers saw her as undermining their candidate (a preview of the feminist candidate wars that would emerge again in 2016), the entertainment and weight loss magnate put together a powerful fundraising and campaign apparatus, now known as the "Oprah effect," that some social scientists have credited with putting Obama over the top.[7]

"I think what Oprah can do is potentially bring out the congregants of the church of Oprah," Marty Kaplan, a communications professor at the University of Southern California, told CNN after the Obama endorsement in 2007. "She is a charismatic leader of a lay congregation."[8]

Indeed, Oprah's value added is that she is widely regarded as a spiritual figure, as were many of America's founding fathers, one whose contemporary influence digs deeply into the American soul (and pocketbook). The eager desire to take advice from Oprah,

6 Andy Borowitz, "Trump Warns That President Oprah Would Force Americans to Read," *The New Yorker*, January 8, 2018.

7 Andrew Malcolm, "A Surprise: Oprah Pays a real Cost for Supporting Barack Obama," *Los Angeles Times*, April 9, 2008; and Tarini Parti, "The 'Oprah Effect': Winfrey's Influence Extends Deep into Politics," *OpenSecrets.org*, May 25, 2011.

8 Alexander Mooney, "Oprah Winfrey May Have Larger Role in Obama Campaign," *CNN Politics*, September 6, 2007.

and adopt her attitude toward life and struggle, has caused her to be dubbed a "daytime cult leader," even by admirers. With barely veiled hostility, as Winfrey geared up to support Obama's re-election in 2012, conservative Lee Habeeb described the star as "a New Age billionaire who has evolved beyond Jesus."[9]

Similarly, Yale religious studies scholar Kathryn Lofton has called attention to Winfrey's cultural power by dubbing Oprah Inc. a kind of civic religion. "The products of Oprah Winfrey's empire offer a description of religion in modern society," Lofton argues in *Oprah: The Gospel of an Icon* (2011). "Within the religious pluralism of contemporary America, Oprah extols what she likes, what she needs, and what she believes," Lofton writes. "These decisions are not just product plugs, but also proposals for a mass spiritual revolution, supplying forms of religious practice that fuse consumer behavior, celebrity ambition, and religious idiom. Through multiple media, Oprah sells us a story about ourselves."[10]

So, what *is* that story – or what is it now, in 2018? Unfortunately, perhaps, it is that liberals want a strongman (or strongwoman) presidency as much as conservatives did in 2016. Indeed, commenters on both the right and the left now seem to take Oprah's sacred or royal (another form of divinity) status for granted, something that should cause us to pause on how dramatically the last twenty-five years of Bushes, Clintons, Trumps—and yes, Obama—have changed our assumptions about what a legitimate political culture looks like.

This essay was originally published at Public Seminar on January 10, 2018.

---

9   Andrew Malcolm, "A Surprise," *Los Angeles Times*, April 9, 2008; Lee Habeeb, "Obama's Oprah Problem," *National Review*, May 18, 2012; Ross Douthat, "Oprah: Prophet, Priestess, Queen?" *The New York Times*, January 10, 2018.

10   Kathryn Lofton, *Oprah: The Gospel of an Icon* (Berkeley: University of California Press, 2011), p. 2.

Photograph by Morgan Gwenwald

RUSA LGBT holds first Russian speaking Pride March in the US, in Brighton Beach, Brooklyn, May 20, 2017

DEMOCRACY OR TRUMP: OUR CHOICES NOW
Teresa Hommel

It is an old truism that people rob banks and steal elections because that's where the money is. But in America today we are facing a president and many congress people who want to steal our whole government, gut it, and shut down its services and protections that enable most of us to enjoy a decent life—public education, health care, social security, environmental safeguards, you name it. As documented by Nancy MacLean in *Democracy in Chains*,[11] some wealthy individuals have been working toward this for decades, intentionally in secret because they knew their objectives would be rejected by most Americans, conservative, liberal, and middle of the road.

President Trump serves the financial elite who would prefer oligarchy to democracy. Was he elected? I doubt it, but he was proclaimed the winner because we, the people, had already been shut out of our role as active participants in self-government and our right to oversee our election infrastructure. Will Trump get a second term? That's up to us, and how hard we work between now and 2020 to prevent it.

I worked for six years as a full-time, unpaid, independent activist against electronic voting because I knew computers could produce any election results their programmers wanted. But along the way I learned so much more about how elections can be manipulated.

I heard about electronic voting for the first time in June, 2003. I was a New Yorker, computer professional, age 59, attending a public forum sponsored by several good government groups: Common Cause, the League of Women Voters, New York Public Interest Research Group, and others. The panelists agreed that America needed computerized voting so people with disabilities

---

11 Nancy MacLean, *Democracy in Chains: The Deep History of the Radical Right's Stealth Plan for America* (New York: Viking, 2017).

could vote independently without direct personal assistance. They said computerized voting would be more modern, as well as more secure and accurate, than the mechanical lever voting machines then in use by most Americans. In fact, the panelists said, computers used for voting would not need to be audited nor the tallies verified.

I had been an Election Day poll worker and loved lever voting machines. They were the size of a huge refrigerator, weighed 700 pounds, and worked like a giant box containing row upon row of old-fashioned, mechanical adding machines. They had rods and gears inside that were as large, visible, and understandable as the parts of a simple bicycle. Invented in the late 1800s to curb cheating in the counting of votes, they could work for hundreds of years with routine maintenance. Thus they were inexpensive.

Each lever machine served a maximum of 999 voters because the counters only went that high, so to change the outcome of an election would require many people to spend many nights in the warehouse with keys to open the machines and tools to move the rods or damage the gears. But that tampering would be easily visible. As a result, after the introduction of lever machines, political parties relied on other ways to ensure the election results they wanted, for example to control who the candidates were, gerrymander districts, or cancel opponents' voter registrations. Partisan employees at an elections board could send broken machines to districts where opponents' supporters voted. Indeed, broken lever machines had been delivered to some New York poll sites in past elections. Strangely, the panelists at the forum insisted this would never happen with computers.

I raised my hand, stood up, and said that I had worked with computers since 1967 and there was no such thing as a secure computer outside of *Star Trek*. In the companies I worked for, computer accuracy was the result of verification procedures conducted 24/7. Information similar to votes on a specific ballot was called a "transaction" and was followed through a computer system and verified via tracking numbers. But tracking numbers could not be used in voting if you wanted a "secret ballot"—any form of voting that prevents a voter's choices from being traced back to him or her. Most states adopted the secret ballot to prevent vote selling and to protect voters from being beaten up, or losing their job or apartment, after voting for the "wrong" candidate.

The international standard for election legitimacy was whether ordinary people could meaningfully observe the casting, handling, storage, and counting of votes, so they could see that procedures were honest. Votes in a computer would be modern, yes, but unobservable.

I'd spent six months on a project with 300 engineers and programmers including some who were wheelchair users, blind, or deaf. They worked as productively as their co-workers by using various assistive gadgets. For example, a blind engineer showed me how to use his text-to-speech reader that looked like a stethoscope; I moved the sensor across his computer screen while a voice read the words to me. Voters with disabilities didn't need computers in order to vote independently because the same accessories they used with computers would work with any voting machine. An inexpensive, computerized front panel with assistive gadgets on one side for voters with disabilities, and mechanical gadgets on the other to turn the levers, would make lever machines accessible.

As the forum ended a man handed me a flyer for an upcoming hearing. I went home and created a voting machine simulation program called The Fraudulent Voting Machine, nicknamed Fraudo, that ran on a laptop. Fraudo conducts an election for president with two candidates, John Doe and Mary Smith. Fraudo works two ways. When you run a "pre-election test" the tallies and audit report are accurate. When you run a "real election" Fraudo falsifies the tallies and audit report so Mary always wins. I thought all those nice good government people were simply ignorant, and I'd educate them.

I demonstrated Fraudo at the hearing; when people saw the corrupted tallies, they screamed. Apparently they had never seen a computer produce wrong results before, unlike the people I worked with who saw it daily and had to fix the errors before their company sent out incorrect bills or statements. Someone gave me a flyer announcing a voting security conference in Denver two weeks later. I booked a flight, and Fraudo and I went national.

Over the next six years I helped New York City comply in the best available way with federal law that required accessible voting for people with disabilities. New York State, which had been expected to purchase unverifiable electronic voting machines, selected recountable paper ballots and scanners with a 3% audit required after each election. I wrote two resolutions on voting equipment that passed the New York City Council, and was credited with writing eight provisions of New York State election law. I spoke before dozens of organizations including political clubs and unions, testified at hearings, and trained hundreds of others to speak at hearings also. I traveled to conferences to speak and hand out information, and saved documents on my website, WheresThePaper.org. Fraudo is still there, but browsers no longer run programs of that kind (Java 1.2). I worked in tandem with an upstate group, New Yorkers for Verified Voting, nyvv.org.

My work against electronic voting was influenced by my parents, Jews who managed to leave Germany before World War II. They taught me and my two brothers to listen to everyone's point of view, pay attention to what the government does, and make sure our democracy represents us by participating. We lived in a semi-rural area near St. Louis, Missouri; in 1952 my older brother Teddy, aged 8, marched down our little street with an "I LIKE IKE" sign; my parents didn't object, though they supported Stevenson.

In 1962, at eighteen, I moved to New York City and got a job as a clerk sorting paper documents and filing them alphabetically in metal file cabinets. Big companies were starting to replace paper files with computers; in 1967 a firm trained me to be a programmer. Later I taught programming. Then I sold mainframe computers for a corporation that trained me in presentation and persuasion techniques. That was a turning point—soon after quitting that job I used my new skills as an activist.

For three years in the mid-1970s I volunteered with the New York State Women's Lobby, a coalition of thirteen organizations that worked to revise New York's sex-biased state laws. I learned about feminism and activism, edited the newsletter, made speeches, and led lobbying trips. I trained women to meet legislators: shake hands; state their name, objectives, and personal reasons for supporting our legislation; and ask for the lawmaker's commitment. We needed people outside the legislative office building to chant, wave signs, and raise their fists. We needed calm, articulate people inside to explain why the crowds were out there and what we wanted.

In 1975 a group called the New York Coalition for Equal Rights formed to campaign for an Equal Rights Amendment (ERA) to the state constitution; it would be on the ballot that November. I made speeches and raised funds. Along with my heroine Congresswoman Bella Abzug I spoke to a crowd of 10,000 in Bryant Park. (My hands shook, I dropped my notes, but I did it.) New York's ERA failed in the election, but the Women's Lobby succeeded, piecemeal, in making our laws fair for both women and men. Mission accomplished! I retired to private life.

After the presidential election in 2000, the nationwide public relations campaign against hanging chads alarmed me. Chads are tiny rectangles or ovals of paper that voters punch out of a ballot card next to their candidate's name. Those that "hang" are ones that don't completely detach. But the purpose of a ballot is to clearly record the voter's intent; punched card ballots did that whether the chads detached or hung. Something bad was happening, though I couldn't figure out what it meant or what to do about it.

The "something bad" came two years later: the Help America Vote Act of 2002 (HAVA) which most states interpreted as requiring computerized voting. I didn't know about HAVA until that forum I attended in June 2003. Nor did I know that a few states had already used such equipment in the 2002 midterm elections when Republicans secured control of Congress—and that some people suspected it had been used to switch votes because over a dozen Democrats, favored to win in pre-election polls, lost with vote swings of up to 16 points.[1]

Fast forward: in 2016 about a third of Americans voted on touch screen or pushbutton machines.[2] With this equipment voters touch a screen or push a button on the face of a computer to indicate their votes, and the computer handles everything after that. Are the votes recorded and counted correctly? No one—voters, election administrators, observers, or candidates—can see. Hence published reports of failure are few and limited to those that cause long lines and frustrate would-be voters.[3] Meanwhile, dozens of computer science studies say this

---

1 Alastair Thompson, "American Coup: Mid-Term Election Polls vs. Actuals," *Scoop*, November 12, 2002, http://www.scoop.co.nz/stories/HL0211/S00078.htm.

2 These machines, whether they let voters indicate their votes by touching a screen or pushing a pushbutton, are known as "DREs" which stands for "Direct Recording Electronic" voting machines. They mimic the function of lever voting machines which are "direct recording mechanical." However, lever machines are single-purpose mechanical devices; in over 100 years of use, a culture of fraud never developed around them because they are too cumbersome to tamper with and a person with brief training can look in the back and see any problems. In contrast, DREs invite fraud because it can be accomplished (1) without leaving any evidence and (2) without requiring physical access to the computer due to its wireless and internet communications capability. Drew DeSilver, "On Election Day, most voters use electronic or optical-scan ballots," Pew Research Center, November 8, 2016, http://www.pewresearch.org/fact-tank/2016/11/08/on-election-day-most-voters-use-electronic-or-optical-scan-ballots/.

3 "Electronic Voting: a Failed Experiment, Direct Record Electronic (DRE) Voting Machine Failures Reported in the News," VotersUnite, March 10, 2007, http://www.votersunite.org/info/DREFailedExperiment.pdf.

equipment doesn't meet basic professional standards and allows easy changes to votes and tallies.[4]

Some touch screen and pushbutton machines have a "paper trail," a paper printout displayed through a window that looks like a cash register receipt and lists the voter's choices. After the voter verifies the printout, it falls into a locked box so it can be used after the election to verify computer tallies. The paper trail idea failed[5] for three reasons. First, most voters can' t verify accurately—in a Rice University study two thirds of test voters didn't notice that eight races they had voted on were not displayed for verification.[6] Second, election administrators objected that they weren't given budgets to count paper trail votes, and those procedures would keep them from certifying election results within the legal timeframe.[7] Third, many of the printers sold by voting machine vendors were so shoddy they couldn't print 200 slips of paper in a 12-hour election day.[8] Because similar printers operated with near

4   Ben Wofford, "How to Hack an Election in 7 Minutes," *Politico Magazine*, August 5, 2016, https://www.politico.com/magazine/story/2016/08/2016-elections-russia-hack-how-to-hack-an-election-in-seven-minutes-214144. See also John Schwartz, "Computer Voting Is Open to Easy Fraud, Experts Say," *New York Times*, July 24, 2003, http://www.nytimes.com/2003/07/24/us/computer-voting-is-open-to-easy-fraud-experts-say.html. See also Rady Ananda, "Annotated Bibliography of Expert Reports on Voting Systems," WheresThePaper, December 11, 2007, http://www.wheresthepaper.org/DecRadyAnandaTechReports.pdf.

5   Teresa Hommel, "Paper Trails: A Good Idea That Failed," WheresThePaper.org, May 26, 2009, http://www.wheresthepaper.org/VVPAT_Idea_Failed.pdf.

6   Sarah P. Everett, "The Usability of Electronic Voting Machines and How Votes Can Be Changed Without Detection," Rice University, Houston, Texas, May 2007, http://www.wheresthepaper.org/SarahPEverettDissertation.pdf. See, especially, discussions on pages 77 and 103.

7   Doug Lewis, "Testimony of Doug Lewis, Executive Director, National Association of Election Officials - The Election Center," House Administration Elections Hearing, March 20, 2007, http://www.wheresthepaper.org/HouseAdminTestimonyDougLewis3_20_2007.pdf.

8   One example is Joe Guillen, "20 percent of election printouts were unreadable, Officials fear disaster in Cuyahoga County during primary vote," The Plain Dealer Cleveland.com, November 28, 2007, http://www.wheresthepaper.org/PlainDealer071128_20PercentElectionPrintoutsUnreadable.htm.

perfection in cash registers and gas pumps across America, some activists speculated that vendors delivered faulty printers to avoid creating evidence of their voting machines' malfunction.

In 2016 roughly half of Americans voted with paper ballots and scanners.[9] The voters use a pen to make a computer-readable mark next to their candidates' names and then insert the ballot into a scanner, a computer that reads the marks and counts the votes. The ballot is a first-hand paper record of the voter's choices, but if the scanner's ballot programming has errors it can credit votes to the wrong candidates ("vote-switching") or not count all the votes. Calibration errors can make the scanner look in the wrong place on the ballot for the voter's mark, pick up smudges as votes, or fail to count marks that are not big or dark enough. A report in 2009 listed 186 scanner failures,[10] and those were only the ones that were noticed and publicized.

If scanned paper ballots are taken out of observers' view at the close of polls, when they are recounted some days later we can't know if they are the same ballots or altered. Think of the many ways paper money can be protected—or stolen—and apply that to ballots. Some scanners produce electronic ballot images to be used in recounts; insiders can leave work with memory sticks from many scanners in their briefcase, and use their laptop at home to switch votes.

In 2016, about a fifth of voters lived in jurisdictions with both touch screen or pushbutton machines and paper ballots with scanners.[11] Only 0.1% of voters lived in jurisdictions using hand-counted paper ballots,[12] where typically at the close of polls the

---

9   DeSilver, "On Election Day."

10   Ellen Theisen, "Ballot-Scanner Voting System Failures in the News – A Partial List," VotersUnite, May 22, 2009, http://www.votersunite.org/info/OpScansIn-theNews.pdf describes 186 malfunctions. Scanners have roughly one-third the number of failures that DREs have.

11   DeSilver, "On Election Day."

12   DeSilver, "On Election Day."

local residents show up to be counters or observers, and produce the tallies within a few hours. The manageability of hand counts correlates to the number of voters served at each table (also called a ward, precinct, or election district), not to the population of the city or state.

We use scanners these days to grade tests for school kids and read marks on lottery tickets. In stores we hold the bar code of a product near a scanner to get the price. We are accustomed to scanners that work. In 2016, however, we were asked to believe that in Michigan, where Trump's margin of victory was 10,704 votes, there were 75,335 ballots with no vote for president.[13] The number of such ballots was suspiciously high in many other states.[14] Did so many people go to the polls and not vote for president? The unlikely numbers nationwide begged for open confirmation; immediate hand-counts should have been done before the ballots could be modified. Manual counts of votes *in a single contest* are simpler and faster than feeding ballots through the same scanners that may have miscounted on Election Day.

In 2016 in Detroit, 80 broken scanners caused errors in 59% of precincts.[15] Voters in Florida faced intimidation; in North

---

13 Philip Bump, "1.7 million people in 33 states and D.C. cast a ballot without voting in the presidential race," *Washington Post*, December 14, 2016, https://www.washingtonpost.com/news/the-fix/wp/2016/12/14/1-7-million-people-in-33-states-and-dc-cast-a-ballot-without-voting-in-the-presidential-race/?utm_term=.ce6f41059f85.

14 Bump, "1.7 million people."

15 Charlotte Alter, "Detroit Voting Machine Failures Were Widespread on Election Day," *Time*, December 14, 2016, http://time.com/4599886/detroit-voting-machine-failures-were-widespread-on-election-day/. "More than 80 voting machines in Detroit malfunctioned on Election Day, officials say, resulting in ballot discrepancies in 59% of precincts...." Jocelyn Benson, former dean of Wayne State Law School and founder of the Michigan Center for Election Law, who noted the large number of voters in the state who were recorded leaving their ballots partially blank [said,] "When you have 75,000 votes for president that are blank, that could be because 75,000 people didn't vote for President, or it could be because you have 75,000 votes that weren't counted."

Carolina and Colorado electronic voter lists (called "poll books") failed.[16] Voter ID laws disenfranchised some *200,000* voters in Wisconsin where Trump won by 22,748 votes.[17] Nearly 30 states used a program called Crosscheck to delete the names of likely Democratic voters from voter rolls, disenfranchising *millions* of eligible voters.[18]

My focus as an activist was observable handling of votes and tallies, but a wide variety of corrupt tactics were used in 2016. Why would cheaters work so hard when they could just switch votes? I believe their strategies fall into two tiers, visible and invisible. Visible fraud holds people's attention, while invisible, computerized fraud is the backup guarantee that pre-selected candidates are declared the winners. News commentators can ponder, "How did our pre-election polls get it wrong?" and "Why did so many voters change their mind at the last minute?" Jonathan Simon's *Code Red* supplies evidence of vote-switching, as well as how some corporate news media adjust opinion and exit polls to support announced election results.[19]

---

16   Mark Berman, William Wan, and Sari Horwitz, "Voters encounter some malfunctioning machines, other headaches on Election Day," *Washington Post*, November 8, 2016, https://www.washingtonpost.com/news/post-nation/wp/2016/11/08/election-day-voters-report-long-lines-intimidation-and-confusion-in-some-parts-of-the-country/.

17   Ari Berman, "Wisconsin's Voter-ID Law Suppressed 200,000 Votes in 2016 (Trump Won by 22,748)," *The Nation*, May 9, 2017, https://www.thenation.com/article/wisconsins-voter-id-law-suppressed-200000-votes-trump-won-by-23000/.

18   Greg Palast, "The GOP's Stealth War Against Voters," *Rolling Stone*, August 24, 2016, http://www.rollingstone.com/politics/features/the-gops-stealth-war-against-voters-w435890. A study completed after the 2016 election showed that Crosscheck purged approximately 300 valid voter registrations for each invalid one: Alison Bruzek, "Mass. Ended Its Participation In Controversial Voter Fraud System In March," WBUR Boston Radio, November 3, 2017, http://www.wbur.org/radioboston/2017/11/03/massachusetts-crosscheck-system. The study can be accessed through a link in the seventh paragraph of the article.

19   Jonathan Simon, *Code Red: Computerized Election Theft And The New American Century: Post-E2014 Edition*. (www.CODERED2014.com, 2015).

American elections have regressed to the wild days before lever machines were adopted when, at the end of the election day, poll site captains turned in empty ballot boxes with tally sheets reporting a large number of votes for one candidate and none for the other, judges wouldn't open the ballot boxes, police chiefs told officers at poll sites to look the other way, and so on.[20] A cartoon in *Harper's Weekly* in 1871 shows Boss Tweed of New York leaning on a ballot box on which is written "IN COUNTING THERE IS STRENGTH" while Tweed says, "As long as I count the Votes, what are you going to do about it?"[21] But Tweed had to do more than count votes. Similarly today, those who control our elections and nation use many strategies. We have to recognize, understand, and resist them all.

Concealment of votes and procedures is not inherent in election administration. Columbia County, New York, secures the ballots after each election via a simple, effective, bipartisan chain-of-custody protocol,[22] then hand-counts 100% of them to confirm scanner tallies. Many countries use paper ballots and

20 Joseph P. Harris, *Election Administration in the United States* (Washington: The Brookings Institution, 1934); Tracy Campbell, *Deliver the Vote* (New York: Carroll and Graf Publishers, 2005).

21 Thomas Nast, Caricature of Boss Tweed, *Harper's Weekly*, October 7, 1871, https://commons.wikimedia.org/wiki/File:Boss_Tweed,_Nast.jpg.

22 Virginia Martin, Election Commissioner, Columbia County, NY, "You can't count paper ballots. (Want to bet?)," The Election Verification Network 2017 Annual Conference, REFOCUS. RENEW. RE-INSPIRE, March 15–17, 2017, Washington, DC, https://electionverification.org/evn-2017-conference/. The presentation is described in part: "[T]he word is, even among election administrators, that you 'can't' count paper ballots. But Columbia County has been doing just that since 2010.... It isn't that hard, it doesn't take that long, and it doesn't cost that much. ..."

public hand-counting; in Germany[23] volunteers hand-count votes in front of observers as soon as the Election Day ends so authenticity of ballots and tallies is ensured by continuous observation. The Democratic and Republican election commissioners of one of New York's upstate counties, two elderly women, once told me, "We tell everyone what we're going to do. We tell 'em when and where. We tell 'em, you better show up and watch, because we don't want you coming around later and telling us we did it wrong."

Can computers be secured?[24] The 2005 FBI Computer Crime Survey—at that time the largest computer crime survey ever conducted—reported that 87% of organizations had security incidents within the last year; 44% had incidents perpetrated by their own insiders.[25] If these numbers hold true for election boards, it means that most will have intrusions, two in five by insiders.

---

23 Brad Friedman, "Democracy's Gold Standard, Hand-Marked, Hand-Counted Paper Ballots, Publicly Tabulated at Every Polling Place in America..." *Bradblog*, September 16, 2009, http://bradblog.com/?p=7417. In March 2009, Germany's highest court effectively banned computerized voting and vote counting, finding that (1) "No 'specialized technical knowledge' can be required of citizens to vote or to monitor vote counts." (2) There is a "constitutional requirement of a publicly observed count." (3) "[T]he government substitution of its own check [or what we'd probably call an 'audit'] is no substitute...for public observation." (4) "A paper trail ...does not ...meet the above standards." Dagmar Breitenbach, "German election: Volunteers organize the voting and count the ballots," Deutsche Welle, September 19, 2017, http://www.dw.com/en/german-election-volunteers-organize-the-voting-and-count-the-ballots/a-40562388. Photographs and text explain the conduct of the German federal election on September 24, 2017, by approximately 650,000 volunteers.

24 In the information technology industry, computer systems achieve accuracy (also called "security") via routine, continuous, independent verification. The word "audit" describes any procedure that proves that the results of normal computer operation are accurate and not accessible to unauthorized persons. Independent audits are a universally accepted standard practice where people want accurate, private record-keeping in business, industry, and government, but America's computerized voting and vote-counting systems are not audited.

25 2005 FBI Computer Crime Survey, Federal Bureau of Investigation, January 2006, http://www.wheresthepaper.org/FBI_ComputerCrimeSurvey2005.pdf, pp. 7–8. See also http://www.wheresthepaper.org/YahooNews060120FBI_Most-CompaniesGetHacked.htm, 2005.

Although the vast majority of election officials I met impressed me as committed to honest elections, the use of computers enables a single employee to corrupt an entire election.

Computer insecurity has worsened since 2005. Most people who put their personal data online are now worried about its security or know it has already been compromised. IBM President and CEO Ginni Rometty called cybercrime "the greatest threat to every profession, every industry, and every company in the world."[26] Verizon's "2016 Data Breach Investigations Report" warned, "No locale, no industry or organization is bulletproof when it comes to the compromise of data."[27] Of 1,000 IT leaders polled by Invincea, 75% reported that their networks had been breached in the last year.[28] When companies that know the most about security, more than any election board, can't protect their own data, it means that computers introduce unmanageable risks into our elections. What we need instead is huge numbers of people—as voters, poll workers, observers, and vote-counters.

Many election boards don't actually know how to program their own electronic equipment. Without vendor support, they would not be able to hold elections.[29] This has led to price gouging and spiraling costs.[30] Dependence also means that opportunity for cheating has been outsourced to vendor employees whom we

---

26 Bill Laberis, "20 Eye-Opening Cybercrime Statistics," *SecurityIntelligence*, November 14, 2016, https://securityintelligence.com/20-eye-opening-cyber-crime-statistics/.

27 Laberis, "20 Eye-Opening Cybercrime Statistics."

28 Laberis, "20 Eye-Opening Cybercrime Statistics."

29 Ellen Theisen, "Vendors are Undermining the Structure of U.S. Elections," VotersUnite, August 18, 2008, http://www.votersunite.org/info/ReclaimElections.pdf.

30 M. Mindy Moretti, "State and County Elections Offices Struggle with Economic Crisis," Electionline.org, February 20, 2009, http://www.wheresthepaper.org/Electionline090220StateCtyElecOfficesEconomicCrisis.htm.

have no reason to trust—they have not been elected or vetted, and are not answerable to the people.[31]

Regardless of technology over the years, election cheating has taken place when observers and investigators were not allowed to protect the vote.[32] But cheating in the past was localized. Each local boss controlled a limited territory—a neighborhood, city, county, or in rare cases a whole state. Today we have an infrastructure for nationwide control of election results. Over 90% of our election equipment was sold by three vendors who have continuing access to it because they provide the support services and ballot programming.[33] These machines have communications capability that allows votes and tallies to be modified by insiders or outside hackers anywhere in the world. Our corporate news media's focus on Russian hackers is, in part, a denial of our vulnerability to insiders.[34] You will hear the reassuring line, "there's no evidence our

31 Jennifer Cohn, "States have used taxpayer money to buy election systems from vendors with close past and/or current ties to a foreign dictator, a sophisticated cyberfelon, a Congressman, and the far-right Council for National Policy," *Medium*, January 28, 2018, https://medium.com/@jennycohn1/updated-attachment-states-have-bought-voting-machines-from-vendors-controlled-and-funded-by-nation-6597e4dd3e70.

32 Harris, *Election Administration in the United States*. Campbell, *Deliver the Vote*.

33 Lorin Hitt (faculty director), Simran Ahluwalia, Matthew Caulfield, Leah Davidson, Mary Margaret Diehl, Alina Ispas, Michael Windle, Matthew Caulfield, and Michael Windle, "The Business of Voting Market Structure and Innovation in the Election Technology Industry," Penn Wharton Public Policy Initiative, 2016, https://publicpolicy.wharton.upenn.edu/business-of-voting/. The report assessed market shares in the election technology industry: Election Systems and Software ("ES&S") 43.8%, Dominion Voting Systems 37.3%, and Hart Intercivic 11.0%.

34 A video suggesting our broad vulnerability is: Matteen Mokalla, Taige Jensen, J. Alex Halderman, "I Hacked an Election. So Can the Russians," *New York Times*, April 5, 2018, https://www.nytimes.com/video/opinion/100000005790489/i-hacked-an-election-so-can-the-russians.html and https://www.verifiedvoting.org/verified-voting-hacks-into-voting-machine-in-new-video-from-the-new-york-times/.

voting equipment has been subject to fraud." But you will rarely be told that smoking gun evidence was concealed or destroyed.[35] You will *not* hear the strong, pervasive forensic evidence activists have gathered—numerical, statistical, and pattern analysis with the same quality relied upon routinely in aerospace, economics, epidemiology, and other fields, and used by the USA to evaluate elections in other countries and call for investigation and election re-dos.[36]

There is a broader picture. Election administration is only one of many areas that have come under corporate control in the last five decades. An overview of what happened can help us understand how to reassert government by the people. In 1971, Lewis Powell, a corporate lawyer who later served fifteen years on the US Supreme Court, wrote a memorandum for the US Chamber of Commerce urging business leaders to use their money to exert more influence on American culture and government.[37] His memo is useful for study because it is a brief and explicit blueprint. The history behind it is revealed in books such as Kim Phillips-Fein's *Invisible Hands: The Making of the Conservative Movement from the New Deal to Reagan.*[38]

Powell called for pro-business influence on news media, universities, colleges, law schools, business schools, high schools,

---

35 Frank Bajak and Kathleen Foody, "Georgia official discounts threat of exposed voter records," APNews, June 16, 2017, https://apnews.com/b96f4825faa7439a-b85af1d2459673c4. See also Frank Bajak, "Georgia election server wiped after suit filed," APNews, October 27, 2017, https://apnews.com/877ee1015f1c43f196 5f63538b035d3f.

36 Simon.

37 Lewis F. Powell, Jr., "Attack on the American Free Enterprise System" (Confidential memorandum written for and internally published by the US Chamber of Commerce, 1971), http://www.wheresthepaper.org/PowellMemoForUSCham-berOfCommerce1971.pdf.

38 Kim Phillips-Fein, *Invisible Hands: The Making of the Conservative Movement from the New Deal to Reagan* (New York: W. W. Norton, 2009).

textbook revisions, and staffers and elected officials at the national, state, and local levels. His memo was followed by unprecedented political organizing by business executives, detailed in Ted Nace's *Gangs of America*.[39]

Electronic voting arose in the context of corporate and financial interests' increasing activism and power. Our leading good government groups[40] appeared to have been influenced at their national levels during the 1990s. By the time HAVA passed, authorizing nearly four billion dollars for states to purchase new voting equipment, these groups had somehow forgotten that election integrity depends on observation. They insisted that computers were secure, and that new voting technology should be selected based on modernity, convenience, quick election results, and accessibility for voters with disabilities.[41] They advocated open government and oversight by the people in other areas but not in elections: the computers they touted had proprietary, trade-secret software; even if the software had been released to computer scientists for inspection, no one could guarantee that the same software would be used on election day; moreover, election legitimacy depends on average people observing understandable election procedures, not computer scientists evaluating software.

39 Ted Nace, *Gangs of America* (Oakland: Berrett-Koehler Publishers, 2003). For Chapter 12, see http://wheresthepaper.org/GangsOfAmericaCh12TheRevoltOfTheBosses.pdf.

40 Groups I unsuccessfully tried to inform about computer vulnerability included ACLU (national and New York State levels), Common Cause (New York State level), PFAW (New York State level), Leadership Council on Civil Rights (national level), and the League of Women Voters (national level; at the 2004 and 2006 national conventions I helped craft their position on voting technology. The New York State LWV was responsive.).

41 For example: Teresa Hommel, "ACLU Position on Electronic Voting Systems, 20 Comments by Teresa Hommel," WheresThePaper, November 23, 2007, http://www.wheresthepaper.org/ACLU_Policy_comments.htm. A copy of the ACLU policy is at http://www.wheresthepaper.org/ACLU_Policy_322b_Electronic_Voting_amended_10.2007.pdf.

In December 2003, the National Institute of Standards and Technology (NIST) held a conference called "Building Trust & Confidence in Voting Systems."[42] Jim Dickson, the leading spokesman for accessible voting for persons with disabilities, who is himself blind, represented the American Association of People With Disabilities (AAPD) and addressed a plenary session.[43] He advocated touch screen voting because "Voters can hear the ballot using headphones & cast their vote in complete privacy. Voters who are paralyzed, using adaptive tools, can cast their vote in complete privacy." He didn't say that the same adaptive tools would enable such voters to use any type of equipment. Whether or not Dickson knew that courts had never allowed inspection of electronic voting or vote-counting equipment after its use in an election, he repeated the mantra "There is no documented case of an election being changed with computer tabulation." He opposed paper trails, asking, "How does the voter know the paper ballot he sees accurately reflects what is recorded in the computer?" He didn't ask how a voter knows a touch screen accurately reflects what is recorded in the computer.

Dickson and the groups that used similar talking points could have demanded accessible equipment that did not shut out observers or depend on false ideas of computer security. They could have supported accessible ballot marking devices along with publicly observed, hand-to-eye vote counts at close of polls, a solution advocated by most election integrity activists nationwide. Blind voters in Rhode Island were already voting independently using *tactile ballots*. The VotePAD, a tactile ballot usable by blind

42 "Building Trust & Confidence in Voting Systems," National Institute of Standards and Technology, December 10–11, 2003, www.nist.gov/itl/voting/building-trust-confidence-voting-systems.

43 Jim Dickson, "Voter Verified Paper Ballot: De facto Discrimination Against Americans with Disabilities," National Institute of Standards and Technology, December 11, 2003, https://www.nist.gov/sites/default/files/documents/itl/vote/1-Dickson.pdf.

voters as well as 80% of voters with mobility limitations, was in development.[44] Other accessible devices could have been easily implemented, such as the front panel for lever machines described above.

But the money did not flow that way. The National Federation for the Blind received a million-dollar donation from Diebold, then a prominent vendor of touch screen voting machines,[45] and used disability lawsuits to force companies and election boards to purchase Diebold equipment.[46] Dickson's organization AAPD received generous donations from large corporations who were thanked on AAPD's website. Some persons with disabilities objected that computerized voting might not be voting at all, but they got no traction.[47]

I kept lugging my laptop with Fraudo to meetings and conferences. Some good government groups ignored me, others criticized my message, saying it would discourage people from

44 I received sample tactile ballots from the Rhode Island Board of Elections and the developers of VotePAD. For online images and description of a tactile ballot, see Douglas W. Jones, "Handicapped Access to Mark-Sense Ballots," 2006, http://homepage.divms.uiowa.edu/~jones/voting/access/. "Toolkit on Disability for Africa," United Nations Division for Social Policy Development (DSPD) Department of Economic and Social Affairs (DESA), 2014 or later, http://www.un.org/esa/socdev/documents/disability/Toolkit/Participationin-Political-Publiclife.pdf, includes instructions for use of tactile ballots in Africa.

45 Opinion, "The Disability Lobby and Voting," *New York Times*, June 11, 2004, http://www.wheresthepaper.org/NYT/NYT06_11DisabilityLobbyAndVoting.htm.

46 Bev Harris, "Diebold and the National Federation for the Blind," BlackBoxVoting, June 16, 2004, http://www.wheresthepaper.org/Diebold_NFB.pdf. "Late-Breaking News Diebold and NFB Partner to Develop Next Generation Voice-Guided ATMs," *The Braille Monitor*, November 1, 2000, https://nfb.org/images/nfb/publications/bm/bm00/bm0012/bm001202.htm. Devin Shultz, "Blind group withdrawing voting machine lawsuit," *Lancaster Eagle Gazette*, June 15, 2004, http://www.wheresthepaper.org/EagleGaz06_15BlindWithdrawLawsuit.htm.

47 Brad Friedman, "BLIND AND DISABLED VOTER ADVOCATES, GROUPS CALL FOR 'IMMEDIATE BAN' OF DRE VOTING SYSTEMS!," *Bradblog*, March 14, 2007, http://www.bradblog.com/?p=4270.

voting. When I said that electronic voting equipment would allow undetectable tampering with elections, I was called a conspiracy theorist. I couldn't make sense of it all. I could see the connection between the campaign against hanging chads and old election equipment, passage of HAVA, vendor competition for HAVA money, and intent to establish an infrastructure for invisible control of elections. But the large number of people, good government groups, companies, and governmental entities that all mouthed the same lies was evidence of an overarching context that I couldn't fathom. Frankly, the situation could not have existed without some well-organized, long-range planning, whether you called it a conspiracy or not.

Our nation's ideas about what makes a good election seemed to shift. We went from "get it right on election night" meaning "have enough election staff and observers to determine accurate tallies as soon as the polls close" to "if the tallies are potentially verifiable we don't need verification." We went from knowing that observers are the only way to get honest elections and people have to show up in person to do that work, to thinking that watching election returns on TV is good enough and we should "trust" our election administrators.

After all our talk about verification and recounts, we need to step back and ask whether recounts are really a safeguard. In many states recounts are allowed only for extremely close races, are prohibitively expensive, and can't be obtained by a non-candidate or non-affected candidate. We can rarely observe the chain of custody of ballots before recounts occur, and many jurisdictions recount by feeding ballots through the same questionably programmed and calibrated scanners. The routine recounts that most states mandate are too small to discover most fraud.[48] Some

---

48 Thirty-two states require audits of some kind. National Conference of State Legislatures, "Post-Election Audits," March 28, 2018, http://www.ncsl.org/research/elections-and-campaigns/post-election-audits635926066.aspx#state req's.

election officials simply refuse to allow recounts or inspection of ballots, or destroy evidence, regardless of the law.[49]

Jill Stein, 2016 Green Party presidential candidate, sought recounts in Michigan, Pennsylvania, and Wisconsin, hoping to uncover evidence of almost certain fraud. She cited, for example, the high number of ballots from black, Democratic-leaning Michigan precincts with no vote for president. In Michigan and Pennsylvania Trump petitioned the courts to stop the recounts, and they were aborted. In Wisconsin, counties with large anomalies only fed their ballots through the same scanners again. In all three states the election boards and state officials used financial, legal, administrative, and delaying tactics to prevent meaningful recounts or visual inspection of ballots. They asserted that no problems had been revealed, meanwhile doing everything in their power to prevent revelation. Jill Stein described our situation: "[A]n un-recountable election is a blank check for fraud and malfeasance."[50]

To prevent a president unelected by voters in 2020, we have to look at voting equipment from another viewpoint. I believe our most important task is to preserve the Electoral College; it keeps hackers and insiders from making full use of our national infrastructure for vote-switching because falsely inflated tallies for a candidate in one state can only affect the Electoral College votes of that state, not the Electoral College votes of other states.

But what if all the people's votes nationwide were reported together, one total number per candidate, and the Electoral

---

49   For example: Warren Richey, "Why did Broward destroy 2016 ballots? Sanders ally seeks US probe.," *The Christian Science Monitor*, December 15, 2017, https://www.csmonitor.com/USA/Politics/2017/1215/Why-did-Broward-destroy-2016-ballots-Sanders-ally-seeks-US-probe.

50   Jill Stein, "Recount Update: January 25, 2018," Jill2016, January 25, 2018, https://www.jill2016.com/recount. See also "With Multi-State Presidential Recount Over, Stein Campaign Ends Fundraising Drive," December 13, 2016, https://www.jill2016.com/fundraising_ends.

College had to give the presidency to the candidate with the most votes? Greatly inflated tallies from some states would outweigh more accurate tallies from other states. Further, as Jonathan Simon explains, getting rid of the Electoral College, if not coupled with observable vote counting, would enable election riggers to shift votes anywhere in our country with equal impact, and more easily escape the minimal scrutiny that we currently give to battleground states.[51] The math for such a coup was published by four Yale University students who show that switching one vote per electronic voting or vote-counting machine can change the outcome of most national elections. Changing two or more could "establish, or overcome, a considerable margin of victory."[52]

After the 2016 election some commentators urged us to get rid of the Electoral College because it was created in 1787 to limit the power of the people's votes to elect the president, and is a vestige of slavery.[53] To me, history is less crucial than keeping vote-switching from electing our next president. If the Electoral College affected baseball, we would be analyzing how it helps or hurts every player and team, and their game strategies past and future. Elections are more competitive, the secret plays more complex, the stakes higher—but we have no drug tests for the equipment or slow-motion replays. We have seen no in-depth analysis, nor will

---

51 Simon, p. 46.

52 Anthony Di Franco, Andrew Petro, Emmett Shear, and Vladimir Vladimirov, "Small Vote Manipulations Can Swing Elections," *Communications of the ACM*, October 2004, Vol. 47, No. 10, http://www.wheresthepaper.org/ACM.pdf.

53 Dan Kennedy, "Yes, The Electoral College Really Is A Vestige Of Slavery. It's Time To Get Rid Of It.," WGBH, December 6, 2016, https://news.wgbh. org/2016/12/06/news/yes-electoral-college-really-vestige-slavery-its-time-get-rid-it. See also Akhil Reed Amar, "The Troubling Reason the Electoral College Exists," *Time*, November 8, 2016, http://time.com/4558510/electoral-college-history-slavery/. See also Rich Barlow, "The Electoral College Was Born In Racism. Let's Drop Out," WBUR, December 30, 2016, http://www.wbur.org/cognoscenti/2016/12/30/abolish-the-electoral-college-rich-barlow.

we because the elephant in the room—vote-switching—is taboo to mention.[54]

National Popular Vote (NPV) is a group that has worked for years to persuade states to sign a legal agreement to award all their electoral votes to the presidential candidate with the most popular votes nationwide.[55] The agreement will come into effect after it represents enough Electoral College votes to control a presidential election. By the end of 2017, the agreement had 61% of what it needed. Groups such as Common Cause and Daily Kos advocate for it.

NPV has no interest in observable elections. They use economic arguments: candidates spend more money in swing states, which also receive more federal money and benefit more from presidential policy decisions. NPV also uses feelings-of-voters arguments: battleground states receive more attention, so people living elsewhere feel politically marginalized and muted.[56] These are real economic and emotional issues, but bypassing the Electoral College is not an appropriate solution. Further, NPV says our state-based winner-take-all Electoral College system

---

54 The publicity against the Electoral College since the 2016 election resembles that in 2000 against hanging chads and for computerized elections. Both campaigns ignore democracy's need for the people's oversight of elections; both rely on the people's ignorance of election administration as if elections ran themselves or were run by angels. Our computerized voting now prevents oversight, but one state's tallies don't affect other states yet. Eliminating the Electoral College will end that limitation. So far the public is not asking why America's history of slavery is being used to anger and distract us, why modernity is being touted as a panacea like it was in 2000, and why we are being urged again to make a major change in our election administration without analysis of its *current* strengths and weaknesses and without discussion of how this change will make things better or worse.

55 https://www.nationalpopularvote.com. The District of Columbia, although not a state, has three Electoral College votes and has signed the NPV contract.

56 John R. Koza, "At the next presidential election, the popular vote must win out," *The Guardian*, November 10, 2016, https://www.theguardian.com/commentisfree/2016/nov/10/at-the-next-presidential-election-the-popular-vote-must-win-out.

makes some people feel like not every vote counts.[57] Note that NPV doesn't urge states to allocate their Electoral College votes proportional to their statewide tallies, which might make those people feel better without enabling switched votes to elect our president.

The folks at NPV are undoubtedly aware of America's infrastructure for computerized nationwide cheating, the potential for nationwide fraud published by the Yale students, and the role of the Electoral College in limiting the effect of vote-switching to the state in which it occurs.[58] But are our state legislators equally informed? We need to share this information with them. States like New York that have already passed a law to participate in the National Popular Vote agreement need to be lobbied to repeal their law and withdraw from the compact. We also need to inform individuals who support NPV without awareness of its context or implications.

NPV won many converts after the 2016 election because Clinton appeared to receive 2.7 million popular votes more than Trump, yet he won the Electoral College. The situation is presented in simplified, inflammatory terms: let's get rid of our *old-fashioned* Electoral College that put Trump in the White House. But the frantic efforts to avoid recounts or visual inspection of ballots requested by Jill Stein suggest that Trump's win resulted from dishonest single-party election administration behind locked doors that prevented likely Democrats from voting, disqualified tallies from heavily Democratic precincts due to minor errors by poll workers, deleted votes, and employed myriad other tactics to ensure Trump's win. The solution we need is multi-party election

57 Koza, "At the next presidential election, the popular vote must win out."

58 "Biographies," NationalPopularVote, February 2018. John Koza, originator of the National Popular Vote agreement, has a PhD in computer science and a long-standing interest in the Electoral College. He published a board game involving Electoral College strategy in 1966. https://www.nationalpopularvote.com/about.

administration that facilitates citizen participation and oversight, and voting technology that facilitates meaningful observation.[59]

New York State requires bipartisan election administration with one Democrat and one Republican in each job. This can be unwieldy, but it minimizes insider opportunities for malfeasance. New York City's election commissioners meet in public, their meetings are online, and many pre- and post-election procedures are open for public observation. But even New York is not perfect. Over 126,000 voter registrations disappeared in Brooklyn in the 2016 presidential primary; there was fast recognition and response, however, rather than stonewalling and denial.[60]

Democracy is more than elections; it requires more from citizens than voting. There are many ways we can work to revitalize our democracy. We can spend more time discussing and analyzing governmental issues. Our social divides might become less rigid if we talk about policies on which we seem to disagree and try to discover common ground. There are books on how to discuss difficult subjects and reconcile with those from whom we have been estranged. Many people have a sense of what is fair or unfair; often we can form alliances even though we face different types of unfairness. Practice on your family and friends, who are both the hardest and easiest people to talk with. It can feel more comfortable to spend time with "people like me" and more important to work against our own oppression, but our relationships with others give us more strength. Further, we must

---

59 Other election issues include activists' fight against Instant Runoff Voting which is advocated as a convenience but requires computerization as well as mathematical knowledge beyond that of the average person; internet voting and overseas voting by fax which are the most insecure votes, and failure to consider that the data for most voting systems is on the internet at some time during the election process, despite common knowledge that nothing on the internet is secure.

60 "Officials investigating why 126,000 voters were purged from NY rolls," PBS, April 23, 2016, https://www.pbs.org/newshour/politics/officials-investigating-why-126000-voters-were-purged-from-ny-rolls.

distinguish between others who listen, show respect, and find compromises that allow us to move forward, and those who use dissention or disruption to prevent us from doing the work of self-government.

We need reliable sources of information about governmental policy and action. America once had many small, independent newspapers with differing points of view; their editors stood behind what they printed. Our anonymous, photoshopped internet content is not a replacement. Some Americans today favor British news sources such as *The Guardian*, others like political comment presented as comedy by Stephen Colbert, Trevor Noah, or John Oliver. Rachel Maddow, Amy Goodman, Thom Hartmann, and *Bradblog* are sources. In addition to simply receiving news, we must write letters to the editor, articles, and complaints when news is partial, biased, or not reported. For example, in 2016 our corporate media failed to report Jill Stein's daily struggle for recounts and the evasive tactics of officials in the three states.

Learning civics in school, age-appropriate starting in kindergarten, would help our children prepare to be active citizens. If families talk about governmental policies and how they affect us, our kids can develop skills to discuss, question, and evaluate. Democracy requires that kind of thinking. We can encourage those who are interested to prepare for careers in government.

Using elections as an example, we can see that people need to register voters, get out the vote, work and observe at poll sites, and campaign for candidates. In addition, some of us must work at the infrastructure level to ensure that voter registrations don't disappear, and watch the procedures before, during, and after elections. We need to monitor state and local laws and regulations, policy changes, and failure to follow legal procedures. We need to know who our candidates,[61] legislators, executives, and judges are,

---

61 Candidates may lie about their principles and party affiliation. For example, Matt Volz, "Green Party candidate was on state GOP payroll," *AP News*, March 13, 2018, https://apnews.com/aae15528a9fe415282402c4e14090c75.

and pay attention to what they say and do. By staying involved over the years we can develop a historical perspective so we know what questions to ask, how to interpret the answers, who is involved, and how to respond.

We can join a political club, work our way up, become the voice and decision-makers of our parties, and participate in making laws, policies, and procedures.

Doing things for the first time can be challenging, but if we persevere, the work of self-government gets easier and more interesting and exciting. We will meet and learn from role models. One critical skill to develop is time management so we don't neglect ourselves, or our family, friends, or jobs. We can tithe our free time to take care of our government—it's a kind of maintenance chore, like washing dishes.

It is probably true that some people may stop voting if they think our nation's elections have problems. If we don't educate people and make changes, however, our elections will become a mere ritual. Corrupt elections do not support democracy. Dictators have told us that: Josef Stalin declared, "It's not who votes that counts; it's who counts the votes." Anastasio Samoza of Nicaragua boasted, "You won the vote, but I won the count."

I've been told that Americans won't show up to do the work of self-government. Yet in November 2016, I ran a poll site in New York City that served 15,000 voters. Knowing that we would be understaffed, I approached some organizations to get volunteers. More people came to help than we needed. In 2012 when Obama was elected for his second term, I ran a smaller poll site that was packed with voters from the moment we opened the doors at 6 A.M.; we could not serve them fast enough, so I climbed up on a chair and yelled that we needed help. Dozens of people changed their plans for the day and stayed to work, some till midnight. I believe people become active when they understand the need and urgency; our silence about problems robs others of the opportunity and choice to work for what they believe in.

Honest government, especially election administration, requires informed public scrutiny, discussion, and participation. The more we study and investigate our governmental bureaucracies that operate in secret, the more likely we are to figure out how to unlock their doors. At this time, as our president and Congress are dismantling our government, its institutions, and the rule of law, the only way to preserve and strengthen them is our persistent engagement and vigilance, and use of the Electoral College in 2020 to limit the effect of vote-switching to the states in which it occurs.

FACE

Kate Conroy and Marty Correia

DAY ZERO: November 8, 2016, East Village, New York
My spouse and I got up early to vote. I had a tall latte and an entire pumpkin muffin as an after-voting indulgence. I was pretty convinced that Hillary had it in the bag. All day and for weeks prior I eschewed any notions that Drumpf would come close to winning.

That night, as Marty and I watched the returns roll in, I believed the early polls that Hillary would take it. When some East Coast states started turning red, I worried. Marty intimated she thought Drumpf could have it. I dismissed her comments completely—not out of knowledge, or research, or political analysis—but out of faith. I believed that a '99 Bush/Gore scenario could never again play out. I believed that Democrats were savvier strategists. I went to bed expecting an overnight miracle.

When I got up the next morning, Marty already had the news on. With sleep in my eyes and aches in my bones I stood in the living room transfixed by the announcements. Marty let me soak in the results. I was stymied. I was zombied. I felt as if a clock was broken at my core—the time clock of progress re-winding in a dark downward spiral.

I don't remember much of the next hour. I know we had breakfast. Marty headed to work, I showered and dressed. But my feet could not take me out the door as they did on any ordinary day. I couldn't face this day as any other. This backslide was visceral. I couldn't pretend otherwise and pondered how I could step outside in a way that would be neither hysterical nor phony.

For "inspiration" I visited the memory of the Bush/Gore race. I'd gone to bed on that election night with the news that Gore had it and woke up to news that Bush had won. I was disillusioned. But, because I had a corporate contract job with conservative colleagues, I had to put on a face and get to work. I was out of it all day and when people asked why, I didn't feel safe saying my guy lost. I just said that the election was a real nail-biter and I'd been up all night.

Now I work at a university, where my colleagues' politics and mine are more in sync. Although I feel that I can be honest about my political views, I couldn't see myself making small talk, discussing political opinions, or being supportive if someone needed it. I needed time to orient myself to this outcome. The rewinding feeling continued and its presence became stronger and louder in my thoughts. Its voice produced a word. Backward. It echoed. Backward. Backward. Backward. The echo led me to an idea, which became a decision. I would walk backwards to work.

Even though the half-mile walk is almost a straight line, I cross several avenues, which I knew would worry my protective lesbian husband, Marty. So I dug out the construction vest we keep in our roadside emergency bag. I Sharpied on a white swatch from an old T-shirt "WALKING BACKWARD to WORK" and I pinned it to the vest. I donned the vest over my coat and headed out the door—backward.

Photograph by Marty Correia

Walking Backward to Work
DAY 1: November 9, 2016
Pleading Brow: "Why?"
i shrugged in return
Unnoticed Stranger: "Walking Backward to Work."
Earnest Young Man: "Ma'am, can I ask you why you're doing this?"
i woke up this morning and it's the only thing i could do
a small wave
choked up by a nod
palm to heart
walking backward
checking over my shoulder
watching my step
breaking custom of pleasantries
keeping the lights down
taking a tissue
feeling it
deep
tomorrow?

From MARTY

When Kate told me she had walked backwards to work my first thought was about her safety. We often joke about the side of me we call "Safety Sam." It's when I morph into the old school butch who alerts everyone when the floor is slippery or when that last step is a little higher than the rest. While Safety Sam was concerned about street crossings and curbs, another part of me, we'll call her "Prissy McGhee," worried what people thought of a safety vest-wearing middle-aged lesbian shaking it up in the East Village.

Was this the time to worry about what people thought? No. But that New Englander in me pops up now and again just so I can tell her to get lost. As I get older I care less about those things. I no longer get fully dressed to do laundry or get mail in our building, and it works as a people deflector. If I had only known this years ago, I could have saved myself hours of awkward hallway chatter.

Kate's action that morning reminded me of a piece of art I saw in the 1980s or 1990s. It was a room that had been cut in half. Or maybe half the room had been ransacked. I don't remember exactly. But I am sure that it was a response to someone losing someone they loved – maybe to AIDS. It was during that time when it seemed almost all art was about AIDS. The idea of that room is stuck in my mind. The details are not. That room was created to shake up the illusion that everything is okay. Even though everything looks like you expect it to, it shouldn't. Loss and grief can ruin everything while nothing appears to have changed.

The morning after the United States elected Donald Trump as president I showered and had some kind of breakfast, because that's what I always do. I left for work and clocked in by 9am, because that's what I always do. Sometime between when I left our apartment and Kate left for work, she came up with a way to cope with the disgusting election results. Kate threw herself backwards into the flow of traffic – the traffic of the workaday morning, of St.

Mark's Place, of Broadway, of the mo(u)rning commute and the traffic of the minds of everyone who saw her. She changed what these people saw; she forced them to see what she was feeling, just by walking backwards to work. By not doing the safest thing, by not doing the usual thing, by not facing forward, she walked into her grief, her unrest, her rage, her fear. I worried if she would do it again the next day, the day after that. What if she became the woman who walked to work backwards every day of this presidency?

DAY 2: November 10, 2016
Passerby: "Walking Backward?"
yes
to work
    sanctimonious prattle
    apathy
    business as usual
"Keeping it cool."
awww, thanks!
proud
Blue Eyes: "Can I ask you why you're walking backward?"
yes, it's how I face the day
practicing for the future
Luxe Suit: "Oh. Interesting."
Darting Glance: "Scary."
walking backward
crossing Broadway – Lenapeway
pleasantries resume
so soon
wave
chatter
lights up
get to work

DAY 3: November 11, 2016
i had developed a method
    meet eyes
    share nods
    acknowledge smiles
Ponytail: "Why are you walking backward?"
to meet the future, what are you doing?
"I was on a job interview"
the future
did you vote?
Shyly "No."
Why?
"I can't. I'm not from here."
Canadian?
Nervously "No."
"Israeli."
good luck
Focused: "Thanks for making me think."
home stretch
Phone-In-Hand Enthusiast: "I got you"
i appreciate it
bumped into wall

After bumping into a wall on Friday, I took the weekend to decide if I needed to keep up the practice. It had given me a sense of purpose and freedom to enter the day in a manner consistent with my frame of mind while shielding me from expectations that I should treat the days as if they were any other. By Monday I felt I should face reality forward. I needed to productively focus on the future. I retired the vest and walked to work, face first, praying for justice to prevail before inauguration day.

From MARTY

It's a year since Trump's inauguration. Kate stopped walking backwards to work well over a year ago now. It's been a year of stress eating and drinking. This morning we confided to each other that we've been waking up every morning wondering if we have hangovers, grateful for the days when we wake up with clear heads. My newest tactic is to drink only on the weekends. This might mean I have to not look at the news or listen to people talk about Trump during the week. That's not a bad idea. I'll start tomorrow.

Over the course of the past year, we've come up with many ways to cope: drinking, protesting, talking about our anxieties and anger with friends, taking walks, throwing ourselves into our creative lives. I've been eating as if the world is going to end and am now twenty pounds heavier. This year I need to reel everything back in. The world hasn't ended and probably won't any time soon.

We are barraged with fake news about fake news. We are enraged by how far this administration has gone wrong. We know there is no end in sight. Black people are still being shot by civilians and cops, right now 1.5 million people in Puerto Rico are still without power and we are fighting to defend DACA and the Dreamers. Hundreds of other worries surge through my heart and my news and social media feeds. Now that we are burdened by all of this plus deportations of long-time neighbors and a possible nuclear war with North Korea, I feel silly that I was worried about Kate walking backwards to work on the streets of New York City.

WHAT MORE CAN I DO?

Katia Perea

Tuesday, November 9, 2016:
    Take in those that are in danger, organize the resistance, fight the powers of injustice, keep doing the important work of education and peace – now more than ever.

Today, 2018, who cares what day it is:

There is an anarchist bookstore upstate that sells mugs made by a local potter (of course they do); the mugs read Kill Your Local Misogynist.

I live in New York City, my local misogynist became President.

What more can I do that I have not always been doing?

More marches, more workshops, donate more money to the cause, be more sex-positive, dismantle gender more, deconstruct racism even more, graffiti more insulting subway ads, speak up more against jerks in public spaces, in the classroom, at work, write more inspirational poetry, write more scientific research, write more counter-hegemonic theory, argue more with the family during the holidays when they mention their conservative politics, comment more on posts that are offensive, make more posts that call out offenses, make more phone calls to my local politicians, sign more petitions, volunteer more time and more services for needy folks, more support to detox, make more visits to the sick, send more letters to the jailed, offer more help to reforest, to clean up, campaign more to save them, foster them, adopt them.

Kill Your Local Misogynist, well, mine became president, so that is off the table, and now I want to know – what more can I do that I have not already been doing?

Photograph by Saskia Scheffer

Fight the Cistem

INAUGURATION DAY

H. Ní Aóдagáín

Six a.m. Joan Berrigan was glad she awoke early. Sitting with a cup of tea, she watched the morning come through the bare branches of the maple that grew outside her bedroom window. She and Marta had planted the tree to celebrate their fifth anniversary, the same year they bought their home. That maple was almost thirty years old.

Marta had been gone for thirteen of those years, but Joan continued to talk with her every morning, as if Marta sat beside her in the bed.

"Well, darling, this is the big day. I believe I'm ready. I've walked through it several times. Everything is in place. I'm going to need your strength today. I'll be pulling on you."

Joan still questioned whether some vestige of grief and the absence of Marta—which once caused her unbearable pain— influenced her decision. In the last ten weeks, she had chewed on that thought, analyzing it from all angles, and each time she arrived at the same conclusion.

Her motivation came from a much larger place than her own personal loss or the need to escape her loneliness. It had been born as she stood on Pennsylvania Avenue at age six, her small hand tucked into her father's giant one, while John F. Kennedy's motorcade drove down the street. She looked up to see her dad's face lined with tears, and became alarmed.

"Da, what's wrong? I thought this was a happy day."

"It is, lass, it is. The first Irish Catholic to be President. Our people have achieved the unthinkable."

She was twelve years old when she heard about the priest who burned draft cards to protest the Vietnam War and was to be imprisoned. His name was Daniel Berrigan.

"Da, are we related to him?"

"Oh, my colleen, that we would be so honored to call the good priest family, but at least we can call him clansman."

"Why did he do what he did, Da?"

"Some are born to bear the sins of others. They choose to dedicate their life in service to the good."

Her father's words rose in her during that interminable night of sleeplessness after she watched the election results. They stayed with her all the next day as she moved in a stupor, struggling to accept the unacceptable. Did the people of this country comprehend what they had just done? Or was she more aware of the potential dangers, having lived with Marta for over two decades?

Joan's passion to speak truth to power had been fully ignited during that horrific night when Marta, huddled in the corner of their bed shaking in fright from a nightmare, had described the gruesome details of the torture that had so damaged her body and mind, while imprisoned in Chile under Pinochet's regime; how the screams of the women in the neighboring cells still reverberated through her dreams; how the faces of the guards who had abused her re-surfaced over and over again in strangers' faces, no matter how far she traveled from her native country.

"You've never truly understood why I love being a postal carrier. The absolute power I have to walk the streets of this city, to know its routes intimately. You've not understood, because I have never told you my deeper truth. I don't ever want to be confined by four walls again. The freedom to walk this city is also the freedom to run from it, should I need to."

Wanting to grasp the horror Marta had lived through, Joan researched those years leading up to Pinochet's rise to power. She was shocked to learn that Chile had been a model of democracy. In 1971, the Chilean people voted in a Socialist, Salvador Allende, but within two years, with the covert help of the US, the Chilean economy collapsed. On September 11, 1973, Pinochet led a military coup, which toppled the Allende presidency and ushered in two decades of brutal dictatorship.

September 11th—always a difficult day for Marta. She mourned the friends she lost, the country she had to escape from, the thousands of people killed during Pinochet's reign.

Each year, Joan and Marta took the day off, and so were home when a friend called to say that a plane had flown into the Twin Towers in New York. Terror filled Marta's eyes, her skin blanched, and she began to gasp for breath.

"Marta, it's okay, darling. You're safe. Come here. Come close to me. You're safe." Joan held her for the next two hours as great spasms of fear took her over, her body shaking uncontrollably. The terror etched on her lover's face still haunted Joan.

No matter how much she searched, Joan never found an explanation for the bizarre synchronicity of those dates and still questioned if there were any deeper connection between the two events. If anything, it fed her growing mistrust of the analyses and rationales of the media, and alerted her to the existence of larger, unseen forces at play, about which the common person had no knowledge.

Fifteen years later, on the morning after the election, those same suspicions resurfaced as she paced back and forth in front of the bookshelves that filled the three main walls of her living room, scanning the titles, looking for answers.

How could the pundits and pollsters have been so wrong? How could the Clinton campaign have so miscalculated? How were the American people duped by a con man of such epic proportions? Was it possible that the tables were turned, that a foreign power interfered in the electoral process, as the US had in Chile, Guatemala, and other countries for decades?

Joan had anticipated the election of the first woman president of the US, a dream that all feminists of the second wave yearned for, but never thought possible during their lifetimes. Instead, she confronted the starkest of realities, the election of a man whose morals, ethics, and beliefs were anathema to everything she had worked for.

She had always been a prolific reader, ever since the first time her Da took her to the Library of Congress. "All of these books are yours. They belong to you and every other American. Use your privilege wisely."

Standing in front of her bookshelves, she saw herself as a twenty-one-year-old student traveling home from Boston. Engrossed in one of her assigned texts, Mary Wollstonecraft's *The Vindication of the Rights of Woman*, she became horrified by the idea that the rights Wollstonecraft demanded for women in 1792 were still being fought for, two hundred years later. Then and there, Joan vowed to devote her life to the liberation of all women, and spent the next four decades as a feminist historian, rescuing women's stories from the forgotten pages of history. Her bookcases were a reflection of her work, and the names of her heroines began to hum in her brain. Christine de Pisan, Elizabeth I, Olympe de Gouges, Constance Markievicz, Emily Davison.

And that is when her mind froze. In the next moment, the image of what she must do seared itself into every cell of her body. Immediately, she understood it as inevitable. This was her destiny.

She spent the next several weeks considering the feasibility of her idea. Having lived in the city her entire life, she'd experienced Washington DC on high alert innumerable times. A policeman on every corner, helicopters overhead, anything out of the ordinary immediately suspect. She watched hours of footage of past inaugural ceremonies, trying to imagine herself among the throngs of people celebrating the new president, dissecting the images to find those places where the crowds were the thinnest, where security might be lighter.

As the days passed, she felt a sense of renewed purpose, indeed a renewed joy, as she returned to that mental state she so loved during her working life—completely immersed in the intricacies of a given construct to which she applied her highly developed critical thinking and her ability to see the larger framework. At the same time, she also was cognizant of each minute detail. Such was the stuff of historical research and she reveled in it. Each day opened before her, filled with to-do lists that propelled her out of the door and into the cold December mornings, the fog lifting off the Potomac, the chill giving way to a crisp, bright winter's day.

The only regret she had centered on Jim. He would have yet another reason to hate her, not because of the action she would take, but because he would be thrown into the limelight as her only surviving kin.

They had always been markedly different. She loved accompanying Da to the union hall, to sit among the journeymen as they argued politics and strategized how to gain the ear of their Congressmen who walked the halls of power twenty blocks away. Jim eschewed their father's world, refusing to participate in the weekend fishing trips, the Redskins' home games, and the trips to the Library of Congress to bone up on Irish-American history. She was certain that her father favored her, as she thrived in the role Jim never wished to have—her father's sidekick.

Maybe it was the loss of their mother, when they were both so young, or maybe it just came down to personalities. She'd assumed Jim's disdain for her was rooted in sibling rivalry; but as he grew into adulthood and his hostility toward her deepened, she recognized her brother as someone who regarded intimacy with suspicion, and camaraderie as a waste of time.

The breaking point was the vileness he flung her way when she came out as a lesbian. She and Marta had met in an all-women's hiking club, and Joan was smitten from the start. Feelings and fantasies she carried since a teenager, in love with the captain of the volleyball team, coalesced as Marta's charcoal brown eyes met hers on a hike through Rock Creek Park. Wiser than she, Marta explained away her brother's enmity.

"You two have more in common than you think. He's just not willing to claim his own inclinations."

Thirty-three years later, Jim remained a secluded bachelor, married to his work as a computer analyst in some national security apparatus in Bethesda. They rarely communicated, and he would be at a loss to explain her actions. Nothing inside her wished him to be harmed by what would transpire in the next eight hours. The less he knew, the better.

The same was true of the women who had been part of her life for decades, and with whom she and Marta had forged life-long friendships. Had they even an inkling of what she was considering doing, they would have stopped her. She laughed at the thought of them setting up vigil to keep her from leaving her house, or kidnapping her so that she would not be in town today. She sent out her love to them, trusting they would ultimately honor her decision.

The morning sun seeped through the fog that gripped her Georgetown neighborhood. She could hear Marta say, "Enough musings, Ms. Joan, time to get on with it."

She placed her teacup on the night table and climbed out of bed. Midway between plumping her pillows and pulling the thick winter duvet up over the sheets, she abruptly stopped, overtaken by the realization that she would never again awaken in her own bedroom, walk to the closet to choose her clothes for the day, and step into the shower.

A sob of protest rose in her, which she squelched immediately. "Now, none of that. You have a job to do today. Joan of Arc shed no tears before she was led to the stake." Even as she squared her shoulders and drew in a conscious breath to ready herself for what was to come, she felt a shift inside. Some part of her mind took special note of the photographs that lined the stairwell as she descended the steps and turned into the kitchen. It listened with a sharper ear as the egg sizzled in the frying pan, and felt keenly the weight of the fork she held between her thumb and forefinger.

Everything became a bit sharper in the morning light. The wineglasses perched on the sideboard seemed to glimmer, and the clock above the sink ticked louder as she sipped her second cup of tea. All that came within her sight shimmered in significance. The vase her mother had bequeathed her called out to her, its fluted edge resembling a flower opening, "And what of me? To whom will I belong, come tomorrow?"

She shook her head vehemently to stop the thoughts. Her papers were in order, her executor named. She had taken care of everything. It was time to leave. If she stayed much longer in this house she so loved, filled with cherished objects gathered over the course of sixty years, she risked losing her resolve. From the hallway closet, she took out the ankle-length coat she had bought for the occasion. White wool, she had chosen it for its warmth and its color. Today she walked in the footsteps of the suffragists, many of whom had risked their lives to further their cause; she would wear white in their honor.

She picked up the canvas book bag lying by the front door, secure in the fact that she'd prepared well, packing and repacking it several times in the last few weeks, refining her check list after each dry run. She had carried that bag to work for the last five years before retiring. It didn't quite match the snow-white newness of her coat, but she needed its familiarity, as much for comfort as for its role as decoy.

She stepped outside, invigorated by the rush of cold air that enveloped her. Turning to lock her front door, she couldn't prevent the words, "for the last time," from flashing in her mind. She took two steps back, looked up at her beloved home, and whispered a "thank you" for the years it had sheltered her.

An hour later, she stood on the steps of the Library of Congress, her back to the Capitol Building, waiting for the doors to open. She'd decided early on that a visit to her old stomping grounds, the morning of the Inauguration, would help her remain strong and cloak her actions in an appearance of normalcy.

"Dr. Berrigan, well, aren't you here bright and early. I didn't quite expect to see you today, of all days." Ernie, the door guard, who'd swept her through security each morning during her tenure as a resident researcher, gave her a wink as he waved the wand up and down over her coat. They held similar political leanings, and had shared their profound despair in the weeks following the election.

"It's a travesty, Dr. Berrigan, a travesty. To allow such a man to follow in the footsteps of Lincoln, FDR, and Mr. Obama. I am ashamed of my country, I must say it, I am ashamed."

She'd nodded and reached out to take his hand. "So am I, Ernie, so am I. We just have to keep fighting, do what we can to resist, to speak out, but you know that."

"Yea, I know. I just thought, maybe we were getting somewhere, but it seems two steps forward, a mile backward."

"Keep the faith, Ernie. We work in the most important institution in this city, in my opinion. This library holds our history, as flawed as it is, but it also holds the principles by which this nation needs to be guided, especially in times of crisis. I know I sound preachy, but it's true. Only through the education of the citizens of this country can minds be opened, can change occur."

Today, bantering with him as she walked through the barricade, she felt a moment of shame that she had used their friendship to carry out her scheme. She silently apologized to him as he bid her a good day.

"You too, Ernie. I hope it's not too busy!"

Stepping into the Great Hall, she was overcome with emotion. This beautiful building had been Joan's second home, with its magnificent staircases, domed ceiling, giant columns. She had first stood in the Great Hall as a young girl at her father's side; she'd run up and down the stairs with schoolmates while teachers scolded them to be quiet; and Marta had perennially perched herself under the mosaic of Minerva while waiting to accompany her home after a day of research.

As a feminist historian, she was acutely aware of the fact that the statues, paintings and decorations celebrated the preeminence of Western civilization, while omitting the narrative of those cultures and peoples, women included, who were subjugated, colonized, and destroyed by it. She hoped her work as a researcher had contributed to the weaving of a different, more diverse, more inclusive history of this country.

In formulating her plan, she'd chosen the Library because of its proximity to the Capitol Building and because she knew it so well, its hallways and reading rooms as familiar to her as the nooks and crannies of her own home. What she hadn't realized was that by going there that morning, she'd be saying goodbye.

Tears stung her eyes, and for a moment, she felt disoriented. Her mind searched for ballast, and she conjured up Marta's face, which held a serene and loving look. "Find your feet, mi amor. Find your feet," she heard her say, the mantra Marta chanted in times of crisis, in moments of uncertainty.

She did as Marta taught her, pushing the balls of her feet into the floor, which brought her back to where she stood. She took a moment, once more, to relish the splendor of the Great Hall, and then turned toward the Main Reading Room.

"To work," she said half-aloud, just in case someone was within earshot.

She needed to arrive at the Library when the doors first opened, to ensure that it was Ernie who checked her through. For the next three hours, she would peruse the Library's databases, sit with a stack of books at her side, and act the part of researcher. She found the book she saved to read that day: *Phoenix, Letters and Documents of Alice Herz.* She would wrap this courageous woman's words around her, like the arms of a loving friend.

The clock of the rotunda chimed, pulling her from her reading. She checked her watch. 11:00 a.m. She gathered her things and left the reading room. Climbing up to the second floor, she reached the Visitor's Gallery where she found a seat near a window. She would sit and empty her mind of everything except the sight of a nearby tree and the clouds that rolled across the morning sky. She had thought it all through, weighed the implications. Now she sought a sense of peace that would buoy her in this final hour.

A half hour passed. She stood up, her book bag in one hand, her coat draped across her shoulders. She took the elevator to the ground floor and entered the bathroom. In the largest stall, a baby-changing table stood against the wall. She placed her bag on it, and emptied its contents. The pencil case held the scissors she needed, and with them, she opened a bag of coffee beans and shook some onto the table to release their odor into the room. She then took out the vacuum-sealed bag that, from the outside, looked like it held a carefully folded raincoat.

Another officer might have confiscated the scissors, the coffee beans (as no food or drink were allowed) and the sealed bag. But in the three different dry runs she had done, Ernie hadn't blinked an eye. Thank you, friend, for the part you played, she thought as she cut open the thick plastic bag.

Tucked in the folds of the raincoat were an oversized long-sleeved cotton shirt and a thin pair of pants, still wet from the solution they had been soaking in for over a week. She pulled them over her clothes, rolling the pants legs up to her knees. She then reached into her bag and pulled out the sash she had sown, emblazoned with the words, "Rights for Women." As she placed it over her head, images of the Pankhurst sisters, Susan B. Anthony, Alice Paul and the thousands of women who had proudly worn such a badge flooded her mind. She smiled. She was not alone.

She grabbed her coat from its hook, and quickly buttoned it from top to bottom. The slightest chemical smell, reminiscent of nail polish, escaped from the open collar of the coat. To disguise the odor, she scooped up two handfuls of coffee beans and deposited them in her coat pockets. She took out a plastic ziplock bag that held her invitation to the Inauguration and poured the remaining beans into it, shutting it tight.

She bundled the raincoat, scissors and empty bag into a garbage bag she had packed, knotted it and threw it in the trash. She reached inside her book bag, took out her wallet, and a small brown paper bag, and then placed the book bag on the floor next to the changing table. She left the bathroom and moved down the corridor that led to a back door of the library. Fixing her eyes on the end of the hallway, she willed herself to walk, not run, so as not to garner attention. She finally reached the exit available to researchers only, walked through the automatic scanner, leaned against the bar of the door and stepped outside. As she rounded the building, she breathed an enormous sigh of relief. No one had seen her; no one had stopped her.

All of a sudden, she felt the presence of her father, as if he were walking alongside her. "Da," she cried, and the grief she always carried for him overtook her.

"You're a brave lass, Joanie girl." Words he had used to describe her since she was small echoed through her mind.

And then he was gone.

Shaking, she stopped in the middle of the sidewalk and looked around. She was alone, the back of the massive building to her right rising like a fortress.

"Okay, no more visitations, please. This is difficult enough as it is," she said aloud as she began her ascent up Second Street.

At ten minutes to twelve, as planned, she approached the southwest entrance of the Inaugural Grounds. Sitting down on a bench some feet away, she watched the few stragglers line up to walk through the metal detectors. From the brown paper bag, she took out a packet of cigarettes and lighter. She lifted the invitation—her ticket—from its plastic bag. Choosing the moment when no one else was in line, she got up and walked toward the entrance, leaving the small empty bags behind.

She smiled her brightest smile at the officer who reached for her invitation.

As the officer motioned for her to walk through the metal detector, Joan addressed her. "I just realized I'm carrying my cigarette lighter. Will that be a problem?" She opened her hand to reveal the pack of cigarettes and lighter.

The woman silently took them from her, nodded for her to step through, and handed them back on the other side. Joan flashed her another smile, even as she concentrated on not letting the woman see that she was trembling. She walked forward, adrenaline coursing through her body. She had just passed the last hurdle. There was nothing else to stop her.

She followed the inside of the stone wall that edged the Capitol Grounds, walking behind the hundreds of people sitting in neatly arranged rows of chairs or standing in designated areas. She came to a stop under an enormous tree, from where she could look out and see the ceremony displayed on the massive screens installed for the event. She solemnly removed her coat, placed her wallet and the sash she wore in the crook of the tree, and stood watching. At the moment the Chief Justice appeared on the screen to administer the oath of office, she took ten steps forward, and laid her coat on the ground. She sat down, the cigarette lighter in her hand. As the president-elect placed his hand on the bible, she flicked the lighter, and lit the edge of her shirt.

Bystanders later said they heard the woman scream, "Marta!" as the flames engulfed her.

"PARABLE OF THE SOWER"

Pamela Sneed

If you want to know the ending
how it's all gonna turn out
the aftermath of trump's presidency
don't turn to analysts, wall st. or cnn
for an accurate portrait of where it's all going
what it's gonna look like
reread Octavia Butler's *Parable of the Sower*
set in California around 2027:
people in fear/behind walls/gated communities
a woman raped so much
she can't stand
gun violence/addiction/fires that can scarcely
be put out
people scavenging for food/trying not to become prey
compassion gone
the main character named Lauren a hyper-empath
can feel others' pain
a metaphor for artists
whatever you think of Marina Abramović
her show title is right, the artist is/was always present
from the beginning of time until now.
Look again at the *Hunger Games*, the districts are
actually concentration camps with gray garb
                                    and barbed-wire fences
that nod to Nazi Germany
humans pitted against each other to survive.
Sometime after Trayvon Martin was shot
I finally understood
something deep about Star Wars

I've always rooted for good guys/always.
Once I heard a friend at the movies rooting for Poison Ivy/
Batman and Bat Girl's nemesis
I was shocked that anyone could root for a bad girl
but after Trayvon was killed by George Zimmerman
who walked free
I finally understood what could turn a character's eyes dark
(you could become so disillusioned)
and then I understood in the Star Wars franchise
what made Darth Vader, Vader
I felt that again after Trump's election
No more green, blue light
Only gray, dark drab, white bones, war.
Last week, I worked with a class I hadn't met before
On the subject of Black Lives Matter.
I repeated something Gregg Bordowitz said to a group of students
"What if the only justice we have right now is here
in this room?"
One student said, "Nothing ever changes."
So responding, I ask, "Are you telling me then
you can't change?"
They were all surprised, shocked by my question.
At the end, I asked the class, "What have you learned today?"
A Black girl answered as if she were channeling Octavia herself,
"Change.
Is up to us."

UPRISING

Pamela Sneed

16 years old
from the suburbs, Boston
I'd go into the city shopping
with my cousin and friends
we'd venture into Boston Commons, the Park.
There were hustlers there with a set-up table,
I didn't know then.
They played some sort of game with shells
hid money under a shell or a plastic cup
moved their hands real quick
made it purposefully look so easy
naïve 16 years old, I bet
50 dollars, a lot of money for me then.
They made it look so easy.
You just had to pick the right one.
Of course, it was rigged
I lost
felt dizzy,
sick to my stomach
lost my gaze.
On Tuesday night after the election
I felt the same way heisted in a shell game.
Walking outside on Wednesday, in my neighborhood
a white woman who barely ever speaks was crying
asked, "What do we do?"
I answered earnestly, teacher, artist, professor
who always tries, "I don't know."
Later, I walked up the street, a white man in an SUV
with the window down drove by.

He wore an expensive business suit
had a big brown cigar
like when babies are born
expensive seen only in gangstah films like *Goodfellas*
or on the *Sopranos* after a kill.
He looked happy, smug,
that's when I realized the Trump Presidency is a hustler's game
Ballers club
Players only
Pimp paradise
Wives with teased hair and lots of plastic surgery
on the white BET.
They made it all look so easy
like a choice
Who knew
The American Dream was a side hustle for big businessmen
with all their ugly red white blue striped flag merchandising
available at Walmart and Target, I'll never buy into again.
Who knew freedom was a marketing idea/consumer product
hallucinatory drug cooked up in some rove-ian as in karl type
                                                    of laboratory
sweatshop maintained by the architects of apartheid
freedom like air if you're white and male and rich enough
to keep breathing.
Today, I started to cry as I wrote
to my students
knowing that in everything so far, I've tried to protect them
and realizing there are places in this world
even my maternal hands can't reach.
In Poland, the Warsaw ghetto against a Nazi fascist regime
on Southern Plantations, in fields, in Haiti,
on shores of Africa.
Uprising:

The 6os
The streets
James
Nina
Bayard
Miriam
June
Nikki
Lorraine
Audre
Pat
Malcom
Martin
Betty
Sekou
The unnamed
Artists
Poets
Teachers
Always
Uprising.

POST ELECTION

Pamela Sneed

Like trinkets sold at gift shops
near former slave sites
masks carved for tourist consumption
paper promises given to those getting off the boat
from somewhere
those who crossed the desert, dehydrated
raped, throat slit, still
arrived by foot
Like dollar off coupons at Target
going fast/buy now.
Hope and democracy are a poor woman's
last pennies spent to buy Christmas lights
and ribbon at Rite-Aid
like children's drawings with multi-colored crayons
displayed in elementary school windows
are what mothers fight for when their children
are killed in a school shooting by an imbecile
who had easy access to guns
all the shooter wanted was to be like Kim K. and Kanye, a star.
Like, when hearing the testifying of the family members of
the 9 black congregants he shot
while their heads were bowed in prayer
in Mother Emanuel Church in Charleston,
Dylan Roof shouted in the courtroom:
"It's not fair,"
After, the cops took him to Burger King.
Like Jeffery Dahmer who ate the flesh and hearts
of young Black boys.
He was killed in prison/stuffed in a broom closet.

And like the leader of the Rwandan massacre.
Like a poet once said of an abusive father
I'm glad
So glad
He's dead.
Like candy spun by politicians
dissolving as soon as your tongue reaches to taste it.
Hope and democracy are just words
evading Walter Scott
Trayvon Martin
Emmett Till
Mike Brown
Akai Gurley
Gift
and Sandra Bland.
Hope and democracy are like old Harlequin romance novels/
                                                    extinct.
As my friend says, "There's no more love,
only drama."
Hope and democracy are slogans
written on cups in souvenir shops on 42nd St
having nothing to do with our lives and
reality.

Photograph by Morgan Gwenwald

(untitled)

JOIN THE MAGICAL RESISTANCE

Fran Winant

"*A merican democracy was never supposed to give the nation a president like Donald Trump. We have never had a president who aroused such grave and widespread doubts about his commitment to the institutions of self-government . . . and to the need for basic knowledge about major policy questions and about how government works . . . who daily raises profound questions about his basic competence and his psychological capacity. . . and whose victory came with the assistance of a foreign power. . . a president who, from his first day in office, plainly showed that he had no business being president . . . a presidency devoted to the . . . will to power of one man, not the needs of the nation . . . a threat to our democracy and the product of its weaknesses.*" — One Nation After Trump, by E.J. Dionne, N.J. Ornstein, and T.E. Mann*

Some form of magical alliance with nature and the universe, such as Wicca, is believed to be the original religion of humankind, and Wicca remains a viable spiritual alternative for modern feminists, especially in times of distress. The Bind Trump Wicca Ritual performed monthly on the date of the waning crescent moon is a form of spiritual activism focusing the power of group intention to alter reality. It mobilizes the same energy as prayer, affirmation, spiritual healing, visualization, manifestation, and positive thinking. The tone of the ritual is joyful, not negative or angry. The word "bind" could be interpreted as "restrain without harm." The idea behind the ritual is to stop the energy of Trump and his Republican enablers from doing harm and to encourage them to leave the political stage, restoring the nation to Us the People, or as someone I knew would have said, "Don't go away mad, just go away."

People understood from the person Trump had shown himself to be during his campaign what they could expect from him as president, an autocrat who "praises strongmen ... freely demeans whole groups of Americans . . . [often expressing a] hostile attitude to long-standing alliances. . .[and who] shamelessly demeaned women and bragged about assaulting them . . . [someone who evokes] fear for the future of . . . freedom and democracy. (cited above) Soon after his inauguration as president on January 20, 2017, an outline of the Wicca ritual began circulating on social media under the heading, "A Spell to Bind Donald Trump and All Those Who Abet Him" (https://extranewsfeed.com/a-spell-to-bind-donald-trump-and-all-those-who-abet-him-february-24th-mass-ritual-51f3d94f62f4). The reader was instructed to gather certain paraphernalia and perform the ritual alone or with friends at the time of the waning crescent moon. The ritual was to be repeated monthly, as indeed it has been, with its one-year anniversary in February of 2018.

Happily, a group made a video on that first night that is still available. Thus, to participate, you can follow along with the video starting at 11:59 pm ET on the designated night. The date gets magically changed each month on some copies of the original video, but in case you do not find that to be so, you can get a list of monthly waning moon dates on https://www.facebook. com/notes/bind-trump-official/waning-crescent-moon-ritual-dates/745096415640153/. Dates for 2018 are: 1/13, 2/12, 3/14, 4/13, 5/12, 6/11, 7/10, 8/8, 9/6, 10/6, 11/4, 12/4. The video of the ritual is available on that same Facebook page or on https://www.youtube. com/watch?v=4Tr6oqAlRCQ.

The instructions mention that part of the value of performing the ritual is personal because it contains "an embedded self-exorcism" to help release us from the anguish of being subjected to a force that seeks to crush our will. In speaking about the ritual with friends, I was asked how it was possible to overcome your revulsion at having spiritual contact with such negativity for even the few minutes required to perform the ritual. I realized that I had found my way around this by thinking of the group in the video as an ongoing thoughtform that continues to exist for as long as needed. My part in the ritual is to focus on empowering the group as it continues to do its spiritual work. I have strong positive feelings about them and want them to succeed. This helps to balance the negatives surrounding the reason why the ritual is necessary.

The ritual is intended to build power by being performed simultaneously by many people. As someone who has been following along with the ritual for the last year, I feel that if you miss the date or time it is still alright to do it anyway as a form of personal prayer, visualizing the waning crescent moon and willing that your intention join with, support, and reinforce the intention of the group. Your intention will find its path to where it needs to go.

In case, when you are reading this, the video is unavailable, the following is what you would see and hear as you watched and added your energy:

A group of women and men is standing outdoors in a circle around a fire whose windblown sparks are everywhere. The area is further lit by strings of clear holiday lights. Participants hold candles and small pictures of Trump. The leader holds a large book containing the words that he will read aloud. An altar between him and the fire contains a picture of Trump, a bell, an upright Tower tarot card, and representations of the four elements: a candle for fire, a goblet of water, a bowl containing salt as a symbol of earth, and (unseen but probably there) the feather mentioned in the instructions as a symbol of air. As the ritual begins, someone leans forward to take a light from the altar's candle.

The leader says: "A Spell (group repeats) to Bind Donald J. Trump (group repeats) so that his malignant works (group repeats) may fail utterly (group repeats), that he may do no harm (group repeats) to any human soul (group repeats) nor any tree (group repeats), animal (group repeats), rock (group repeats), stream (group repeats), or sea (group repeats). Bind him (group repeats) so that he shall not break our polity (group repeats), usurp our liberty (group repeats), or fill our minds with hate (group repeats), confusion (group repeats), fear (group repeats), or despair (group repeats), and bind too (group repeats) all those who enable his wickedness (group repeats) and those whose mouths speak (group repeats) his poisonous lies (group repeats). I beseech thee, spirits (group repeats), bind them all (group repeats) as with chains of iron (group repeats), bind their malicious tongues (group repeats), strike down their towers of vanity (group repeats)."

The leader reaches down and inverts the Tower card on the altar. "I beseech thee in my name (group repeats), in the name of all who walk (group repeats), crawl (group repeats), swim (group repeats), or fly (group repeats), of all the trees (group repeats), the forests (group repeats), streams (group repeats), deserts (group repeats), rivers (group repeats), and seas (group repeats). In the name of Justice (group repeats) and Liberty (group repeats) and Love (group repeats) and Equality (group repeats) and Peace (group repeats)"—he takes the bell from the altar and rings it— "bind them in chains (group repeats)"—rings the bell again—"bind their tongues (group repeats)"—rings the bell again—"bind their works (group repeats)"—rings the bell again—"bind their wickedness (group repeats)." He takes the picture of Trump from the altar. He and the participants lift their pictures of Trump upward, as though showing them to a watching spiritual presence, then bend toward the fire, casting the pictures into the devouring flames.

Leader and participants point at the crumbling pictures and say together, "You're fired, you're fired!" The leader then says, "Our ritual is ended, brothers and sisters. May we go in peace, harming none, and continue our magical resistance under the waning crescent moon until Donald J. Trump is driven from office!" All say together, "So mote it be!" They laugh strongly, "Ha, ha, ha, ha, ha, ha, ha," laughing Trump and his enablers away as though they are part of some cosmic joke. All whoop and cheer and jump up and down, prescribed in the instructions as activities to help participants re-ground themselves. Some raise their arms in victory, "We did it!" Everyone applauds and music begins to play: "Light My Fire," by The Doors, the perfect ending.

FRESH PINEAPPLE

Freesia McKee

The drunk man downstairs video chats with his girlfriend at night, pressing the phone against his window to show her our walk by.

Another year of politics pressed against your cheek. Can I kiss you again in this parking lot? Is it early enough that no one will see?

The neighbors with their grill, our weekend bedroom filled with the smell of cooking meat.

Say you'll stay with me. Say we'll celebrate this year. Say you'll make sure to lock our door with all three keys. The beach's fourth wall, this little home.

The space I desire inside of you. The space you make for me. The world we want between us. Nothing is so far when the cat scratches the edge of the bed to get our attention.

The piles of hurricane debris on dozens of our daily walks, debris from the hurricane and all the lesser storms.

I am not sure how to describe the disaster, still a fresh wet wound, especially since in ways I can't count, this year has been good for you and me.

All class privilege political.

You remind me, in many ways for us, this year has been hard. But most current events I see from a balcony, through the radio and our news apps.

App: Like an appetizer, harbinger of the forthcoming courses. We know those courses are coming. How much can we control? Deadly decisions we view from far away. We shake our heads.

I don't want to confront the ways I create and perpetuate harm. It's easier to be an either/or.

The man downstairs opens the door of his place to air out his stale smoke. We close our bathroom window. What would I do, I think, if I lived with someone like him. And this question is why I don't smile at him anymore.

On one of our daily walks, we encounter a fresh pineapple sitting in an abandoned shopping cart. Where does this image come from? A stranger with a syringe of poison injecting ripe fruit.

You ask me if we should take it home. To me, the risks don't seem worth it, though the realest dangers may be the ones we're used to ignoring.

There is nearly never a man in the bushes. There has always been a man in the white house. These men don't need to hide.

Another neighbor leaves her shoes between the sidewalk and the street. The shoes have been there for days. Because they're broken, a strap ripped from the sole, I know she's throwing them out, leaving them for someone who can use them, someone like me.

If they were perfect, I would know she was setting them out to dry.

I wear my neighbor's shoes when you and I take the bus down Biscayne to a place we will dance together. Only one of the straps is broken, and the shoes are just my size.

No matter what city we live in, I know you and I can find a place, and this particular place-ness is related to our whiteness, our class, the paper degrees stacked in our closet.

When you find a fishhook on the ground in front of a neighbor's door, you are careful when you hand it off to me. I feel self-satisfied when I wrap the ragged hook in tape, adding it to the safe trash at our place.

Only problems like these have an easy address.

You remind me of the litany: *he believes people who are trans are a burden; they crafted the tax bill in self-service; they're limiting access to doctors and medicine. We are governed by sexual assault. His utter incompetence towards North Korea and Russia and every country in the world. Jerusalem. The privatization of schools, the privatization of knowledge. Harder and harder to get a safe abortion. Deporting Haitian people who are climate refugees. The FBI's growing file on Black Lives Matter; Erica Garner gone at 27. Puerto Rico. The money from oil pipelines, more valuable than Native sovereignty or safety. The press secretaries who climb through press conferences lie by lie. The president's patriarchal narcissism. These old, old problems.*

We start making a list and can't stop.

REMEMBER

Grete Miller

Remember
It is not usual
The fake this, fake that, Twitter
Document it all

Abnormalities
Verbal Volleying Warfare
Torpedoing Truth

Nefarious and
Unabated behavior
Yes, that just happened ...

Marginalizing
Art, science, news, education
End the bludgeoning

We must build a strong
Counter offense based on truth
Call out the extremes

Do not tip-toe side steps
Have the courage to stare it down
My camera. My weapon
We eat our future
It keeps me up at night
My Pen. My weapon.

It keeps repeating
My body no longer rests
My pulse. My weapon.

The world turns to blood
Comfort and peace have run off . . .
Our lives. Are weapons.

I am just asking you
In case we come out alive
What will you do now?

Photograph by Morgan Gwenwald

Edie Windsor at 25th Annual NYC Dyke March, June 24, 2017

QUEER SUICIDALITY, CONFLICT, AND REPAIR
Morgan M. Page and Sarah Schulman

On October 10, 2016, QED hosted its first live Queer Conversation at Le Cagibi, in the Mile End neighborhood of Montréal. This conversation featured Morgan M. Page, a Montréal-based writer and artist, with Sarah Schulman, a New York-based writer and LGBTQ rights activist. In this Queer Conversation, Page and Schulman read the eulogies that they gave at the funeral of Bryn Kelly, a friend of both who took her own life in January 2016. Prior to the event, the Facebook event page included information about several suicide prevention resources including Suicide Action Montréal, Trans Lifeline, and the Trevor Project. Because it was a live event, we decided to purposely include in the published version the engagement among Page, Schulman, and the audience. We were heartened by the turnout and the deeply engaged audience participation that ensued. We hope, as was noted by Schulman and Page toward the end of the event, that this conversation about Bryn Kelly's life and death will motivate us all to reconsider conflict, care, and community.

Morgan M. Page (MMP): I'm Morgan. I'll more fully introduce myself in a minute. I just wanted to, like, say "hello" and get the attention of the room and let you all know that this event is "Queer Conversations: Suicidality, Conflict, and Repair." Obviously, this is a very emotionally loaded subject for probably most of us, right? So if you feel like you need to leave at any point, don't feel bad, just, you know, do what you need to do to take care of yourself. We've also posted, albeit not a comprehensive list, a small list of resources for follow-up afterwards, if you feel like you need counseling or anything like that. I also wanted to begin by saying by acknowledging the fact that not only is it Indigenous Peoples' Day today, we're also, obviously, I hope obviously, on occupied indigenous land, the traditional territories, I believe but I may be wrong, of the Haudenosaunee and Algonquin, and any conversation that is about conflict on occupied territories really shouldn't ignore the fact that these conflicts are happening on conflicted land, right? That makes sense to everybody? So I want to make sure that that was kind of the first thing we broached and hopefully it will also continue to be part of the conversation that we have later this evening. So should we begin? Are we, are we good?

Sarah Schulman (SS): Hi, everyone. I just want to say I'm really, really happy to be here with all of you. Morgan and I met in an airport and we clicked like crazy with a beautiful conversation and the beginning of a really authentic friendship that I'm really honored to be part of, and I'm so happy that we're doing this together today. Thank you.

Tom Nakayama (TY): Hi, my name is Tom Nakayama. I'm at Northeastern University in Boston and with Chuck Morris who's at Syracuse University in New York, we co-edit a journal called *QED* and I'll pass around some information about the journal. It's one of the features of the journal—it's a journal that tries to bring academics and activists in conversation about GLBTQ worldmaking and one of the features of the journal that has been sort of a regular has been what we call queer conversation and so this evening we have queer conversation with Sarah Schulman and Morgan Page. And so to begin this queer conversation, I wanted to ask them about their experiences at Bryn's funeral. Do you want to introduce yourselves first?

SS: I'm Sarah Schulman and that's Morgan Page [laughter].

MMP: So if you don't know us already [laughter].

SS: So I thought that I would tell a little bit about—a little background—to the eulogy that I wrote and maybe Morgan would like to do the same and let you in on what was happening for each of us, and then we're gonna share our eulogies with you. And just to let you know, mine is seventeen minutes long, so just keep that in mind. So let me just start. After Bryn Kelly killed herself a group of her close friends—closest friends—who were in New York organized the funeral for her. This group included her partner Gaines, myself, and Kelly Dunham, Anna, Alice, a little bunch of us that organized the event and the decision was to made to have it at St. John the Divine Cathedral, which is an iconic enormous cathedral in New York City because Bryn was a church person. We had gone to some other churches that were more in her religious tradition, but they wanted to charge us and St. John the Divine felt that they weren't doing enough to support the trans community and so they gave us the space. So the decision was made that I would give the central—a large—eulogy, and so I wrote the draft and I submitted to the other people who were organizing the event. And we had about three rounds of corrections and comments on the phone and through email and then we met as a group in person to go over the text one more time, and at that point, we read the guidelines for people dealing with public events related to suicide and particularly the guidelines for describing the way that people killed themselves and what we felt that the guidelines said was not to give people instructions on how to kill themselves, that the guidelines said do not say, you know, take this number of this drug and mix it with this about of that. But that saying the way that the person killed themselves was not the same as telling people how to kill themselves, and the way that she had killed herself was such a big part of the experience. A lot of us were in the house with her right after that. So the group went through and changed a lot of things, we all agreed on the text, then a few other people vetted the text. Morgan read the text and also the minister at St. John, which is an Episcopal church. So then we had the service and about 700 people showed up, many of whom did not know Bryn and when I gave the—sitting in the front it was mostly women and then Ted Kerr sitting up in the front. So there was Ted, there was me, there was Naomi, who had been Bryn's roommate, Eva, her girlfriend whose name I don't remember, Morgan and then Red Durkin. Those were the speakers and we were all seated together in the front. So when I went up to give my talk—like I said, it was seventeen minutes long—and I really couldn't tell, I really couldn't see, the audience, but I could hear Red crying while I was talking. And when I came down from the podium I passed here and she was going to the bathroom and I could see that she was crying. Then I went back and sat next to Naomi, and when the service was over, Naomi turned to me and hugged me and said "thank you for your words." Her girlfriend, Eva and her girlfriend hugged me. Morgan I knew had already read it and told me that that was exactly what she wanted from the service. So as far as I was concerned, the people that were closest to Bryn, this was something that they could feel good about.

There was one person who that it wouldn't be good for Bryn's family to hear the way that she killed herself, and he was opposed to me describing that. However, after the service, Bryn's sister said that it was the most powerful thing she had ever heard, so it turned out that that was something that was meaningful to them. Anyway, I got about ten messages from people telling me that they appreciated the honesty, and a few people telling me that they had recommitted to staying alive. But the next day there was people online and on Facebook, who were not close to Bryn but who really objected to my eulogy, and very, very, very much so objected. So I just wanted to say how I understand the objections, what I understood them to be, and how I processed them or understood them.

So one of the biggest objections was that people said that they had come to the funeral to feel better, and for me, one of the things I realized, what I should have realized before, is that I come from the AIDS generation, I come from the ACT-UP generation, and I have been to many, many political funerals. And the concept of the political funeral is present to my mind that it never occurred to me that there are one or two generations that had never experienced a political funeral, and didn't recognize it for what it was, and now that I realize that I would have contextualized that at the top, and I did not understand that. The other thing was that I think there were a lot of people who are not used to being live in a room with 700 queer people. I think there's a generation of people who have not had that experience before, and that's very overwhelming. And I also think that there were people who were so young—and also that because they haven't had the AIDS experience—even with the level of suicide that is present in our community, there were quite a few people there who had either never been to a funeral at all, or had only been to, like, an elder relative or something like that and they were used to a kind of nicety of a formal, traditional funeral, so that thing that for me is very natural, which is to use the funeral as a gathering place to talk about the things that are really going on in our lives, some people felt that that was inappropriate. So that, I would say, was the major arena of objection.

Another arena of objection was the assumption that some people made that I had just gone rogue, that I had just gone up there and just said all this shit. People didn't think that we had all vetted it, that it had been discussed, that the minister had, you know, and it was interesting that that assumption was made, but not one person asked me, what was the discussion, what was the prep, nothing. So there was just this assumption that I had done something terrible on my own and all of that, which is also something that—this has to do with the book I've just written, which is how come people don't ask questions. Why do we just assume the worst? Why don't we just ask the person? You know, and part of it has to do with us not being in person with each other and I think that's one of the reasons we don't ask.

The final objection had to do, I think, with religion. So I'm Jewish, and I'm very culturally Jewish, but I'm not religious. This was in an Episcopal church, and there's this concept of ascension. Bryn was religious. And so one of the criticisms was, why did you have to say her death was a waste? Why couldn't you say: Bryn, you did the best you could. And the reason I couldn't say that is because, for me, Bryn is not addressable because, for me, her death means that she's gone. I do not have a religious concept of her looking down on us or hearing me. And this is something that is really—and this is something that I didn't understand until I heard the objection—and it's just a cultural, religious framework that we each come from, some of us have rejected them, some of us haven't, and for some people that was very offensive on those terms.

So that's what happened there. But in the end I felt like our community of people who were closest to Bryn were united by the service, and I do feel good about my participation, so that was my experience there.

MMP: Just to back up a little, before I go into my little spiel, for those of you who don't know, Bryn Kelly was a prominent trans woman artist living and working in Brooklyn, New York. She was 35 years old, she was a theater maker, and she was a fantastic writer. You may have read some of her blogs without even knowing it because she often used anonymity and constructed characters as an online form of writing, so she's the Hussy online, which if you've ever gotten to read is incredible, one of my favorite pieces of writing ever. She also wrote about her experiences as an HIV-positive trans woman accessing social services through another blog called Party Bottom, which was also wildly popular. You may have seen posts from it a couple years ago called "How to Be a Good Roommate to Someone with HIV," that went viral; it was quite large.

I guess I'll start by acknowledging that we are in the middle of a suicide epidemic within queer and trans communities that reaches across all segments of our community and has very disproportionate impacts on the most marginalized in our community, particularly indigenous people who often cross over with our communities and in Canada have the highest suicide rates of any group as well as black and other people of color. It is a large and extremely sensitive topic that we can't possibly hope to unravel in one evening but we're hoping that through discussing one person's suicide this can be fruitful as we move forward to future events which, hopefully, there won't be too many of. I've been very active within the trans community within the past ten years, and Bryn's suicide was not first suicide of someone close to me that I've seen. Suicides happen very regularly within the close community around me. Whether they're friends I have, coworkers, or community members I've shared space with, they happen with an astounding regularity that contributes to many of us who see this happening feeling hopeless and ourselves feeling suicidal ideation, right? So on January 14th, when I heard about Bryn's death, I was actually on the tail end of one of my deepest periods of depression and suicidality that I've ever gone through in my life, which was about four months long and were the cumulative effects of grief and trauma, including seeing many of my bright and incredible people that I know take their own lives through suicide, and also including the sudden death of my boyfriend, Jack, in 2013, and the deaths of about half a dozen people since then that I've been close with. Bryn's death and the pain caused for so many, particularly her close friends and partner, were a wakeup call to me about my own suicidal ideation and escalating behaviors. In fact, when I read Sarah's eulogy for the first time—I was part of the organizing committee for the memorial, but I was living up here in Montreal and Gaines, Bryn's partner, emailed it to me and said "What do you think of this?" I didn't know that there were conversations happening about this piece. I was just like, oh, what do I think of this? So I read it and the effect on me was very immediate, that I felt that it dissuaded all of the suicidal ideation that I'd been feeling for me personally, and I really respected what a bold statement it was as you all will hear shortly. I did have some objections, whereas you know, like, what I think this is great and I support you on this with going forward on this, however... [laughter] there are, like, one or two little things that I think may be not appropriate for this space and this time so let's, you know, edit [laughter]. And that's when I was told about the conversations that were happening and contacted by all the other people in the organizing committee that was doing this and we had a lot of intense discussions about the purpose of what Gaines, Bryn's partner, called a political sermon. He kept referring to us to stop calling it a eulogy and to start calling it a political sermon because that's what it is, which is, I think, a really smart way of summing it up.

Anyway, through all of this process, I was traveling down practically every couple of weeks to help with the organizing and just be supportive, and I was asked by other people in the organizing committee if I would write a eulogy myself so that there would be a more "traditional" eulogy that would happen, so that's what I did. And I'm gonna read it to you in a little bit.

I think the—I also want to say about the event, so for those of you who haven't been there, the cathedral of St. John the Divine is the third largest Christian Church in the world. It's gigantic. If you look up at the ceiling there's practically clouds, like it's so big and it was full, as Sarah said, with 700 people, many of whom didn't know Bryn, which was a very interesting thing to negotiate emotionally to be in a place of mourning and to have to interact with people who were mourning someone who they didn't know. But something that was very, that wasn't new to me because in 2012 I was also involved in the organizing for the funeral of trans activist Kyle Scanlon in Toronto, who, I don't know if any of you are familiar with his work, but basically if you're a trans person in Canada, you owe him so much in terms of how you're able to access hormones, how you're able to access shelters, very basic things that, in some ways, we're still fighting over today. We wouldn't be as far without Kyle, and I felt that the situations were very similar. Anyway, it was a big, weirdly alienating, large event that was very anxiety producing in the ways that queer and trans events are often are anxiety producing. I'm sure there are some of you today who are having internal freak-outs because someone you had an argument with on the internet two years ago is sitting in the back of the room, and you can just feel their presence. I know I feel that way [laughter]. Just me? Ok.

But um, anyway, I think one of things I found really interesting to the response to Sarah's piece—and we'll probably get more into it after we actually go into the pieces—was that those who were reacting to the piece online who had not seen it being read in person had missed an incredible amount of nuance and tone to how the piece was actually delivered. In person, when I walked up to Sarah in the cathedral, there were tears in her eyes from the moment that I walked up and throughout the entire eulogy, or as Gaines called it, political sermon, it was very emotional. And to me that—I really felt like those emotions were hard to discount and that they were important to the experience of the eulogy. Of course, the words are very important and words matter but also an idea of where it was coming from felt very important and really affected me. My speech went off without a hitch. People loved it [laughter]. People still share it on the internet [laughter]. Not to rub it in [laughter]. But I guess those are my introductory thoughts on this exciting topic that we have to share with you in a moment.

TY: Ok so why don't both of you read your eulogies.

SS: Ok and then we can open it up.

MMP: Would you like to go first?

SS: Sure. Relax. [laughter]

I had the honor of being Bryn's creative writing teacher at the Lambda Literary Retreat. As a writer, she was an organic intellectual, funny, deep and her work grappled with things that matter. Our relationship evolved into a loving, enriching friendship—I called on her a number of times, and she was always there for me. She knew that I loved and respected her.

I am not a religious person, and I do not believe in an afterlife. Instead, it has been my experience that heaven and hell take place on earth. And so, our lives provide us with opportunities for depth of meaning and understanding IF we face and deal with difficulties honestly. It is that uncomfortable, sad and overwhelming work that can bring us to the revelations we need to survive, thrive and be accountable to others. For this reason, I approach this earthly catastrophe with openness. This tragic waste of our beloved friend, Bryn, is a challenge we have to face. Many people today will tell the story of her life. Bryn Kelly's warmth, her genius, her deep, soft beauty and kindness. But I want to take this time to talk, in detail, about Bryn Kelly's death. I want to make a contribution to this ongoing conversation about how to end the terrible idealized fantasy of suicide that has overtaken our community. A falsity of distorted thinking, that has become, not only an option, but in fact an expectation.

Several suicide attempts ago, Bryn ended up in a terrible Brooklyn hospital where she was told that they only had room for her on the men's ward. They also confused her HIV medications, endangering her ability to continue her regimen. And instead of administering her hormones, they gave her Depo-Provera, a long-lasting form of birth control. These kinds of cruelties, and acts of hostile, dehumanizing indifference do not make a person want to ask for help. In fact, like all forms of shunning they exclude people from help. Then, about a year and a half ago, Kelli Dunham called and told me that Bryn had taken an intentional overdose, and that Gaines and Nogga—ever loving and vigilant—had found her checked into a fleabag hotel in Bushwick, arguably a better choice than a men's ward at a bad hospital.

Gaines and Nogga and I agreed that they would take her in a car and meet me at the NYU emergency room. I stood outside with a wheelchair, they pulled up, and we swooped into the ER with Bryn groggy and hovering on unconsciousness. In addition to the pills, she had drunk a lot of beer. NYU triaged her in eight minutes. She was treated with kindness, decency and care. Her friends and partner were respected and engaged with support and care. They brought her to a beautiful private room, placed a full-time nurse in the room. And we—her community—started the process of repair.

A few events: Gaines wisely asked the doctor if NYU had a Trans Patient Advocate. Bryn became very upset. "Gaines", she admonished, as though he had done something wrong, when actually he did exactly the right thing. She was angry that she had been revealed as trans—even though she had just tried to kill herself—because she'd already learned the hard way, many times over, that this exposure, in an institutional setting, could lead to more pain than she could bear. The doctor, with recognition and responsibility, acknowledged that NYU did not have a Trans Advocate, but that they should have one.

I then tried to phone her therapist. The public clinic she attended for therapy was a disorganized bureaucracy with no provision for emergency contacts. I was given an endless run around, for hours. Finally, Kelly Googled the whole staff list until she found someone's home phone, and in that manner, I got to talk to the therapist directly. It did not take long for me to realize that she was completely inadequate to the task. She was young, inexperienced, had never had a suicidal patient before, and didn't even bother to come to the hospital. The situation was clear. Despite all the love in the world from her friends and partner, Bryn Kelly had not been getting the quality of professional care that she needed in order to solve the pain of her life enough to fully live it. Some hours later, Bryn beckoned me to her bedside. She was soft, vulnerable and open. She held my hand. "Why did I do this?" she asked. "Why did this happen?" We started talking. She told me that she had become so angry that she couldn't think of anything but hurting the people close to her. As she described it, she experienced small events: normative conflict or normative frustrations in close relationships as these hugely threatening, catastrophic assaults. This anger was not focused on hostile institutions, inadequate services, or incompetent and indifferent practitioners. It was tunneled into anger at the people who loved her and a desire to punish them. I would call this process "cumulative pain"—a combination of anxiety and oppression—where the pain of one's life becomes focused onto the person or people right in front of you, the ones who are there to be blamed because they love you. And therefore, the pain gets expressed by destroying these people, these relationships and ultimately one's own life, thereby leaving the exterior structures of oppression fully intact, unburdened, and unaddressed. After recovering medically, Bryn spent some time on the psychiatric service at NYU. I visited her there and she seemed to feel it was a beneficial experience. But when she was discharged, I was concerned. Bryn's doctors wanted her to go into a program to deal with her substance use, and she did not want to go. That is when I knew, truly, that this cycle was not over.

This time, when Bryn finally took her own life, the path to destruction engaged these same unresolved issues. She had been doing very, very well. The last time I saw her she was energetic, engaged, caring, fun. We danced outside Saint Mark's church to a Christmas band. Just two days before her death we planned a group dinner at my house. Friends were commenting on how happy she seemed, that her medication seemed to be working. How well she was doing.

Then, as in every person's life, Bryn had a normative conflict with her partner. But the pattern of trauma combined with anxiety, and long experience with depression, of course kicked in. And because no method had been developed in her life of what to do when it kicked in—she became very distressed and began to destroy. She drank a bottle of vodka. And I want to say here, that no one I know has ever killed themselves sober. She wrote an extremely angry and punitive suicide note that expressed a kind of tunnel vision of rage at the people closest to her. And the note was so focused on hurting other people that it contained no real recognition that she was actually ending her own life. Her note showed an interior logic, way out of sync with what events were actually occurring in the exterior world. Many times I have wished that she could have spent the day in 12-step meetings, called her sponsor, and asked her friends and doctors for support to hospitalize herself back to the positive environment at NYU. But, because of alcohol and depression, the fact that these conflicts were entirely resolvable eluded her completely. That there were many options eluded her. While she did invoke the many suicides and deaths of trans and queer women in recent years, listing their names in her letter, it was only to momentarily claim in her rage and pain, that ultimately these deaths had no impact, which is the opposite of the truth. These deaths have devastated us and, clearly, they contributed to Bryn taking her own life.

No, the drunken, anxious, tunnel vision of her letter was a singular, one-note designed to hurt a few people, the ones who loved her the most. In fact, the note assumed that when Gaines came home from work, and found the door barricaded, and discovered her dead, he would call the police, who would be the ones to deal with her body and the death scene. But in fact, Gaines forced the door open, saw that she had hung herself, and then he and Nogga cut down the body, cut off the noose, and tried to resuscitate her through chest compressions and mouth to mouth. But she was dead. Then they called the paramedics who laid her out on the floor of the front room.

For the rest of the night, those of us who came over were confronted by Bryn's corpse on the floor of the apartment, her arms extended and her hands open. I sat with her body for hours, dealing with the police, the detectives, the medical examiner and then the transport workers, identifying the body. At each interview level, to the officer, to the homicide detective, to the medical examiner, I said that same sentence. "She was a wonderful person, with a beautiful partner and many caring friends." "So what happened here?" the police would ask. "She didn't have a system for tolerating frustration," I said. I signed the body identification form. And in that time, I spent most of the night looking at her lying dead on the floor. This was not her suicide fantasy—lying on the floor with a police detective scotch taping her noose to her leg, her loved ones crushed, her sisters and community threatened by her example. The police officer stepping on her bed with his shoes.

There were many acts of kindness that night. I particularly remember Elias volunteering to call Bryn's mother, and tell her what had happened. He had a deep, caring sense of responsibility, kindness in the way he communicated this terrible information. I saw Nogga and Jax gently clean up after Bryn's body had been removed by the police transport workers. Nogga's loving mother and sister, making tea. Dr. Zill Goldstein, who Bryn called "the only doctor who ever listened to me," giving her history, privately, to the medical examiner. And all the friends who came to love Gaines, to hold him, to be truly with him and to give him all the love that he well deserves. This is what we do when our friends take their own lives. These are the details of those consequences. This is what suicide really does. It causes nothing but despair. It does not get revenge. It ends a life filled with love and promise. It deprives the world, and it causes more death. Just as the suicides of queer and trans women before contributed to Bryn's death, we must make sure that Bryn's suicide does not continue to cause the deaths of others. Please stop this idealized fantasy that suicide will satisfy any need, when all it does is cause more pain. We must stop killing ourselves. It is an act of violence, helping to create a violent future.

After her body was finally removed, we started the well-worn, modern ritual—now habitual—of calling people around the world so that they would understand what had happened, before they saw it on Facebook. We all spent the next day taking care of people, letting them know gently, and in person, that Bryn had taken her own life. As I had this multitude of conversations, each one causing pain, I kept thinking back to that time in NYU, Bryn in her hospital bed, holding my hand, asking "Why did this happen?"

Finally, late in the day, I talked to Morgan Page on the phone, and she illuminated something very important for me. Morgan pointed out that Bryn had never stopped seeking a solution. That she had repeatedly attempted to find treatment. She went to many different kinds of clinics, and engaged a wide range of therapists and doctors. She tried enrolling in many different kinds of classes. She constantly tried to find a way out of the problem and into her own real and rich life. And then I realized the obvious. Bryn Kelly died, not because of a lack of community—she had a wealth of community. She died because she was poor and could not afford the sophisticated level of treatment and support that someone so intelligent and complex needed in order to fully live her life.

I now believe that Bryn Kelly died of poverty, of lack of services. That had she been able to be sure of secure housing, had she been able to enter an immersive, individuated full service environment that recognized and valued her, as we here all recognize and value her, perhaps her life could have been saved. But without it, she could not get to a place where the frustration provoked by normative difficulty did not become an emblem of all the grotesque institutional oppression and erasure and burden that she had been asked to bear.

I do not view Bryn's death as a failure of our community, but rather as a wound on our loving, caring yet fragile community assaulted regularly by a punitive and indifferent system. We must stop destroying ourselves, while letting the institutions that are hurting us, stand, unopposed. In this case, our love could not overwhelm that institutional cruelty and abandonment. But that does not diminish how much we all give each other, and the beauty and the power and the wealth of how much we all love and care. We have to stay alive, and fight like hell for the living.

MMP: So here's my eulogy. Much easier to get through, I promise.

Of all the hussies in this whole rotten, hussified world, this Hussy was my favourite. Even before I knew her personally, I was obsessed with Bryn. Her pseudonymous writing struck a chord of recognition in me that I'd never felt before. It was as though she were writing directly to me, a feeling I think many of us here shared in one way or another.

Bryn and I were, in her words, "pretend rivals/frenemies or whatever." I've never met anyone else I felt so directly in competition with, not only artistically, but also often for the attentions of the very same trans mascs. The first time we dated the same man, I was green with envy. I thought, in horror, "she's prettier than me." In a short, two year, fit of jealousy I even grew out my undercut to compete with her voluptuous locks. And by her own admission the jealousy was a two-way street. I was the Eve Harrington nipping at her heels. But for all of this, our friendship never turned sour, as it so easily could have.

Bryn's wit was a rapid-fire mixture of high and low brow—a complex bricolage seamlessly pairing Dolly Parton with Preciado, Halberstam with Stevie Nicks. Around her more than anyone else I felt like I needed to keep on my toes—to step up my game as an artist, as an activist, and as a fellow MTF4FTM masc hunter.

Many knew her as a party girl, as a performer, as a hairstylist, and as a writer—an aloof and sometimes capricious social butterfly. But to some of the luckiest of us, Bryn meant so much more. Her presence in the world, as the first trans woman I've ever met whose whole thing was so close to my whole thing, made me feel like it was possible for me to exist in the world uncompromising.

To those who were close to her, Bryn was not just the brilliant raconteur and beautiful artist. She was a keen listener and emotional support. In 2013, when my boyfriend died suddenly, it was Bryn who called the ambulance and stayed up for hours dealing with both the cops, who didn't want to take the call, and my own shell-shocked reaction. Throughout the most painful thing I have ever experienced, she showed me incredible kindness. It takes a lot of hurt to make high-riding bitches like us, but that same hurt endowed her with a deep well of compassion.

When all was said and done that night, she wrote these words to me, which I think are relevant for all of us here this evening. "So, this is going to be hell, I can assure you. But you will get through it, because you are strong. End Oprah-talk." Thank you.

TY: What we would like to do next is to open the conversation to all of you, if you have questions or comments you want to ask either or both of them.

MMP: Or just want to say.

TY: Or just comments you want to say.

Q1: This is for Sarah. It's Sarah, right? There's a couple of things that you mention in your political sermon that I understand your point of view—I understand what you wrote—from your position or from the other side, like as a friend so close from Kelly and for so long, and I've been helping her for so long, I can understand what you went through yourself and what brought you to write all of that.

I've been suicidal for twenty-five years—actually right now I'm going through a crisis, with the help of some friends. And I think it's interesting what you said, but if I may, I think there's a misunderstanding about what being suicidal means. Some people have it as an obsession, some people it's revenge, some people it's sickness, but it is more than—you said she didn't have a system to deal with frustration. It's true if we see it at a binary level, but it's so much more complex for some people, like myself. It's an obsession. It's like I live with it every day. Every day if you give me the choice between death and life, I will choose death. But I stand up and live because that's the option that I think is relevant, because it's the good thing to do. But this doesn't mean that this is something that my soul is torn about. Sometimes it can also be physical, it can be cognitive. It can be something that I'm missing from the youth that I cannot even . . . ah, my English is not perfect so I don't have all the words to say so. I think it's way more than that for Bryn. I understand the revenge that Bryn had, that somewhere it was just a way to yell this suffering that she couldn't explain or express and that the only way that she found was to hurt because she was so hurt, but I don't think it was just because of the system. And I understand the goal is to discourage youth to kill themselves, and it's true it's a violence process, but I do that the love—I really, really think that Bryn could not make it to twenty-five years old if she did not have all that love. I already told a best friend before a suicide attempt I wanted to do, "if I did please cry, but remember I'd been successful to get through that until that time." Because for me, I didn't even know I could get to that point. And since that day, I'm still alive, and I'm like "oh, I'm alive, whoa that's awesome." But for a suicidal person it's like a sickness, it's like cancer. Every day you make it, it's wild. So, I don't feel like it's a waste—it's not a giving up. It's the end of a battle, yes, and it's hurtful for everyone around. But that person had fought for so many years, that person had failed and succeeded but that thirty-five years? She made it. And that for me, it's awesome. So, every time someone dies from suicide, I cry because it's like, "man this is the end of a battle," but me I'm still standing up so I'm going to continue to battle until I fall myself. But we continue fighting, and that love that you've all given to her? That's what make her get to there. That's the way I see it.

SS: Thank you.

MMP: Yeah, thank you for that. I really agree with you that it's not a failure of a person, that it's the end of a very long struggle, generally, and that is the community around a person that enables that person to continue going on. I think that's very, very true, and I think one of the things that I think a lot about because so many of the people that I know have committed suicide is the responsibility we have to each other to provide that kind of love and that kind of support, even, and especially, when, as Sarah speaks about in the eulogy, or political sermon, even when there are no services available or when the only available services are transphobic or racist and inaccessible because they're expensive and all these things I think that's why I think as a community we need to be showing people love and helping people through extremely difficult times, you know? And I think this is one of the things we wanted to get to, that part of that responsibility is not just when someone comes to you and is like "I'm feeling suicidal." It's a responsibility that carries through all of our interactions with each other where we, I feel, you may not feel this way. Your mileage may vary. But I feel we have a responsibility to each other all the time to de-escalate all kinds of conflicts that a person is having. When someone is having obsessive thoughts or suicidal ideation, for example, to be that sounding board, to help bring that person back into a way of looking at the reality of their life, or the reality of whatever situation is going on, and making responses that are equal to that reality, you know? And this goes beyond when someone is having suicidal ideation, when we're having community conflict. Queers love, we love yelling on the internet and we love going on Tumblr and tearing each other apart. One of the things—I have this friend who is a poet. His name is Stephen Ira; he's a trans guy poet, he's super brilliant, you should follow him on Twitter. He's @supermattachine on Twitter. And he says that—I'm loosely quoting him—because we're in a suicide epidemic, it's irresponsible of us to, essentially, try to destroy each other. The responsible choice for all of us, since we're all at risk, is to actually have the difficult conversations, where we sit down with people and try to de-escalate conflicts and try to respond with responsibility and accountability to each other in ways that are fair and equitable for all parties involved, you know? That's some of the things that came up when you were speaking, so thank you.

Any other thoughts people want to dive into? I can talk all night. I have, like, pages of things I can talk about. Been makin' notes for days [laughter]. Yes.

Q2: My question's for Morgan. I just wanted to dig in a little bit more to your initial reaction to the draft that you first read. I've known Sarah for a while. I've always known her to be a considerate person who is about the conversation, so I guess the most disturbing thing that came out of this for me, as someone who didn't know Bryn but who did know a lot of the people who were very much affected by this suicide was that somehow she was using this as a political line to centralize herself within a situation that no one would want to center themselves in. And so when you guys talked about the difference between political sermon and eulogy that was really striking to me because perhaps there's an irreconcilable chasm between those two concepts, like, would it be more appropriate for Sarah to talk at someone's funeral if she were trans and that was the political sermon and would it be more appropriate as someone who was very close to Bryn to only talk about what was good about her as a person rather than as a part of the larger socio-cultural matrix. And so I guess my question is for you because you're central within those matrices as someone who really cared about this person and as someone who hews so closely to that identity politic, that sense of who can speak for whom. I guess I wanted to know what were the things you thought were inappropriate and, like, what was you're—if you don't mind, sharing them.

MMP: Totally. Um, so when I first read Sarah's speech, I read it, and my eyes just like opened like "whoa that's a lot." I thought it was a very, very powerful piece of writing, which is unsurprising because I've been a follower of Sarah's writing, I generally find it to be quite powerful. There was only one thing—well two things, really—that I objected to that I asked to be changed. And one of them was—it was just one sentence. It was kind of a gruesome sentence about the state of Bryn's body, and I understand why Sarah would include this because the point of this is to dissuade suicide. One of the conversations we were having as the organizers were going back and forth about whether or not this is appropriate and who should be saying what was the idea of suicide contagion and suicide clusters. So as some of you may know, but perhaps some of you don't, when a person commits suicide—particularly a prominent person—it tends to trigger suicidal ideation in many, many, many people around them and because Bryn was so prominent we, in particular, wanted to take pains to make sure that a suicide cluster, as it's referred to in the literature, did not occur, and I felt like the rest of Sarah's speech without this one line that was kind of gruesome could adequately convey that. That was kind of the consensus we had as organizers. I mean, I can't speak for everyone else, but this is the impression that I got. You know, we asked Sarah to change it, and she did.

The only other thing I asked her—I didn't ask her to change it— but I talked to Gaines about was the mention of Bryn and Gaines having what Sarah calls a normative conflict, essentially a big argument. Because I had a really tricky experience when my boyfriend died and the reactions I received particularly from people who didn't know him, of like blame in these weird ways, which makes no sense. He died of an unexpected medical condition. You know, it was a very weird experience. So, I was like, "just as your friend who want to protect you, Gaines. Have you thought about the reaction people could to hearing that you had a fight with Bryn?" Because as we all know, sometimes queer community is a really intense game of broken telephone, where one phrase can suddenly be drawn out of proportion and suddenly two weeks later we can hear, like, "Gaines hit her! And the police were called!" And all this, which none of this happened and none of which is at all the root. So, it was more of a like, "let's think carefully about this." But to me, one of the reasons I—it was Gaines and I who were so fiercely and strongly advocating amongst the others for the inclusion of this. One of the reasons of this was that Bryn and Sarah were close, closer, I think, than I was to Bryn, and Bryn held Sarah's, what I've called her steel core of moral fiber and her insight really on a very high pedestal in her life. And Bryn was not a person to mince words if she had something to say and I felt in reading the speech that this was something Bryn would defend if she heard this being read at somebody else's funeral. I felt like it was something in line with her own thoughts. So, I felt like that was good.

Some of the reactions that happened centered around the fact that Sarah is not trans. And I found that really interesting because they all came from people who were not close to Bryn, which is always interesting to watch, when you're close to a situation and then you see people who you don't even know reacting to a situation that you're actually a part of. And, for us, Bryn's whole life wasn't just being trans. She was a very active member of the queer fun community in Brooklyn. She was—even though she did not identify as a lesbian—very active in the lesbian community. In fact, she once judged lesbian fiction at the Lambda Literary Awards, and she posted about it on her blog. She was like, "my favorite activity is judging lesbians" [laughter]. And so, to me, I think sometimes we fall down a bit of a rabbit hole where we think that only a person who is exactly like this person can talk about this person and I think that doesn't talk about the truth of who that person's community was. You know, it doesn't talk about the many different communities that a person can be part of. You know, god forbid, I ever succumb to my various thoughts, but I don't think that it would only trans people saying interesting things or difficult things at my funeral if that happens, god forbid. In fact, one of the things that I posted in response to Sarah is that, well, I hope when I go, Sarah has something really intense to say about it [laughter]! But that's my punishing impulse deep inside my head and the fact that I think her insight is so valuable. I don't know, does that answer your question?

Q3: Sarah, so I wanted to thank you for posting your eulogy online, because that's where I read it. And it really, and fairly dramatically, changed the rhetorical relationship I have with rhetoric of suicide, like it really helped shift the frame for me. And one thing that was really quite powerful and awesome about hearing about your conversations with Bryn's partner was that it really felt to me that the act of that eulogy and the way you built the service was that you really wrapped love around Gaines at a really crucial moment. So, I wanted to hear you talk a bit more about that, the community act of caring for someone in such a difficult position.

SS: I don't think I can say anything as articulate as what Morgan just said. I mean, you know, queer people, our culture, we're locked in blame. We're locked into finding out who is the bad person, finding out who they are and making sure that they get punished. And I wish we could change that to trying to understand what's happening. I just think that trying to understand what's happening will help us a lot more because I'm old—I'm fifty-eight years old—and I've never seen punishment do anything positive. I just don't think punishment works, and I don't even understand what the goal of it is, to be honest. And so, that was part of the—and also Gaines is very, very young and it's very traumatizing, and we just wanted him to feel the love that is there for him.

MMP: To piggyback off that a little bit, right before we jump into you. Actually, no, I'll just let it go.

Q4: Actually, it's kind of along the lines of the last question, but kind of, and I guess it's for both of you, there's just been a lot of talk, like, outside this talk there was a panel on Black Lives Matter and one of the speakers was talking about how we should be shifting from a space of self-care to a space of collective care. And I guess in talking about this, especially from your positionality, being so close to this person, but also having to do this work in thinking about it as a political sermon rather than maybe as something for yourselves as the people who were close—maybe my question's getting a little bit off—but just in talking about the idea of self-care versus the idea of collective care and what that means to you.

SS: I haven't gotten to the self-care part yet. I've never gotten there. No, you know, it's because I'm coming from AIDS. That's influencing everything, and, you know, I do experience Bryn as an HIV-positive person. And I think that is part of her death. This was my instinct, was to do it this way because this was the way everyone I knew in ACT-UP or whoever who died of AIDS that was how we handled their death. When a person dies for reasons that are social as well as personal, and you're talking about an oppressed community, it's my natural impulse to articulate both of those moments.

MMP: I think, in terms of self-care versus community care, I think it's really difficult for people in my age group, not that I can speak for all of us, but I think it's very difficult for us to understand generationally what the AIDS crisis was like and the very different way that people were interacting with each other in care relationships. One of the things that a lot of people don't know is that the lesbian community in particular stepped up to be in person caregivers for so many people before better medications were available. And I think this is something we can learn from, in terms of suicide and in terms of so many other things going on in our community, that we can step up for each other in ways that can affect the outcome. And that stepping up doesn't just mean— though it does mean—showing up to the hospital. It also means being a patient advocate, and it means taking that advocacy even further to ensure that someone like Bryn isn't put on the men's ward ever again, not just in her case, but in all cases, you know? I think, to me, that's what collective care looks like, when we not only show up on the actual day, we don't just show up on the night Bryn dies to take care of Gaines, we also continue to show up to make sure that the social conditions that Sarah outlines so eloquently are not reproduced, that we do everything in our power to stop them.

I think one of the other things about Sarah's political sermon that I so valued and also found shocking was how political it was. You know, I've been to so many funerals. I'm twenty-nine years old, and I've been to fourteen funerals and that's not all the people I know who have died. That's just the funerals I could get to. And I've never seen something like this happen before, where people were willing to stand up and say what actually happened, especially for, I don't know how it is in other communities, but I feel like in white communities we have a very delicate way of speaking about tragic events that have happened so that no one gets upset anymore and we can slide it back under the rug where we keep the racism and all the other things we don't want to talk about, and I feel that what Sarah is to take away the rug and make us not look away, you know? She describes the scene that night so that you're not idly imagining it, so that you have a concrete idea of the effects that your loss, in my case—I'll just speak for me—I had a very strong idea, then, of what would happen if I did the same thing, which in the four months preceding Bryn's death I had been thinking about every day, you know? And to me, that made me stop and think, as much as sometimes life feels unbearable to me, I can't bear to put the people that I love, even if I'm in a mood where I'm like "I want them to feel pain and I want them to know how bad they hurt me." Even in that moment, I can't imagine putting those people through that. Like knowing the details of that takes the wind out of the sails of that for me personally. Again, I can only speak for my own experience, but that's what comes to mind.

Q5: So, I just wanted to echo back the brutal honesty of describing suicide attempts and suicide and how much that helps the community to talk about what's happened. And the next thing that I want to say is that I feel that I'm hearing two conversations here. I'm hearing a main conversation about suicide and what that looks like and how that affects our community and another conversation is sort of like one that we're all laughing at about conflict and how everybody at one point in their life has had a conflict with someone in this room. And I want to know if you two can connect those two. I know that when I came to this event, I did a lot of thinking on that and I realized that every suicide and suicide attempt that I've ever witnessed has involved alcohol and also a normative conflict while somebody's in a mental health crisis. So, my question is specifically for both of you: How can people in the framework of knowing that everybody is possibly suicidal and trans or oppressed or anxious or just bad at conflict can support each other in a collective way that prevents suicide, that prevents eviction from housing, that prevents all these things going in the community every single day?

SS: Well, I mean, you can't fix all those things, right? A lot of people here know that you can't control people's alcoholism and their addictions, right? However, we can make things worse for each by, I'm gonna quote myself here, overstating harm, which is the subtitle of my new book, by acting as though things that are difficult, uncomfortable, and upsetting are cataclysms and crimes of the highest order, when they are not. And if we can take down the accusations, and the condemnations, and all of that, we can make each other's lives a little easier. We have control over that.

MMP: I see it as the critical importance of de-escalation in our lives. Again, I'm very influenced by this book Sarah keeps referring to, which just came out. It's called *Conflict Is Not Abuse* and if you want copies, we have copies you can buy later. But I feel like we have these conflicts, and this is very true of my own suicidal ideation, I have what I would describe what I would describe out of the state as a normative conflict—like, someone disagrees with me, or someone yells at me on the internet, or a boy broke up with me and was a dick about it. I have these normative conflicts and then my mind spirals out of all reasonable scale of what has happened. So, for example, someone dumps me for a cis woman and I lose it. And I'm calling my friends and I'm like "he's the worst person who ever lived, I hate him, I'm so mad." And I'm just like freaking out to everyone I know, when in reality it's just a break-up. It's not the end of the world; it's not like we have children together, which even then would not necessarily be the end of the world but might be a heightened thing compared to two people around thirty who don't have children and don't live together who, you know, were just seeing each other for a few months. But I think that it's really important for all of us to step in and de-escalate these conflicts, including when we see people blowing up at each other and when we see ourselves blowing up at each other we need to able to step in and be like, "what is the actual problem here?" Like if a person made some political faux pas, which no one is saying, is a great thing, just that justify socially isolating them? I think this is one of the big problems we have in queer community. We pay a lot of lip service to prison abolition, but we don't actually internalize that in our lives and how we interact with each other. The logic of the prison is isolation, and the number one danger to queer and trans lives, other than outside violence, is social isolation. I work in the social services, I've provided services for trans people for many years, and every one of my funding applications the number thing we're trying to reduce is social isolation, because when you're isolated you become hopeless and you despair and you also have no access to resources and people who care about you. In the queer and trans community, unfortunately right now in this moment, we have a tendency to, as Sarah says, catastrophize small conflicts which, again, no one is saying there's no bad things happening, but often we're taking very small conflicts and catastrophizing them and calling for the removal of this person from community spaces and saying, "oh, you can't come to this queer space anymore because you said something transmisogynistic and that was hurtful to us so you're not allowed to come." Often, this isolationist move comes without terms, so there's no terms for repair, there's no room for nuance about what each party thinks is happening, so, for example, recently someone didn't know I was a trans woman and exploded at me on Twitter for making a joke about trans woman stuff because they thought I was being transmisogynist, and they, like, blocked me and made all these horrible jokes about me and photoshopped pictures of me. It went completely berserk and there were all these other people feeding into it, and I was like, "I'm sorry to disappoint you, but I'm not cisgender. I am, in fact, transgender, and I'm pretty sure that means I can say whatever I want about my own body." And I feel like this is one particularly ridiculous example, but there are examples where there are genuine conflicts going on where a person has done something shitty, or has been accused of doing something shitty whether or not they understand it as something that's shitty, and things just spiral out of control. I think, again, I would just call it the importance of de-escalation. We need to be able to step in and say to our friends, "I see that you're having a huge blow-up with this person. How are you? Can we talk about this? Can we meet in person and talk about this? Can I help the two of you sit down and talk about this?" I don't know what we can do, but we all have to deal with each other. I don't know if you've noticed, but Montreal is a small island. It is a very small island and you're going to run into these people at events like this for the rest of your life.

SS: Morgan, you recently wrote on Twitter, and you suggested that we reintroduce the word heartache and I think that's right, you know, instead of saying, "that person did this terrible thing," just say, like, "my heart is broken. I feel really sad. I feel really upset. I feel really frustrated."

MMP: Before we get to another, I just want to talk about this specific one. What I was thinking about when I tweeted that was that I see every day, especially on Tumblr, people who are having normative conflict with their partner—again, abuse is very real and that is not what I'm talking about. I'm talking about people who have break-ups, and I'm implicating myself in this because I feel the same way when I go through a break-up sometimes, where you break-up with someone and the only terms we have to talk about it are that this person has done something to me, when in reality it's just a break-up. Sometimes, I'm like, "what would straight people call this?" Oh, right, it's breaking up. That's what it is. I feel like there's a resistance to talking about our own psychology when talking about conflict in queer community, because we are very, very invested in only looking at things on the kind of identity politics or socio-political levels. We're not often willing to talk about thoughts and feelings and how they influence situations, because everything is so politically clear-cut and is only political, including our break-ups, which are always political, that we can't really talk about, "oh, I'm really upset, or this really hurt my feelings. I am mad at this person. I feel disrespected by this person." We can't ever talk about that, so we always—it's almost like a distancing technique where we step outside of it so that we can just deal with the anger part of it and the punishment part of it, by being like, "this is the biggest political crime that has ever happened!" This trans man dumped me for a cis woman and he's clearly being the biggest transmisogynist who ever existed and he should never have friends ever again, Which is not really a reasonable expectation when you step back and look at it a little more objectively. And I think it's the role of friends of community members to sit us down and be like, ok, let's look at the order of events, let's look at what happened and figure out a response that's in scale to those events, you know? That's just my thought.

Q6.a: What I was going to ask, in regard to what you were talking about before, I feel like I see a lot of queer activism-type stuff in my surroundings of basically white university queers that feels very etherealized almost or like—I guess if we're talking about the distinction between political and personal stuff, I guess it's almost more personal than political. I feel like I've heard you talk somewhere, Sarah, about how we talk about it about in terms of personal stuff rather than the structures that exist which is kind of to an extent what you were getting at in the sermon. And that's something that I think about a lot going around Concordia or whatever—it's like no one ever talks about AIDS, you know? Like ever. So, that's what I was thinking in terms of how I feel like it's almost too personalized or like detached from, like, structures and whatever that suck. But then on the other hand, I agree with what you just said about how when we talk about our personal conflicts we make it very political so it's like, on the one hand, when we should be talking about the political structures that make things hard we instead talk about the personals, or not necessarily personal, but like less concrete stuff, like we don't talk about this law sucks, we talk about . . . I don't know! I just feel like I see so much Concordia queer stuff that's just very, like, airy and like, I don't know, I feel like you get what I'm saying. Like, not to do with an actual concrete thing you can do. But on the other hand, when we talk about, like everything you just said: When we talk about personal conflicts, they get super highly politicized, so it's like a weird . . . so anyway, I guess the question here is, like, do you have anything to say about this seemingly opposite direction or movement between activism and personal stuff or between political and personal stuff?

MMP: Small question! Sarah, do you have any immediate thoughts? Well, sometimes I think we displace what's going on in our lives, and I think this is part of the root of this catastrophizing of normative conflict where we walk through the world, especially those of us of particularly marginalized identities, where we are dealing with so much garbage 24/7—we're dealing with it from people on the street, we're dealing with it trying to access medical institutions, from trying to deal with the government on any level in any way, and we have basically zero power to change that, or at least we feel that way, most of the time. And then in our personal relationships, and this is part of what Sarah talks about in her speech, is about how we move all the pain and anxiety of that onto the people closest to us because we know we have an effect on them, because you can see the hurt in someone's eyes when you tear into them, and there is some part of our lizard brain that finds that very satisfying in a way that we will never find trying to deal with an institution satisfying because you can't hurt an institution. You can't get an institution to understand that you felt pain. You can't get an institution to empathize with you. And you rarely can get an institution to apologize to you, and when you do it's always like Stephen Harper trying to apologize to indigenous people. It just comes of real awkward and does not address the real problems and does not come up with real solutions, you know? So I feel like sometimes our politics can be very vague in terms of what to do because we honestly don't know most of the time, especially— you're talking about people at Concordia, people on campus who are like eighteen to twenty-two mostly, there are some people who are older, but mostly eighteen- to twenty-two-year-olds who are very smart and very earnest but who do not have often access to an older generation and a legacy of activist tactics that could be used to change these situations, right? Like it takes a long time to meet the Sarahs of the world who tell you, "OK, now this is what we're going to do," or, like, "let's brainstorm about what we're going to do to change this bwaaah horrible thing" or whatever, you know? When you're like eighteen to twenty-two and you're like a first-year university student, who's just become politicized, you don't have access to those tools yet. It takes a while to make those connections and get those tools. I don't know. I'm just rambling now.

Q6.b: Yeah, I'll be fast. I think basically, what I realized, as you were talking, was that I was phrasing it as if it were an opposite movement thing, but I think it's more of a thing, as you were saying, where we want to unload the political stuff onto the personal stuff, right? In both activism, in like talking about immaterial things, and in like conflicts in terms of like unloading the political stuff . . . anyway . . . yeah, sorry.

[audience deciding who will ask a question next, and in what order the questions will be asked]

Q7: Yeah, what I wanted to say was, going off of what you were saying, Morgan, about how we're socialized into a prison-industrial complex culture where punishment and punitive measures are the go-to, and that for me means that these aren't really skills we're born with, and, in fact, our human compassion toward each other and our lovingness and our kindness get sort of clouded over by all of the trauma and exploitation and oppression that we're experiencing. I live and work in Ottawa, and one of the things I've been trying to do and a bunch of us are now starting to do are gaining skills around conflict mediation and conflict coaching and affirmative listening, getting to what's actually going on underneath the content and conflicts, and then we are bringing them into the queer community, so we've paired up with a conflict community conflict mediation organization that is now doing a training for just queer and trans people and that will give us access to practice nights with them and long-term we have a goal of building a queer conflict mediation team. A bunch of us are going to do like respectful confrontation training. Basically, what I'm trying to say is that it's actually really hard to put these de-escalation skills into practice especially because there's so much personal involvement. Like when people that I know and love are in conflict, I'm really stressed out. Sometimes, the skills that I do have just go right out the window because I'm in my feelings and not able. Basically, what I'm trying to say is encouraging people to say, like, "I don't have these skills and that's ok," because none of us are born with them, and as part of a community practice of strengthening our community and strengthening our relationships with each other, that should be something we intentionally invest in.

MMP: I completely agree. This is part of why I'm trying to shove Sarah's book down everybody's throat in my personal life. Everybody's who's been around me has heard about Sarah's book nonstop, because I've been like "we have to talk about this!" Not because I think you have to agree with everything that's in it, but because we need to have this conversation desperately, and I think the things that you're doing in your community in Ottawa are incredible and exactly the direction we need to take and it takes a lot of deprogramming to take out these ideas we have that the only conflict resolution we have is punishment, you know? And that's really hard! We've been taught that for hundreds of years, you know? And it's reinforced on every level every day, and it's a really difficult but really, I think, fruitful thing to do. I have said on Twitter several times that I have this rule now—several of my friends have started referring to it as the Morgan Page rule, which makes me feel like such a jerk—where I will not talk shit about trans women in public. Period. Because it's not helpful. It's not helpful to anyone. If I have a problem with someone I'm going to go to them and have a conversation with them, and if it's not worth have that really difficult and awkward conversation, then it's not worth freaking out about. But also, part of the reason I say I will go to that person is because I do not think it is useful to try to mediate conflicts on social media in front of eight million other people who are not on the same page about conflict resolution. That doesn't end well. I've never seen that end well. So that's what I have to say about that.

Q8: I just wanna say thanks to you guys. I feel a lot wiser, but I also think it's really brave to bring forward political eulogies that are contentious. And I thought it was also a really brave intervention for you because we don't always agree in our communities, and I feel like I really learned a lot from the discussion. But I guess I'm just curious because I'm personally very scared of making political errors when I'm speaking and I wondered how you folks weather when people disagree with you and how you continue to be courageous in bringing forward interventions that speak to when we disagree with each other and hanging in there when we don't, understanding that folks have been really gentle and kind tonight, but it's still kind of feels hard even in those situations and then kind of how do we continue to do that. I myself hate to make political errors, or just to say things that people politically don't agree with, and that makes it really hard to have difficult conversations in our communities.

SS: I have no fear of in person conversations. But some stuff online is way too much for me. It's just very overwhelming. But you can get to a point, for example, I'm a very strong pro-Palestine activist, and I get in discussions with other Jewish people who don't agree with me all the time. At a certain point it's not worth pursuing. You don't have to keep going until you're screaming at each other. You can see right away that it's not gonna go, so you can let it go, like, I made my point clear. So I know in person when to stop trying to convince the other person, or when I'm not listening anymore. Online it's just so much harder. For me, part of it is, again, this generational thing. My relationship to technology is very different to someone in their twenties, and I find it really dehumanizing sometimes.

Q9: Just on the topic of internet conflicts, and sort of responding to that, and another thing is that, you were talking about how, for you, conflict on the internet is harder than conflict in person. I just wanted to talk about another chasm that exists between people is that for many people because of things like political status or social capital or race or reputation or body of work, it's really hard, if not impossible, to address people in person. I think the internet is amazing in how it bridges that gap and allows, like, a person of color with comparatively little or no social capital to address maybe the most politically significant and well-known person in rad queer circles right now and I think that's something to be celebrated and is really amazing, so, yeah.

MMP: I think it can have that power. Where it can have problems, for me personally—where it kind of breaks down—is the kind of "dogpile" effect that happens, where one person has a critique and has something they want to challenge another person, and then eighteen million other people who aren't involved in the situation come and escalate. Where suddenly it goes from this person said and did something that hurt me or was politically fucked up, to now, five people coming on in increasingly catastrophic language saying that this person is the worst person who ever lived, or on Tumblr saying that this is a trash person, this is a garbage person, and these people should not exist anymore in community. This is why I definitely think the internet can be—I'm from a different generation than Sarah; I'm obsessed with social media, even though it gives me total anxiety all the time but I'm totally addicted to it. I'm surprised I haven't been tweeting right now: It's because I'm concentrated on being present with you all today [laughter]. But I think a problem for me is that these conversations are done for the public, sometimes, more than they're done for resolution, that there are instances where people are trying to make a point to other people uninvolved in the situation rather than trying to resolve a conflict with the other person. I don't blame people for that because sometimes I feel that way, too, and I feel we are very encouraged to do that all the time. But I think that this is maybe not the most helpful way to de-escalate and resolve a situation is basically my hot take on that. But I do agree with you that it can be a very democratizing force, by ensuring that those who feel voiceless have a less anxiety producing way of getting their voice heard. I think that's really important. I just think it's complicated and difficult.

Q10: You were talking about institutionalization, and you were talking about the health care that Kelly was seeking, and you were talking about collective care. Do you think that there's a way that what you're doing tonight could be a beginning of the renaissance of collective care? Because the truth is we have been fighting for legal rights, and we do have enormous progress socially, and when you come to helping each other, we are not that strong. That conversation right there is a start on a subject we should discuss more often as a whole community. Do you think something can be done—because we cannot change the institution, you know? We are the victims of it. So, what can we do?

MMP: I think collectively, over time, we can change institutions, but I do think that this often begins with changing our personal relationships, the ways that we react to interpersonal conflict and the ways that we move through the world. I think that's very real. I feel like my head would get very large if I thought that this night was the beginning of a renaissance in the trans and queer community to change all of our ways of interacting. But I do hope that it's the beginning of a conversation here in Montreal for all the people in this room (and our fabulous friends from Ottawa and Toronto) to take these conversations back and try to engage people with them, I guess, to try to continue this conversation.

Q11a: My thing is kind of like picking up on some things that have already been said. I wasn't sure what to expecting by coming tonight, but I'm really appreciating how I'm hearing a lot of different things coinciding, because for me, the presence of suicidal ideation in my life and the lives of people around who we're mutually trying to keep alive—it's a lot of things that coincide all at the same time. And it just feels like you're just sitting in this wind tunnel that is life all the time. I really appreciate bringing up the role of alcohol and addiction, particularly in a community where you feel like you have to participate in consumption to be anybody or in order to go to anything that happens you need to drink, and if you don't drink, then you're alone or you feel like you can't go to things. And I appreciate talking about how we create or escalate conflict, and I guess that what I'm having all these realizations about as I'm sitting here that the number one thing that leads me to those dark places where I consider suicide is two feelings. One is feeling isolation and when it's combined with feeling overwhelmed. It's like I feel super isolated and I don't know what to do because everything feels like it's too much. And it's not just that my problems are too much. It's that the solutions are too much. It's that everybody's throwing a million solutions at me, fucking online memes about self-care twenty-four hours a day, or, like, fucking start a Wicca practice and that might make you feel better. And it's like I can't handle the enormous amount of work it would take to solve the problems in my goddamn life, and I think that the thing that sometimes makes me feel better is realizing that I'm not really gonna solve the problem that is my life. I guess that's the number one thing that makes me feel better is when I realize that my feelings of isolation combined with being overwhelmed are primarily a symptom of larger systems. For example, I think self-care is a product of austerity, really. I think this moment of self-care comes from austerity, because there's no social services to gain access to any fuckin' shit that's gonna help me and so they're like, "here's a scented candle."

[laughter]

MMP: Take a bath about it!

Q11b: Yeah! Meditate and shit like that! And I'm not saying that none of these things help. I don't mean to tease. If a candle really helps you, then more power to you, but my point is that every time I feel super overwhelmed, when somebody makes that connection to the larger thing, I feel a little bit lighter. Because I realize that I often feel like I'm shouldering everything personally. And having that moment that actually I'm not shouldering it personally, that I'm shouldering it collectively with everybody else who has to deal with life under austerity, with everybody else who has to deal with this world of postcolonial, Christian separation—like all these things. That it comes back from somewhere, I think, helps me and that's why the thing I'm taking away from tonight is that I'm very glad that you did take the risk of doing a political sermon. I know it's a personal risk that you take to stand up in front of people and do something like that. And I think that's valuable, because I think that sometimes being able to connect our personal suffering to larger political frameworks reduces isolation and makes something overwhelming maybe a little more clear. I don't have to agree with everything you say, but I really like that you're saying it.

Q12: I just wanted to thank you so much for the generosity you have about this issue and for me I didn't really know what to expect today as someone living with HIV and actively involved in HIV activism, I've known ten-plus people who have killed themselves in the HIV movement and know more people who have died of killing themselves than have died of AIDS since I've been alive, so connecting that to the structural and political issues, as you did in the political sermon, is really important and has given me some things to contend with, to think through how to connect those dots to a political system which is a lack of care and a lack of support for people. I'm also wondering, because a lot of the people I've know who have taken their own lives have been in these leadership positions, they're stars in the community. Kyle, who was a like a mentor to me, and taught me how to be an HIV activist and claim rights for people with HIV was a major person in the trans community in Toronto. And we assumed he has this network of support and care because he was a leader, and he didn't. I just wanted to thank you first of all for this and I was just wondering what you think about this idea, this gap in support for leaders in our community.

MMP: I think I can best express this through what happened with Kyle. So, Kyle Scanlon—I think I mentioned this earlier—was a huge activist in the community for over a decade. He was a gay trans man in Toronto who did an astounding amount of work to make sure that we had the few social services that trans people have today across the country. He was my coworker. We worked directly beside each other and we talked all day, every day for three years about suicide. We talked about it all the time because we both dealt with it like many, many people in the trans community do, and we had a unique position because we were both in leadership roles. And one of things Kyle talked about that was relevant to him and, I think, relevant also to Bryn was that people in leadership positions and artists and well-known personages are assumed to have access to supports that they don't actually have. In Kyle's case, he couldn't go to any social services because he ran all the social services! There were no counselors for him because every single one of them were his friends and colleagues. He knew, and had to maintain a work relationship with—he didn't have access to the FTM support group that he used to run because he used to run it. He didn't have that access, and additionally, because he was a leader, he was subject to repeated acts of cruelty because we believe that people in leadership positions within the queer and trans community are open season. If you have a problem with someone who is in a leadership position, if they didn't acknowledge you at a party, if they hold a position that you disagree with, or they've legitimately politically fucked up or something like that, we believe that because they are a leader, they must be made an example of. I've had this happen to me. There are a lot of people in this world who don't like me, who have a lot of really mean and nasty things to say about me, some of which are true, and I'm totally willing to take accountability for those things, and I try to move through the world doing my best to not repeat those issues. But that doesn't stop those people from doing cruelty toward me, because they really, really want to see punishment. We kind of put our leaders up on a pedestal. We're like, "where's the leader? Where's the leader? Where's the leader?" Then we elect someone leader, basically, or someone gets a job—this is the Canadian model—where suddenly they're a leader and then everything about their life is open season. This is literally why when I quit my job—I used to run the trans services at the 519 Church Street Community Center in Toronto, which is the LGBT community center—when I quit my job, I, the very next day, moved to Montreal because I knew that I would never not be seen as the person running that job which means I'd just be doing that work for free for now, which happens. I get called on all the time to do this work, support work, all kinds of work for people in Toronto. And I'm just like there are other people who can do this work for you. Also, having had that leadership position, I was always going to have my personal life and everything I touched be examined with a fine-toothed comb. Through that leadership position, I had people file complaints about or go on Tumblr and write long posts because I was dating someone they had a problem with like three years ago. And I'm like, "I don't even know what's happening. Why are you coming after me," you know? This is all just to say that leaders are in a particularly tricky position because we're often the ones who are running the services, who are being the supportive people, and so we don't have access to those service.

And at the same we justify any act of cruelty against leaders in our community because they're an example of how everyone else should live. I don't know. Sarah, do you want...?

SS: We need to consult [inaudible]. Two more!

MMP: Two more questions.

Q13a: Should I do like a turkey thing and talk up to the...?

MMP: It's ok [inaudible]. Let's light a candle about it [laughter].

Q13b: Just to reiterate what you are talking about and what Alex brings up, there are two documents called "Living and Serving 1 and 2" that talk about the problematics of trying to access services as an HIV person when you're part of the HIV response. And part of it is definitely I've had difficulty trying to access because it's like I know this therapist, I've sat on a committee with this person, this person's a former lover, but then it's also the same of having to admit that you need services. So, you get a job, and you get put in a leadership role, and specifically if your work is around social support, then to have social and emotional stuff that you need to work through seems like a particularly personalized emotional failing. That prevents folks from accessing services. I know that it's prevented other people, but I will name that it's prevented me as well. And we talk about—I really appreciate the wonderful humans from Toronto who talked about the work of doing de-escalation and acknowledging that we have a limitation of our skillset, and recognizing that this is a thing that we've been taught to do that harms our communities and our movement building. So, we don't know how to do different, so let's learn how to do different, and that's great! I just wanted to say, for folks who haven't heard before, or wanna do some googling, like restorative and transformative justice are the terms used to talk about to the prison-industrial complex punition model. And I would also just say that using restorative and transformative justice models to respond to intimate partner violence is not always ideal and that it can put a lot of the burden of the emotional labor on the person who has survived an assault. So just being aware that that's a thing?

Also, through this conversation another kind of gap has appeared in some of the—like I work for a community health center and I run a street outreach center for people that are homeless and use drugs—and one of the ongoing conversations that we're having that I feel like has become apparent tonight is about grief and loss. We're talking about how we deal with complex and elevated emotional states. So, I've been hurt and/ or I've been pissed off and/or I'm mourning a loss, so the harm reduction movement is, unfortunately, experts at dealing with grief and loss and multiple loss because everybody fucking dies all the time. So, seeking out training—this is the other thing too. There are just no available mental and emotional health services in Canada, like, it's just not a thing that exists, so we find other ways of coping. But there's also tools that we can learn and we can share with each other about how to unpack and process some of complex stuff that we're handed just by existing.

SS: Thank you! Last one?

Q14a: Super, super psyched about your book. These thoughts have been trailing around for a while. So, I guess I really appreciate the conversations surrounding differentiating conflict from abuse, and also kind of owning your trauma and subsequent reactions. I just sort of wondering, because of the conversations around care and healing that are often happening in Montreal. We often have these circles, particularly queers, that are looking to heal, and we can do so together. And because of the way that trauma functions, and the way that we're recreating our trauma reality, you've got these queers that are basically in the process of retraumatizing each other. And so I guess I'm wondering how to kind of deal and mitigate that while this conversation about community care and accountability is happening and when I'm talking about this I do mean abuse and not conflict. I'm gonna read your book; I'm super psyched about it, so if you can answer [inaudible].

SS: I don't totally understand the question.

Q14b: Yeah, I guess it's like this conversation of like while we're talking about community care and showing up for each other and ensuring that people aren't just [inaudible] and stuff like that when these are happening in our relationships, and especially our most intimate relationships, that stem from trauma and how we often recreate these traumatic pairings within our most intimate relationships and how to deal with both of these happening at the same time. Does that make sense?

SS: It's such a complex construction. I'm having my book launch tomorrow at the Concordia bookstore. It's a three-hundred-page book and I haven't learned how to say "duddle duddle duh," you know what I mean? But tomorrow I'm going to really lay out a lot of tropes and ideas, so that might help. I just don't have a soundbite answer for something like that.

TN: On behalf of QED, I just wanted to thank Sarah and Morgan. Let's all thank them for a wonderful time [applause].

SS: I just wanted to say that I've heard a lot of things tonight that I've never heard before, and I really, really appreciate it and I'm definitely gonna think about it. This was very enriching for me. So thank you.

MMP: Thank you all for joining us, and especially those of you who had to stand the whole time, I'm so sorry. Personal apology for that. Also, we have a bunch of copies of Sarah's book, and some of her other books, and some of my books for sale if you're interested in buying them. If not, that's great. You can probably get them from the library. Well, you can't get my books from the library, but I'm sure...anyway. Just putting it out there!

SS: Is somebody gonna be selling them?

MMP: Yes. Our fabulous friend Asher is gonna be up here wheeling and dealing with you.

SS: And, Morgan, you're going to be signing yours, right?

MMP: Of course. I like to feel like a celebrity. So, thanks everybody so much!

CRACKS IN CIVILIZED LANDSCAPES
Adriana de Luiza and Ife da Sylvia

"Cracks in Civilized Landscapes" (2013): a Project by Adriana
(de Luiza) and Ife (da Sylvia) 13 channel Video Installation
+ performance + photo installation + music + poetry + love

"Cracks in Civilized Landscapes" is an experimental multimedia work that challenges architecture (private homes, religious, institutions, hospitals, military building, monuments, etc.) as a patriarchal authority (sexual hierarchies and distinct gender differentiation). Filming ourselves (me and my girlfriend, in the process of fucking in a church, a castle, a museum, a bank and other monuments, we try to deconstruct their sacred, heroic and sexist dimension). We infiltrate these buildings to decipher the oppressive power beyond their formal aspect. (Spaces determines, control, affects behavior and participates in defining the sexual division of labor.) We use sex as a revolutionary process of desecration, "the phallic nature of modern multi-tower block, concretely, represents an era which has been dominated by patriarchy, authority, and hierarchy, which has been brutally molded by the forces of colonialism, imperialism, and state domination over many hundreds of years. This way large-scale architecture provides the most dramatic visual examples of the relationship between space and power." The project is punctuated by an abstract poem, which recalls how language generates gender. This work was created with a lot of humor.

Some places where we fucked: 1 Camara Municipal do Rio de Janeiro, Brazil (Government building) / 2 Tree Park Slope Brooklyn, New York City / 3 Empire State Building, New York City / 4 Basilica of St. Patrick's Old Cathedral, New York City / 5 Islamic Cultural Center of New York City / 6 San Joao Fort in Urca Rio se Janeiro, Brazil / 7 Metropolitan Museum, New York City / 8 Chase Bank

Wall Street, New York City / 9 Eiffel Tower Paris, France / 10 Arch of Triumph Paris, France / 11 Louvre Paris, France / 12 Limousine, New York City / 13 Castle Switzerland / 14 Church Switzerland / 15 Airport / 16 Brooklyn College / 17 Castle Poland

More about this project here: https://adriana-varella-3h26. squarespace.com/cracks-in-civilized-landscapes.

Photographs that follow on pages 181 through 186 are by Adriana de Luiza and Ife da Sylvia.

NO DIA 30 DE DEZEMBRO DE 1903 O BISPO
D. JOAQUIM ARCOVERDE DE ALBUQUERQUE CAVALCANTI
DA CIDADE DO RIO DE JANEIRO RECEBEU ESTA URNA DE
MADEIRA, DORADA PELO BACHAREL ALBERTO DO CANTO
ELA CONTÉM OS RESÍDUOS MORTAIS DE

PEDRO ÁLVARES CABRAL
DESCOBRIDOR DO BRASIL

ELES FORAM EXTRAÍDOS, NO DIA 14 DE MARÇO DE 1903
DA SEPULTURA DE CABRAL, QUE DESDE 1529 ESTAVAM NO JAZIGO DE SANTARÉM
NA IGREJA DE NOSSA SENHORA DA GRAÇA EM SANTARÉM, PORTUGAL

ROSEANNE BARR VS. ROSEANNE CONNOR
Jewelle L. Gomez

I always enjoyed Roseanne, both Barr and her creation Roseanne Connor. Barr seemed like a genuine character who pushed her way up with wit and brashness, kicked ass and took no prisoners. She had a woman's perspective on marriage, poverty, raising kids, food, and living on the margins. And in her role as a stand-up comedian she seemed to have a flinty-eyed wisdom that suggested she could not be taken in by charlatans.

What was also extraordinary was her willingness to be vulnerable enough to create an alter ego, Roseanne Connor, who reflected the struggles Barr—raised working class—had faced in her life. Roseanne Connor was a full-bodied woman, whose self-love and independence were unapologetic (even though Barr's weight and face were often under construction). But both Roseannes were funny and spoke to women who felt disenfranchised. Barr/Connor seemed to step into a role that might predict she would be narrow-minded but she usually was not.

Watching the revived Roseanne show I am having a difficult time finding the humor, because Barr now represents Connor (and seems herself) as falling for the greatest charlatan of our generation, Donald Trump. She then reintroduces him to us (her old fans) and to the next generation of viewers as the hero.

The danger here is that the current Barr/Connor is funny sometimes. So, those folks still living on the margins, still without health insurance, still worried about having too many children are laughing along with someone who is willing to ignore how their economic disadvantages are being exploited by an egomaniac. Of course Roseanne (Barr, not Connor) is wealthy now just like the politicians who want to erase health care and trick people with fake tax decreases. Unfortunately, a Barr bon mot is clever but does not clarify why working class and poor people should support

188 of Sinister Wisdom 110- Dump Trump: Legacies Of Resistance

someone willing to pull the health rug out from under them to satisfy his vanity and his racism. The Connor avatar is anxiety-provoking because she normalizes this unacceptable behavior.

#45 represents so many despicable issues it is hard to know where to start. So, I will begin where my great-grandmother would: he is ill-mannered, as if he were raised in a barn by the cows (sorry, cows). It goes downhill from there. I will skip the bigotries and chauvinism that infect him, all of which are a reflection of his lack of interest in democracy and any of the institutions that support democracy. My love for the show *Hamilton*, notwithstanding, democracy is a completely imperfect system that continues to disenfranchise too many people. But it is a system which expects citizens to repair it, not dismantle it—that's what all of our social movements have been about. #45 is dismantling our democracy like the maniac in *The Texas Chainsaw Massacre*.

All the while marginalized poor whites think this is their chance to find hegemony again (which they never *really* had) by pushing people of color and independent women back down to their "place." I think poor whites' biggest fear is that people of color and women will treat them as oppressively as upper-class whites and upper-class men have treated them—or even as dismally as some of them (poor whites) have treated people of color. So what does it matter that insurance companies reduce their healthcare options, if they can have a sense of power over some other disadvantaged group. So they turned to Big Daddy to save them and give them legitimacy, so the scary not-smiling-enough woman would not win.

Barr/Connor proclaims support of #45's slogans as if they are true accomplishments rather than noise. The Roseanne Barr/Roseanne Connor I thought I knew would be able to see through the blow-hard and recognize his sleight-of-hand. She would hear the pieces of our institutions being chipped away and clattering to the Oval Office rug, she would hear the Constitution and the Bill of Rights being shredded no matter how #45 tries to deflect our attention with his noise.

Instead Connor goes retro: unable to confront an unruly adult daughter who hogs the washing machine and flies into a fury at a daughter who wants to be a surrogate mother. All this weak, whiny behavior that we do not expect from *our* Roseanne is disturbing. It cloaks #45 in a fog of normality, so that people get used to his noise rather than hearing it and the other "noise" it distracts us from.

She's mute on her gender queer grandson, although the administration she supports has diminished his rights to serve in the military, much less let him to use a public restroom of his choice. (Roseanne Barr has a gay and lesbian brother and sister and insisted in the early days of her show that there be queer characters.) And we do not know where she stands on the Black granddaughter who so far only appears in the opening credits. (Is that so #45s black constituents have someone to relate to?) Since the administration she supports promotes the rights of Nazis and White Supremacists, to whom miscegenation is verboten, even on television. Maybe both Roseannes should get a food-taster.

Roseanne Barr's new Roseanne Connor reminds me how dangerous #45 is, and he is made more so as a former feminist icon normalizes his behavior. He has to go and I am just hoping we are tuned into Roseanne when she realizes it.

INVERTEBRATES

Jean Lee

My mother scurried from kitchen to bathroom to bedroom to bathroom, panting and sweating. She collected every textile thing in a red plastic egg crate to wash at the Laundromat two miles away on high heat. I sat, stripped naked, on our mattress, stripped naked, fixated on a flea. The flea floated above the exposed padding, its body surging from side to side. It had wings but refused to fly away. I sat and watched, and I sat and listened to the sound of my mother's movement, her panting, and whimpering. Then: silence. Then, feeling the static of familiar steps, I turned to see my mother holding a white T-shirt. Her wire-frame glasses drooped down her sweat-soaked face, pinning her nostrils, and she squinted in my direction as I draped the worn cotton over my body. It fell, cloak-like, below my knees.

"Don't go next door tonight," she said as she walked back to the doorway, where she picked up the egg crate full of fabric. "They're dirty."

*****

We existed on the periphery of pastoral backcountry where we subleased one-story houses, connected kitchen to bathroom, surrounded by dense pinewood forest. The houses were maintained by a management company, which administered short-term leases based on the percentage of annual income. Lawns flourished and sidewalks crumbled, revealing loose soil below. My house shared a damp, discolored wall with Bee's house. She lived with her mother who rarely left the bedroom. Burdened by the tenacious ache of dysthymia, Bee's mother stayed in bed, where she slept soundly.

Every night, I opened Bee's unlocked door and entered her dimly lit house where she sat in the living room, the smell of musk in the air and on her skin. I piled the couch with my mother's throw pillows and my plush toys. Then, on her damp carpet at the foot of her makeshift bed, I told her stories about girls in fantastical lands. I whispered until she fell asleep.

*****

The T-shirt's frayed hem swept my knees as I walked to Bee's house. As I approached, I saw her sitting in the open doorway, surrounded by pieces of her looping, curling hair the color of cast iron. Her mother, out of bed and kneeling before her, held her hand and asked, "Why, Seulbee?"

"How could you, Seulbee?"

Bee just sat smiling, fondling her new feather cut.

Her mother, too distressed to deal with it all, let go of Bee's hand and staggered back to their bedroom. I heard the door click shut as she retreated, and Bee's smile vanished. I moved to clean the mess, imagining bundles of hair running through my fingers, faint and subdued like pooled water. But, when I grabbed a fistful, the uneven layers were coarse and brittle.

As I cleaned, Bee watched me, immobile.

Before sleep, I sat with Bee, nestled between pillows and plush toys. I held her sylphlike body while she sobbed. She laid her face on my shoulder, her tears running through the seams of the T-shirt, while I brushed her jagged hairline with my fingertips.

"Are you okay?" I asked.

She looked up and opened her mouth to respond and coughed up tears, unable to swallow.

*****

I returned to a quiet house, clean clothes and cloth on the kitchen floor, separated into two piles. In the moonlight, I saw my mother's jeans and work uniforms, kitchen towels, and sheets in one pile; my play shorts, T-shirts, and school dresses in another pile.

"Were you next door?" My mother's voice stood in the dark. "They gave us fleas, and I spent all day cleaning."

She lifted me up, hands beneath my armpits, an eerie embrace. And then she dropped me onto the cold tile floor.

Photograph by Saskia Scheffer

Lesbians don't owe you SHIT

THIS TIME

Denise Conca

try to eat right try to exercise try to take it easy flax is gone and the little store across the street where i bought my lottery tickets and a sign i don't understand is posted on the building in the next block "proposed plan of development" are they tearing down this building and the hotel on the corner are they building over the parking lot and the other parking lot and the union hall what about that the other day goodwills gone when i pass hydraulic equipment for demolition sits atop a big block size pile of rubble i'd seen the sign here that announced goodwill is closing and then the blue fence that went up around the side on mission and around the entrance on the corner and up van ness and it's all gone and though i'm just a block away i don't think i heard any of it especially not over the sounds of pilings being pounded into a large hole in the ground by a large crane where the flax was and flax's parking lot which is where the building site is accessed by the big trucks and heavy machinery in a gate in the fence off of mccoppin which is where i mail letters i written, typed because the pickup on the postbox is listed as 930am and i have an idea that means the letters will get there faster i'm not invisible but somehow as if i've slipped through the cracks all of us here in this building except the guy who jumped out the window in his apartment on this floor, my neighbor, who the building manager said lived in his unit oh probably fifty years and who landed after jumping out in the middle of the night after calling the building manager and the guy who lived next door to him—the guy who lives between me and him—for help and then landed on our other neighbors who live in tents below on the sidewalk behind our building and who were awoken quite terrifyingly i'm sure by a person on top of them on top of their tent and of course the police came and the ambulance and then the cops even came up here to the fifth floor at which point i also woke did i hear the cops banging and knocking on my neighbors door saying sfpd open up and i got up and out of bed and took a piss i think it's 3am and then watched through the peephole at the activity in the hallway wondering as i stood there watching and listening would i answer if they knocked on my door and then went back to bed at this point i didn't even know what happened until the next morning going to work seeing the sticker over the neighbors doorjamb sealing it in effect by the medical examiners office with a threat of felony prosecution for any tampering and i got a text from my other neighbor on the second floor whose window is right above the tent and landing spot and he wrote he heard a loud crash and then someone yelling "what the fuck?" and the ensuing sirens etc no i'm not invisible not someone as obvious as me but surprising to myself as my female body ages and i find my body rounder with more curves and larger breasts lined face even i have to believe my passing more a result of the current political climate yes even in san francisco than any choice of personal presentation i'm making more and more often being called sir or this man in a wide variety of settings not just the public bathroom of the pfa but in grocery stores on the street in the library and at walgreens where the person was profusely apologetic actually uncomfortably so as i tried to explain to her it's understandable the confusion taking the responsibility for being misperceived myself not feeling as though i had the capacity to explain this moment as a rise in fascism and what that means politically economically and personally and is best described as a disembodiment or a separation of self from physical body in a way individualness cannot be expressed even seen the spectrum of personness so narrowed and limited as to be just as a mere shadow a projection a buyer in the marketplace solely production regulated even of self "severe economic and social regulations" this moment of agonizing harrowing requirements of constant consumption and resulting deterioration of the public sphere including the closing of sam's shoe service on sixteenth volvo repair on valencia mission market on harrison and the countless places that have opened and closed in the past three years which never even came into my consciousness so not intended were they for me who is still living here on market street in this moment of increasing terror and desperation no longer seen as middle-aged butch dyke not lesbian nor even woman but as this man

MISSISSIPPI HOUSE BILL 1523

Amy Lauren

soft rain
    kisses the shore
sunset soil
    nestles the rain
& the bayou
    does not mind
        who I kiss

"TERRIBLE! JUST FOUND OUT THAT OBAMA HAD MY WIRES TAPPED IN TRUMP TOWER JUST BEFORE THE VICTORY. NOTHING FOUND. THIS IS MCCARTHYISM!" @realDonaldTrump

Lorrie Sprecher

Francine and I watched Giant Orange Toddler's first solo press conference since taking office, an unhinged, tragicomedy that lasted seventy-seven minutes. "I'm here today to update the American people on the incredible progress that has been made in the last four weeks since my inauguration. We have made incredible progress. I don't think there's ever been a president elected who in this short period of time has done what we've done."

"Let's see," Francine said. "His travel ban was blocked for being unconstitutional, his national security advisor just resigned for lying to the vice president about his ties with Russia, and he repealed the right of transgender students to use the bathrooms that match their chosen gender identities. Well done, sir."

The toddler berated the media for being "fake news," then turned as usual to himself, bragging about his three hundred and six electoral college votes. "I guess it was the biggest electoral college win since Ronald Reagan." Barack Obama had three hundred and thirty-two in 2012 and three hundred and sixty-five in 2008. "I'll be in Florida on Saturday, and I just heard that the crowds are massive that want to be there."

"How does he measure crowds that haven't gathered yet?" I asked.

"Alternative math?" Francine suggested.

He boasted about his deportation squads who were keeping America safe and mentioned the "forgotten victims of illegal immigrant violence of which there are many."

"You know he wants to deport all illegal immigrants to Mexico," I said, "whether they're from Mexico or not. All brown people in the southern United States originate in Mexico, like the Guatemalan Mexicans and the Venezuelan Mexicans."

President Screaming Carrot declared he was assembling a cabinet "that will be one of the great cabinets ever assembled in American history."

"Is that before or after his national security advisor had to quit?" Francine asked the television set.

"No, Francine," I said. "He's building a cabinet from IKEA. He's putting it together by himself."

"Isn't IKEA a Swedish terrorist group?" Recently Trump had mentioned a terrorist attack in Sweden that hadn't happened, and Sweden, the country, was having a fabulous time mocking him.

When Trump finally took questions, an orthodox Jewish reporter stood up and, after respectfully declaring that no one in his community thought the president was an anti-Semite, asked what the administration was planning to do about the rise in anti-Semitism. Hitler Carrot said it wasn't a fair question and told the reporter to sit down. "Number one, I am the least anti-Semitic person that you've ever seen in your entire life. Number two, racism. The least racist person. In fact, we did very well, relative to other people running as a Republican—quiet, quiet, quiet!"

"Oh, my God," said Francine.

"You heard the prime minister," Trump said. "You heard Netanyahu yesterday. Did you hear him? Bibi?" Then he called the question about anti-Semitism very insulting.

"Well, if Bibi gives you the Jewish stamp of approval," I said, "that's final. It's not as if *Bibi* would ever make a deal with the devil to support the unlimited expansion of illegal settlements."

April Ryan, of the American Urban Radio Networks, stood up, and Trump said, "This is going to be a bad question."

"Because she's black?" Francine squeaked.

She asked him about his remarks on violence in the inner cities, and Trump told her, "That was very professional and very good," as though she was his emotional age of four and hadn't been a White House correspondent for the last twenty years.

"Oh, my God," Francine repeated.

Trump blathered on about the unbelievably high percentage of African American votes he had gotten. April Ryan asked if he was going to include the CBC in discussions of his urban agenda.

"Am I gonna—?" Trump asked, confused.

"Are you going to include the Congressional Black Caucus?" she asked.

"Well, I would. I'll tell you what, you wanna set up the meeting? Do you want to set up the meeting? Are they friends of yours?"

"No, I'm just a reporter—"

"Set up the meeting, let's go. Set up a meeting. I would love to meet with the black caucus. I think it's great."

Francine's mouth dropped open. "Is she his *secretary*?" she blurted out. "And are they her friends *because she's black and all black people know each other*?"

"Happy Black History Month."

Later I read an article in *The New Yorker* describing what had happened after the press conference when reporters were escorted back into the briefing room. One journalist asked, "Do you know every black person in the country, April?"

Another said, "April, I have a black friend in Cleveland—could you send him a message for me?"

Ryan shook her head and said, "I mean, I can't even."

On BBC America, Katty Kay said, "It's only a month in, we should add that. It sometimes feels like it's a year in. I certainly feel a lot older."

Photograph by Morgan Gwenwald

Chase dreams not cash

AN INTRODUCTION TO HANNAH ARENDT'S
THE ORIGINS OF TOTALITARIANISM

Fran Winant

This article began as a project I presented in the class, "Resistance, Subjectivity, and Lesbian Lives," taught by Flavia Rando, PhD, at the Lesbian Herstory Archives. I became interested in totalitarianism and the fear that this might be in our future when Trump was elected, or rather, when he was selected by the Electoral College, an undemocratic US institution, over Hillary Clinton, who was democratically elected by the popular vote.

I had once thought that totalitarianism was something that happened to other people, such as the inhabitants of twentieth-century Europe in the Nazi era. Political philosopher Hannah Arendt wrote about that horrifying world from her personal experience. Arendt's book left me with the sense that, beyond an individual leader's narcissism or autocratic inclinations, traits that practically define Trump, and were, in themselves, frightening enough, there was a formula for bringing about a totalitarian political climate, a sequence of events we could see, feel, and smell developing before our shocked gaze.

The formula begins with crowd psychology, the ways that a crowd can be conned and played, and ends with the obliteration of an individual's power to act against what has finally become an all-powerful police state.

In assembling the following formula for totalitarianism, I also enlisted, in parentheses, slogans found in George Orwell's novel, *1984*, which, for me, has the quality of elements of Arendt's work translated into fiction.

THE CROWD

Anonymous:
-No individual responsibility or blame

-Individuals who felt suppressed, powerless, find strength in the mass, the mob

-Different standards of behavior for the mob than for individuals

Suggestible:

-As in hypnotic or religious repetition, simple statements are sufficient, regardless of whether based on truth or faith, logic or fantasy

-Repeated lies become truth, lies continually build on each other

Contagious:

-Ideas spread fast, unstopped by questions, doubts, or reality checks

-Different standards for belief and acceptance of ideas, including confusion about the nature of truth itself

-NOTE: Mass delusion is not a new phenomenon, as seen in *Extraordinary Popular Delusions and the Madness of Crowds*, 1841, by Charles Mackay, highlighting financial delusions, and *The Manufacture of Madness*, 1970, by Thomas Szasz, linking religious delusions about witchcraft with oppressive medical and judicial delusions about gay people. What is new is the way totalitarianism employs manipulation of media to enforce mass delusion as a basis for modern government.

PLUS (+)
PROPAGANDA

Scapegoats, Enemies:

-Groups historically targeted by hate, suspicion, superstition that can be reanimated

-Individuals with different appearances, beliefs, religion, ethnicity, such as women, gays, non-whites, non-men, non-Christians, non-Aryans

-Suspect groups in society such as immigrants, elite intellectuals, the bourgeois, international bankers

Easy Fixes:

-They are criminals, immoral, get rid of them, stop their crimes, kill them

-Drain the swamp, lock her up

-Make them pay, send in the military, bomb them out of existence ("War Is Peace")

Simple Cohesive Narratives:

-Altered descriptions of reality: things would be better for US without THEM

-I love the uneducated who gut-know the real, hidden, denied truth ("Ignorance Is Strength")

-Conspiracy theories: believe me, obey me, the truth is as I say it is, all others lie, are enemies, are engaged in conspiracies against me, us, the truth

-The most effective propaganda results when people come to believe it is their own idea ("Freedom Is Slavery")

EQUALS (=)
TYRANNY

-Total control able to stop any group opposition even if many people disagree with the Leader

-He can lawlessly delegitimize, discredit, insult and mock, accuse, investigate, round up, arrest, imprison, charge with crimes and force into lengthy and expensive trials, torture, starve, deport, murder

-An absolutely powerful Leader does not have to care what anyone thinks

-Even so, "mere" tyranny is only a step to something more

AND THEN (+)
TOTALITARIANISM

-A new form of government for the technological age, simulating the appearance of popular, mass support

-A one-party system enabled by control of all media and, through control of information and the vote, controlling the legal and political system

-The Leader defines who is an "enemy of the people" and which ideas are real or fake

-Control is further enabled by individual isolation, a by-product of capitalism where individual workers are separated from families and social networks

-An educational system that reinforces powerlessness and submission to authority

-Individuals can no longer trust one another for fear of being spied on and turned in to the state

-Individuals no longer have face-to-face personal conversations and thus are cut off from the human exchange that encourages opinions to be formed and tested through free discussion while allowing people to experience empathy and acceptance of one another's common humanity

-People no longer have private and personal lives, their lives belong to the state

-Powerless individuals agree with the Leader who cultivates this agreement through impassioned rallies including public pledges of allegiance to him and appeals to prejudices, fears, hopes, feelings of inferiority and lack, and wishful fantasies

-In a reign of total, unopposed terror, believers do as instructed, act without mercy toward "proven" enemies, accept a world of victims and executioners where such roles can be reversed should the Leader change his explanations of fact and fiction

-Although mass belief was formed through simple ideas such as "Workers will gain power" or "Life will become much better for us," believers will now accept, as the logical product of these same ideas, a world where workers lose even the power they previously had before the Leader took over and where life becomes worse for everyone, with insecurity and unlivable conditions for all

Hannah Arendt locates her hope in the people of the future, that is, in us. Her work reminds us of the importance of maintaining friendships and inspires us to create community and stay engaged in the political process. As an educator, she shares her knowledge in the belief that no one able to understand the horrors of the twentieth century for what they were would ever again allow them to be repeated.

A VOW FOR PASSOVER 2018

Martha Shelly

In these times
when we're driven
seemingly forever
into another Valley of Death
lashed on, the overseers laughing
stealing the flesh on our bones
to forge bombs

In these times I vow
not to leave the slow-footed behind
not to discard the starving, the wounded
I will not weld a vault of steel
around my disappointed heart
will not retreat behind
the gated communities of avarice

When we who are despised
are forced to kneel in dust
with these cracked hands
we vow to gather up our trampled hopes
and rise, and toss them in the air,
to fly.

WHAT HAPPENED AT THE LORRAINE MOTEL: AMERICA'S DIVISIVE POLITICS DID NOT BEGIN WITH TRUMP

Claire Bond Potter

Tenured Radical, April 4, 2018

Long after the stunning election outcome in November 2016, experts and ordinary voters have been turning over the Rubik's Cube of our great national puzzle: how was Donald Trump able to surmount so many barriers—character, elocution, intellect, sexual behavior—to winning the presidency? Many theories are floating around out there, all of them probably wrong. But what nearly everyone agrees on is that this country is more ideologically divided than it ever has been, whether it is the gender war, racial division, class struggle, regional interests, or so-called native-born people activating resentment against immigrant newcomers.

Most of us agreed, long before we understood that there was a deliberate campaign to spread fake news on social media, that digital technologies exploit social divisions and bigotry for political gain.

But is social media the cause of our new civil war? Despite the power of algorithms to match like with like, and turn us against each other, we can't say these divisions are historically unprecedented. Social media does what all media has always done, only better and more quickly: makes it clear where everyone stands.

No media creates division: it expresses differences, and it amplifies them. To paraphrase my colleague Robin Wagner-Pacifici, what media does is make dynamics that already exist visible, to the extent that a moment of change—rendered in media—becomes an event, interrupting our lives from far away. Such an event is a rupture in time, one that expresses our relationship to a particular moment in history.[62] But does it do that

---

62 Robin Wagner-Pacifici, *What Is an Event?* (Chicago: University of Chicago Press, 2017).

at the expense of suppressing our consciousness about a longer past that made the event possible?

The death of Martin Luther King Jr. was just such an event, a stain on American history that is simultaneously unique and, as we know from the history of lynching and contemporary gun violence against African Americans, tragically commonplace. On the fiftieth anniversary of King's assassination at the Lorraine Motel in Memphis, Tennessee, it is worth reminding ourselves that this country could not be more at war with itself now than it was in 1968. The United States was racially divided, and racially segregated, north and south. Our country was also an extremely violent place, and would only become more so in the next decade.

For those of us who lived in and around major cities, one of the questions that always arose in the 1960s was: would it be a "long, hot summer"? This was the term that had come to describe the toxic mix of poverty, oppressive heat, unemployment, and police violence that put urban communities on a hair trigger. You could drop a match and the divisions in this country would erupt in African American neighborhoods. And people often literally did drop a match once things got going. Whether you want to call them urban riots or insurrections, major cities burned in the 1960s, and many of them—Newark, Jersey City, Detroit are a few—have never fully recovered to this day. Should they return to prosperity eventually, it will not be because the vibrant Black and Jewish neighborhoods of these cities have once again flowered, but because real estate developers, sometimes capitalizing on the storied past of these cities, will have built enough glass and steel towers for the bourgeoisie and *haute* bourgeoisie, along with privatized parks, charter schools, and art galleries.

I remember Martin Luther King's death quite vividly, although sometimes—because I was ten—it gets muddled in my mind with the murder of Bobby Kennedy, only eight weeks later. Although the two were assassinated for very different reasons, and their historical trajectories had been quite different, that eight weeks between April 4 and June 5 represented two crucial events that, for many, also represent the metaphorical death of an American history that never reached its promise. That moment is known by historians as the turn from "the good sixties to the bad sixties." King was moving left, embracing the anti-war movement and a sharp critique of capitalism; Kennedy, a McCarthyite and former Attorney General who had failed to intervene more dramatically in the violent suppression of the civil rights movement, had undergone an even more radical intellectual metamorphosis, and was untangling himself from the calamity that liberalism had become.

Could King and Kennedy together have reckoned successfully with the national divisions that had become hyper-visible in the media, most prominently in the "new" technology of television, in the 1950s and '60s? We will never know, particularly since, if we are being honest, these decades themselves were a stage for playing out the consequences of an even longer past, one in which the separation of citizens by race, nationality, class, and gender had been baked into American history and law. These hurdles to national unity included Jim Crow segregation, laws that had been in place for over eighty years in some places by the 1960s; the formal and informal exclusion of Jews from educational institutions, neighborhoods and public facilities; nativisms once expressed through the early twentieth-century Asiatic Exclusion League and the 1882 Chinese Exclusion Act, which sought to end non-European immigration; the late nineteenth-century confinement of Native people to arid, inhospitable "reservations;" the Constitutional, ideological and racial struggles that resulted in the Civil War; in slavery; and the Naturalization Act of 1790, which limited citizenship to "free White persons of good character."

Who can help but think of the language of that first law to follow the ratification of the constitution today when migrants from nations south of the Rio Grande are routinely characterized as inherently criminal and lazy, and Muslims are targeted by our government as potential terrorists?

Is it not also important to point out that the question of "character" lurks not so far in the background of the long exclusion of homosexuals from full citizenship, and the rationale for turning back Jewish refugees in the 1930s, sending them back to Europe to their deaths? And as we approach the centenary of woman suffrage, can we forget that all women were not granted the vote in 1920, nor did voting advance the legal and economic equality of women as a class for another fifty years?

Furthermore, the project of gender equality is radically incomplete in its own way. Federal affirmative action—largely responsible for my admission to a formerly gender-segregated Ivy League university, and for my career as a professional historian—was transformational for many white women and a few women of color. But that transformation had a cost: the agreement to suppress a far older truth: that all-male, all-white faculties were never the natural order of things, but the outcome of decades of exclusion of women and people of color from jobs for which they were qualified. The failure to confront this moral wrong implicitly makes women, and people of color, second-class university citizens to this day. The sexual harassment scandals of 2017 illuminate the fact that the cost of women's progress has been simmering, unending male hostility.

Similarly, mobilizing angry working-class whites is not a twenty-first-century phenomenon, nor does it reflect a new source of division. The so-called "Hands Ad," produced by conservative political consultant Alex Castellanos for Jesse Helms' 1990 Senate campaign, expressed a toxic racial message: "Harvey Gantt Supports Ted Kennedy's Racial Quotas." It predicted the white identity movements that have been reborn in the twenty-first century, reflected racial resentments that were both kindled and suppressed by affirmative action, and drew on a century of fear that competition with black labor would disadvantage white working-class men.

The viciousness of this, and other political advertisements created during the culture wars of the 1990s, shows that, while every media form has its own dynamic and effects, the argument that social media has caused the eruption of *particularly* toxic divisions in this country is quite wrong. Media, even digital media deployed against us by bots, Russian agents, and corporate political consultants, is not the problem. The problem is our failure to confront the fact that our country is historically—not temporarily—divided. Finding your location across these divisions is a characteristic of what it means to be American, even though each eruption, and each event, is new and surprising—even newly traumatizing. Instead of muting and papering over our divisions, perhaps we need to be thoughtful, together, about what has allowed us all to survive them, how we memorialize them, and what we as citizens are willing to do to put our media tools to use to understand and embrace our common history.

This essay was originally published on January 10, 2018 at Public Seminar. http://www.publicseminar.org/2018/04/what-happened-at-the lorraine-motel/

ONE FOR MIKE PENCE

Blanche McCrary Boyd

It was the kind of night that made you ache, and he was the cutest boy I had ever seen. We were in South Carolina, by the ocean, at a camp for young Christian leaders. Mike Pence was a delegate for his congregation, and I was representing mine.

"How many of you are there?" he asked when we were introduced at the first evening's barbecue. His eyes were so guilelessly blue they dazed me, and I dropped a forkful of potato salad onto my foot. Mike knelt and cleaned my big toe with his napkin, and a thrill of feeling shot through me. "I'm alone," I lied.

"I am too, because we couldn't afford to send more people. Reverend Swaggart was inspiring, don't you think?" Jimmy Swaggart had given the opening invocation, broken only by an incantatory *a cappella* version of a country song called "Some Golden Daybreak."

"When he sang 'Jesus will come', I shivered."

Mike and I shared our political opinions. We both thought the Civil Rights movement had been funded by the Soviets and that Ayn Rand was the most important figure in our lifetimes. But I kept staring into his blue eyes and feeling as if I were falling through space. "There's such an openness in you," I said. "I don't know, it's like . . . a vacancy."

"I've heard that before," he said modestly. "It's my simplicity. My clean heart."

Soon we slipped away from the barbecue and found ourselves down on the beach, stranded in the moonlight. "I can't believe this is happening," I said.

Mike's hand reached for my breast but pulled back quickly. He slapped his palm against his leg, as if he were punishing it. "Tell me your earliest holy memory," he said. "And I'll tell you mine."

I knelt in the sand and motioned for him to do the same. "In Sunday school once I had a headache, and the teacher made me lie down while the class marched around me holding little American flags. They were singing "Oh Holy Night', and my headache went right away."

"Amer-i-caaaaa," he half-sang, leaning toward my mouth.

The surf behind us sounded like a chorus of hosannas. "This seems like a dream."

Soon we lay solemnly on our backs, staring up at the silent stars.

"I am anatomically correct," Mike finally said.

"I'm so glad."

"But it's wrong, what we're thinking."

"It's wrong wrong wrong," I said.

"Do you think anybody else will come down here?"

"No, they're all at the lecture." Another evangelical leader was delivering a talk called "Embrace Your Personal Destiny."

"I already know what my destiny is," Mike said.

"I know mine too. I'll produce perfect children from my precious eggs and take good care of myself until I do. Girls should not do anything too strenuous, because we might damage our reproductive organs."

The word organs made us both shudder.

"I'm going to be governor of Indiana," he whispered. "Then Vice-President. And if God wills it, maybe I'll be president."

"I hate liberals," I murmured. "And Democrats."

We turned simultaneously on our sides, our faces close together. "Have you ever thought about this?" he said. "Girls only get eggs once a month, but boys, do you know how many human beings are stored in that amen stuff?"

"Amen stuff?"

"You know." He closed his eyes. "The stuff that makes babies."

I'd read the book *Life and Love for Teenagers*, but I'd never told anyone. "You mean semen?"

"Semen. Yes, that's what I said."

There was a manliness to the way he misspoke, and uttering the word semen out loud to a boy made me dizzy. I picked up his hand and slid his index finger into my mouth. It was a bit sandy, but I didn't mind.

"Oh no," he said, when I sucked his finger right into the back of my throat. He pulled his hand away and bolted upright. "That's got to be wrong."

"Sorry," I said, embarrassed.

.   "Please don't be mad at me. I like you a lot, I really do." He leaned shyly over and began to stroke my arm. "But I am committed to summation."

"Summation?"

"You know. When you have impure feelings and you take a cold shower."

"You must mean sublimation."

"Sublimation, that's what I said."

"I understand, and I cherish my virginity too. But anything else is okay, isn't it?"

"You must be kidding. What church do you go to?"

"The Holy Redeemer. My minister taught me."

"He taught you?"

"Just the kissing and touching parts. He says it's okay but it has to be private."

Soon Mike and I were lost in the sand, and my elbows were getting raw. My shirt was tangled around my neck, my bra unfastened. Mike lay on top of me, and I could feel his hard lump between my legs, like Ken's when you undress him.

"Tell me your holiest memory," I whispered as he began to pump gently against my Bermuda shorts.

"In church," he mumbled, "we were singing 'Rock of Ages' and I could see down the sundress of a girl in the pew in front of me. Oh, oh."

"Move a little bit to the right, Mike, yes, that's good."

"Oh, oh," he said.

We stayed on the beach till dawn, a serious infraction, but it was the stain on Mike's pants that gave us away. I got sent home and he was allowed to stay. I later learned that he had confessed publicly, naming me, but no one in my church ever found out, except my minister, who said he could forgive me but still felt hurt.

Photograph by Morgan Gwenwald

Trump Tower after the election

TINY HANDS

Laura S. Marshall

I stopped in the middle of the street and lowered my sign. "TINY HANDS TINY" and a drawing of a dick. I hadn't seen one in person yet so I had Gabby draw it for me, to get the proportions exactly right, but I added the glitter myself. To the letters, not the dick.

.I had lost track of the chant. At first it was "Not my president! Not my president!" But I didn't chant that because it has a weird rhythm and, well, he is my president. He's all our president, whether we like it or not. But then people started chanting other things, all at once, and the words all turned to noise and I couldn't follow anymore.

The shouts kept moving around me. The people had all kinds of signs. Some of them were better than mine, with better sayings or funnier pictures, but my lettering was neater than most. Gabby's drawing was good, too. Cartoony, but in a good way. Like a caricature, if a caricaturist would draw that portion of the anatomy.

The speeches were a few blocks away still, and we could hear roars every now and then, but none of the speakers' words managed to snake around the corners of the buildings. "Woo-oo!" Gabby yelled a couple times, grinning, her hands in the air, but none of us knew what she was cheering for.

They were only letting people stay in front of the hotel for five minutes. Then you had to move on—five hundred thousand people can't fit in a single block at once. But people didn't want to keep moving, even though this was supposed to be a march. Once they got to the shiny hotel doors, they wanted to stay and listen to the speeches, or scream over them. And everybody had to get a photo in front of the gold name with their middle fingers up. Five hundred thousand selfies take time.

We hadn't gotten that far yet, but Gabby and Ananda and Arvin were getting away from me. I could still see Gabby's hair. She had been growing it out for months, and it hovered around her head like a snow globe of ideas. I wasn't exactly in love with her, but I wasn't exactly not in love. I watched her fist pound the air, her wristband flashing as she yelled something unintelligible over the crowd. The crowd that was carrying her further away.

I held up my sign again and stepped back into the current, slipping past the puffy jackets and pussy hats, the pale limp hair and the steamy glasses. "Gabby!" I yelled, but my voice was swallowed by the chants all around me. "Gabby!" I yelled again anyway, louder.

"Which one is she?" asked a white woman to my right. She was older, gray at the temples, big round sunglasses swinging on a beaded chain. Her sign said, "KEEP YOUR GRUBBY LAWS OFF MY BODY" in thick red tempera paint. She had a fleck of paint on her cheek.

"Um, up there," I told her. "The one with the hair?" Just a few wisps still visible over the body of the crowd, but the woman nodded, mostly to herself.

"Here, this way," she said, and she used her sign to cordon off a path to the sidewalk. "If you run close to the buildings, you might be able to catch up with her." She guided me with a gentle hand on my shoulder as other women paused to let me through. "If you stay in the thick of things, you'll just get swept along. Go on."

"Thanks," I called, but she had already been consumed by the crowd.

The sidewalk was tricky. In theory, everybody was in the street, but in reality the sidewalks were full of onlookers, counter-protesters, parents plying their crying children with snacks. I dodged strollers and shopping bags, no idea what I was stepping in or on, trying to keep Gabby's hair in sight as much as possible, but the faster I moved, the further away she seemed to get. My breath was coming in uneven gasps. At least I remembered to bring my inhaler.

"Gabby!" I tried again when they hit the corner of Fifth Avenue, and I saw her head turn. She stopped moving for a second and looked around; I waved and jumped, but she turned back. And then she and Ananda and Arvin rounded the corner toward the hotel. "Gabby, wait!"

They were gone. They were going to have selfies together, stories about standing up to that glittery building; I was going to have a story about getting lost in a screaming crowd. I stepped up into a doorway and got out my phone to send Gabby a text: *I got cut off. Where do I meet you?* I pocketed my phone and got out my inhaler. I took a puff of the bitter cloud and held it, held it, released. I closed my eyes and tried to breathe peace down into my lungs.

When I opened my eyes again, he was standing right in front of me, watching me through the glass door. His hair was combed back, shiny with grease like his reddened skin; his clothes were dark, so all I could really see was the pale pink thing shaking in his hand. He didn't even grin, just kept shaking it at me through the glass.

I coughed and slipped off the step and crashed into a group of women who were chanting, "Not today, Satan!" I wasn't sure whose side they were on, but I gripped one of their shoulders for a second before I heard a friendly voice.

"Hey, you didn't find her?" The woman from before, with the glasses and the tempera paint.

I shook my head, my eyes still on the doorway. She looked from me to the building and noticed the guy, and she frowned. "Asshole," she muttered, and she took my sign from me. "You see this?" she screamed at him. "Tiny hands, tiny dick? That's you! That's you, asshole! Tiny dick!" She pointed at him, and people around us laughed. He reddened more and turned, scurried deeper into the building.

People kept laughing around us, but I suddenly noticed I was crying. "Oh, honey," the woman said, and she set our signs down and hugged me. She just held me right there in the middle of the bloated city, in the middle of the chants and the signs and the motion. I closed my eyes. After minute or two, I realized she was crying with me, little angry sobs.

When my phone buzzed, the woman stepped back and wiped her eyes. "That'll be your friend, won't it," she said, reaching into her sleeve for a tissue.

I checked the text: *See you back at home. Too crazy to get food around here.* "Are you okay?" I asked the woman as I put my phone back in my pocket.

She shook her head a few times, and then shouldered her sign again, almost taking out a guy passing by. "Let's go get the prick," she muttered, and she took my hand and stepped back into the throng flowing toward Fifth Avenue.

BITCHES BOOKS AND BRUNCH
Women's History Month Bitchfest 2018

YOU GET #TRUMP ELECTED BUT OUR AD FOR #BITCH-FEST2018 DOESN'T MEET YOUR APPROVAL?!?!?!!?!!?#F UCKYOUFACEBOOK #FUCKTRUMP #FUCKCENSORSHIP-MARKZUCKERBERGBLOWSPUTINSDICK #FUCKTHEPATRIARCHY

To kick off Women's History Month this past March, our feminist book club, BITCHES BOOKS & BRUNCH, hosted our first annual opening celebration, BITCHFEST 2018.

Part fair, part festival, it brought together woman-owned businesses and artists for a FAB evening of shopping and partying.

Leading up to the event, however, when we went to promote online, FACEBOOK, who already had not permitted us to use "bitch" in our official Facebook handle, also would not let us promote our event for the same reason: offensive content.

That's right, FACEBOOK, who now unequivocally aided and abetted Russian interference in the 2016 US Presidential Election, would not let us PAY to have our event promoted on their platform because it contained the word "BITCH," which it deems "inappropriate content."

Welcome to America! Where a social media platform may be used by a foreign government to undermine democratic state elections, but where its user-content may not include "profanity."

Explain this logic of offense to us.

bitchesbooksbrunch

BREAKFAST WITH TIFFANIES

E. F. Schraeder

More than half of them stayed home
or fell in line with their Joes and Johns,
wheeled beside them down the grocery aisle
when changing sides
would've made all the difference.

Take note of that empty feeling,
that sinking hope.
They never shop hungry—
nerves taut with wanting.
Tense edges too fierce to tame.

Get to know the contours of desire.
Like a soft hand wrapped around a tight fist,
a dull ache repeats, *you're not enough. Go home.*
Welcome to throwback Thursday—all year.
Some straight white suburban women laughed,

chose to forget how grabbing hands hurt
their daughters. Their sons. Their sisters.
Now they wait at the cutting block. Watch.
The butcher chops off the head first.
Scholars call it internalization.

I WILL BUILD A WALL

Alexis Clements

"A wall," the farmer thought. To mark my land, to keep my crops, to guard my sheep. "I will build a wall." Toiling for months in the sun, the heat as much as the cold, turning up soil to turn up the stones. At the start and the end of long days, always adding more. But it did not keep out the birds, it did not keep out the fox or the wolves, the deer or the weeds, it did not even keep in the sheep. And it did not keep the forest from returning when the farmer went into the earth. The forest just waited, patiently, knowing all along that it was only a matter of time.

"I'M GOING TO BUILD A WALL"

Lorrie Sprecher

The 2016 presidential election was a freak show. An eerily orange-skinned man with pink goggle lines around his eyes named Donald Trump, a man who considers spaghetti with meat sauce adventurous eating and prefers the "cleanliness" of American fast food to any other cuisine, had won the Republican nomination. Francine and I volunteered for Hillary Clinton's campaign. Though we disagreed with her policies on Israel, we knew that dissent under Clinton was a saner alternative than electing a fascist idiot and careening willingly toward global disaster.

The presidential debates were difficult to watch. I screamed at the television as though Donald Trump, Buffoon-Who-Would-Be-President, could hear me. Each debate left me exhausted with a sore throat and a headache. I would have to pause the debate in order to finish screaming, and then I would have to rewind it to hear the parts I had missed because I was screaming. It would take me three hours to watch a ninety-minute debate. I would stop for five whole minutes at a time to scream "*fuck you, fuck you, fuck you*" at his big, fat, stupid face. Then Francine would call, or I would call her, and we would spend the next hour screaming at each other in disbelief. If we watched a debate together, it would take us even longer to get through it because after the screaming, we would have to discuss and dissect whatever unbelievably stupid, offensive thing he had just said to make us scream.

"Seriously," Francine asked, as we drove to Hillary Clinton headquarters to make phone calls the week of the election, "Why is Trump so orange?"

"According to *Mother Jones*, he has a thing for bad spray tans and a friend who's the former CEO of a tanning company. Can you swing by Erie first?"

Every day I drove down the busy thoroughfare in front of Trump headquarters to take down their signs from the median strip. "You can't keep doing that," Francine said. "It's too dangerous. His supporters are crazy, and they're armed."

"The median strip is city property, and I am perfectly justified in removing his signs. If people want to kill me for taking down a fucking Trump sign, they can just fucking kill me." My car trunk and garage were full of red, white, and blue Trump–Pence lawn signs.

When we reached the gaggle of Trump signs, Francine put on her hazard lights while I ran up and down the grassy incline to yank them all out. Other cars did their best to snake around Francine's red Toyota, and I threw the signs into her back seat. "Let's write 'FASCIST RAPIST' on them in red spray-paint and put them back up," I suggested as she merged back into traffic.

We had all heard the recording obtained by *The Washington Post,* which captured Donald Trump boasting about his ability to sexually assault women and get away with it. "And when you're a star," he said, "they let you do it. You can do anything. Grab 'em by the pussy."

During the second presidential debate, one of the moderators, Anderson Cooper of *CNN,* had confronted him. "You bragged that you have sexually assaulted women. Do you understand that?"

In response, Trump babbled about ISIS, the so-called Islamic State, chopping the heads off Christians and drowning people in steel cages. Then he said, "I have great respect for women. Nobody has more respect for women than I do."

Anderson Cooper asked, "So you didn't do those things you said?"

Trump replied, "I'm going to make our country safe. We're going to have borders."

It was the epitome of—well, everything I had been thinking about for the last four years. He was going to make America safe while assaulting women. Countries had borders, but women's bodies did not. In response to his claim that he had not actually attacked anyone, seventeen women came forward to publicly accuse him of sexually assaulting them.

In a court deposition, his former wife Ivana had accused Donald Trump of raping her after a painful scalp reduction surgery to remove a bald spot. During his campaign, Michael Cohen, special counsel at the Trump Organization, defended Trump by saying, "You cannot rape your spouse." The criminalization of marital rape in America began in the mid-1970s.

There was a federal lawsuit against Trump for raping a thirteen-year-old girl, but it was dropped after the plaintiff's life was threatened. Trump was accused of raping her repeatedly at parties thrown by the convicted pedophile Jeffrey Epstein. "I've known Jeff for fifteen years," Trump had said. "Terrific guy. He's a lot of fun to be with. It is even said that he likes beautiful women as much as I do, and many of them are on the younger side."

The editor's note from the relevant *Huffington Post* article reminded us that "*Donald Trump regularly incites political violence and is a serial liar, rampant xenophobe, racist, misogynist and birther who has repeatedly pledged to ban all Muslims—1.6 billion members of an entire religion—from entering the U.S.*" "Birther" referred to Trump's fanatical and long-held belief that Barack Obama was not born in the United States and was, therefore, ineligible to be president.

By February, *The Washington Post* had added "Democracy dies in darkness" as its sub-heading.

If Trump became president, rape would probably be a misdemeanor, an offense as serious as a parking ticket. And now, once again, I contemplated the dilemma of Charles, the man who had raped my friend. I thought about how not fighting violence with violence had worked out for the women of our country.

At Clinton headquarters, people were talking about FBI Director James Comey's decision, eleven days before the election, to announce that he was reopening the investigation into Hillary

228 of Sinister Wisdom 110- *Dump Trump: Legacies Of Resistance*

Clinton's private email server to see if she had used it for classified information. The FBI was investigating Anthony Weiner, a disgraced former New York congressman who had been caught exchanging sexually explicit messages with a fifteen-year-old girl. His estranged wife was Clinton advisor Huma Abedin, and she had some of Hillary Clinton's emails on his laptop.

"Let me get this right," I said. "They find Hillary's emails on a pedophile's computer, and they're investigating *her*?"

It was demoralizing to make phone calls for the Clinton campaign and reach women who were wholeheartedly supporting a self-confessed—not *confessed* as much as boasting—serial sexual predator for president of the United States. It made me wish I had killed Charles when I'd had the chance.

UNCIVIL WARS (AFTER CHARLOTTESVILLE)
Anne-christine d'Adesky

This week the man I did not elect president, a man who should be behind bars and be subject to a historic shakedown – in other words, a man who should be made to consider the full, ugly, inhumane, terrifying, apocalyptic, nation shaking and shaping and blood staining impact of American slavery and racism on our national story – well, he came out. I mean he came out further from the cover of words and the cloak of the Klan robe that his own father might have worn – we are still finding out how deep elder Trump's extreme racism went in terms of Klan membership. The sins of the father are borne by the son, it seems here.

We all knew – I mean us progressives and anti-racists, us refugees and exiles, us queers and pro-abortion rights activists – we all knew he was a mad racist. We knew his blood boiled. It seemed to make his very white face even pinker to think about the dirty Mexicans, as he is so fond of putting it, legally crossing our borders every day, many to do the work to till our American soil and harvest our food in working conditions we would decry as inhumane if someone asked us to do the same, even for a day. When he talks about Muslims, well, his pallor turns scarlet, his eyes become slits through which he seems to have trouble looking, and all he can see is the end of civilization as he puts it. His views as a Christian Crusader have been on full display. This we knew.

Now Trump has really come out; he sided, publicly, via his favorite social media form, Twitter, and then Fox News, and via his unscripted retort to a news reporter, with the enraged, armed white mostly young men and women who brandished torches to, in their own words, retake America, reshape it back to the land of Antebellum and yoke, to massa and human chattel, to white dominion and white culture and whiteness as all that may exist as legitimate and worthy. He ignored their cries to murder Jews, their promise to lynch blacks, their happiness at the murder of Heather Heyer, a white woman, who – crime of crimes to a white patriarch – was a single woman, pushing thirty, who had dared to exist outside the power and definition of a man by not marrying. She was fat – a cow – said the far-right Nazi website, *The Daily Stormer*; she did not deserve to live. She failed to breed, the only good use for women.

Trump did not talk about that unbridled, unrepentant, unleashed, celebratory violent misogyny, which lurks also under the patina of the white culture the new young American Naziklan – a word I quite like – have embraced with such torch-lit fervor. Maybe because Trump is such a misogynist himself he did not bother to notice that element of the white nationalist celebration of Heyer's murder. Trump did not rebuke the angry, young white man who drove his car into a crowd of Charlottesville citizens saying, "No we don't want to see these statues of Generals Grant and Lee in our town squares anymore, because it's a symbol of pure white domination, don't you see?" Oh, but you do see, and that is why you have showed up with your torches and your faces visible, not even hidden by a Klan robe and hood, with dark slits like Trump's eyes when he goes bellicose at the cameras and swears at the fake news media and wishes he had the power to lock them all up, too.

He came out, and now, we have all heard him. Some are shocked; many are not. They are mostly shocked by so many strapping young white Americans desperate to retain their power, steeped in the yoke of an American national story that, until too recently, did in fact present white people, descendants of Europeans, as the only legitimate heirs to this nation and its future. It is always shocking to hear such unbridled racism, such hatred spewing with such furor, released one feels, after years of being thought and felt and likely swallowed like bile after vomit that leaves a bitter aftertaste, the enduring American hangover of white supremacy.

Even before Trump with all the police brutality cases, with Trayvon Martin and Occupy and Ferguson and one after another dismissal of obvious cases of outright murder by white police officers of black men and women, including trans women, we were seeing the rough seams of the fabric of our national story coming apart, being pulled apart by mostly black and brown hands and fingers, bloodied often, working to unravel the skein of a racist culture. The march of the Nazis in Charlottesville is a reply to that forensic work, a reexamination of the structure and roots of racism and white supremacy culture that form the very backbone of our vaunted United States. We can express shock and refusal at the sight of hundreds of millennial wannabe Nazis, and also, we can appreciate that the wolves are being flushed from a resting place of unexamined racial sovereignty.

We are witnessing a fresh chapter of the ongoing Uncivil War, as we should have titled the battle of slaveowners and those who believe all men and women are created equal and should be treated as such. We are witnessing both the actions and the views of Americans who never accepted that equality, who have raised their children to embrace whiteness as an identify that is right and good – and under threat. It is a profane perversion of identity. It has been fundamental to the creation and shaping of these United States, and we are the denialists, not Trump, is we think anything less. It is our oldest drama in other words, a national crimesong, still unspooling its bloody story.

Still, I am taking heart that, for all the torch-carrying white millennials who feel empowered to embrace their inner racism, there are so many others who are finally ready to be true abolitionists, to recognize the history of slavery and racism they have to confront is not only to be found among David Duke's followers, but in their own hearts and minds, in their own education as white Americans. That is the bigger, more important story unfolding here. The jolting re-education, or refocused engagement, of an American society that never completed the critical task of confronting its profoundly racist soul, its racist bones, its racist statues and monuments, its racist teeth in law that, still today, protect the white who are seen as innocent, and punish and murder the black and brown citizens whose main crime is that they are not white.

Now is not the time for polite words, for a mincing of the truth. Trump came out: he is the son of his father, a boy educated to admire Hitler and National Socialism. He views women as objects of conquest, and regards anyone not white as less worthy of, well, everything: respect, rights, property, legal protection, social equality. We can pity Trump as we can pity the young women and men crying out for the blood of Jews and Black Lives Matter activists and queers and Muslims and immigrants who feel America has abandoned them. But he and they are not worth our pity; they deserve our rage instead. Trump does not give an iota of care for us and instead, he wishes us dead, or gone, or anywhere but here, in the America he hopes to reclaim, an all-white, alt-white America.

Last night, last week, today, probably tomorrow, we will see more previously quiet Americans turn up to support the brave activists who have begun tearing down the extant symbols of that old America, the Antebellum America. Who have begun asking themselves, and us, what other symbols of our nation we might erect in the place of the slaveholders Lee and Grant, and who knows, maybe Washington and Jefferson too? We have a lot of work to do now, and it is all fresh, and the blood is oozing up in every city and town square where the roots of slavery have lain entombed in concrete for decades and now, require many hands to uproot.

As we battle Trump, as we vision, another current of energy flows across America, one of justice, one of determination for the project of America, whatever and however we view that vision of equality enshrined in our constitution. I see it, and I am heartened. I see a renewed national act of historic redress. I see a forensic interest in crimes that still demand justice. I see my own children, barely young adults, already deeply steeped in this national conversation about what it means to be a citizen, to have the rights of a citizen to vote, to be protected by law, and what it means for those who lack such protections, but seek and deserve them.

My children are not afraid of Trump. They look to me and other parents, they look to our grandparents, they look at the literature of America and other countries that fought against intolerance and genocidal thinking and they are paying attention. They are learning, and they are ready. I want to protect them from the young would-be patriarchs who drive their cars into crowds of anti-racist Americans, intent on murder. I, like all of us, worry about the violence that is being seeded with this president, with his embrace of the Klan of white America. I am also confident that they will speak out, and act, and they will do their part to, to resist Trump and his white Amerikkka.

Donald Trump came out. His boiling blood racism is now visible to all. His actions and speech will flush more of his kind from their hiding places in the American landscape. Let them come and let us show them that we are the future. The white America they wish to inhabit is not completely gone, but we are committed to its transformation and disappearance, ever more urgently now. Now is the time for action and for vision – hand in hand. Guided by our sense of the firmament of justice, by what we know in our marrow to be good and right and worthy of defending. Our most profound humanity and our belief in our ability to love.

Trump has come out and so have we, the rest of America. We are the far majority, but most importantly, the inevitable arc of justice is on our side. Let us waste no time to help it bend everywhere it must, in all the public squares that still celebrate the Confederacy, in all the sites that demand historic reclamation. We are here and we are ready. We are awake to our past and our future. As in Charlottesville, as in all of America. Our children, too. Woke. Never going back.

Uncivil Wars was written to be read aloud and presented by the author at a "Hex The Patriarchy: Living Tarot" gathering of political resistance on August 17, 2017, in Portland, OR.

STILL MARCHING AFTER ALL THESE YEARS: PHOTOGRAPHIC PORTFOLIO

Morgan Gwenwald

There was a brief period, sometime after Obama was elected, when it seemed like the country had entered a period where decades of work by social change activists were having a visible impact. There were still many deep and ugly conditions to be changed, but there seemed to be a larger possibility for those conversations and that work. At least this is what I told myself as I worked in my tenured librarian position at a small state college in upstate New York. My activist years in NYC seemed to become part of my past, something I occasionally lectured about recorded in thousands of photographs on my studio shelf.

Then it all crashed. In the nightmare that followed I find myself reaching out to old comrades, rejoining the activist community and again putting huge amounts of my non-work hours into projects to fight the brutal madness that had engulfed our country. My garden and my artwork are suffering, but like during the front end of my life, I feel I have no choice. I must engage in the struggle against fascism. Working on the "Dump Trump" issue of *Sinister Wisdom* is a small piece of that work, along with returning (long distance, like Joan Nestle) to Lesbian Herstory Archives coordinator work. I am sure this is the story of many lesbians of my generation. We were fooled into thinking we had a chance at a gentler ending than our beginning.

It struck me as I photographed the lineup of supporters carrying the LHA banner at the NYC Women's March in 2017 that we had returned to our roots. Our banner was over forty years old, probably the oldest on the line of march, and perhaps the only queer banner. (Although in a march of that magnitude, and attending as a marshal not a photographer, I may have missed others).

Part of what sustains me in these dark days is the memory of all who have fought before us, of how we have always had to fight, and that today is no different... ours is a lifetime struggle. (A lesson I learned watching and listening to Barbara Deming during a weekend visit to her home in Squirrels Corners, outside Monticello, NY, during the summer of Sagaris.)

I have assembled a small group of my photographs documenting that banner and the lesbians who carried it in the streets for so many different actions, events, and marches. I hope these images will inspire you, as they inspire me.

I first marched with the Archives banner in 1979. It was an amazing experience, marching in the streets of NYC with hundreds of lesbians (and thousands of queers of all sorts). I had found a community of like-minded activists with Deb Edel, Joan Nestle, Mabel Hampton and other Archivettes. The sign that says "Dan White Means Fight Back" is in reference to the murder of Harvey Milk the year before. Harvey was one of the first publicly elected out officials in the US, who, along with San Francisco Mayor George Moscone, was shot to death by former SF Board of Supervisors member Dan White. When White was not found guilty of obvious premeditated murder (but only of two counts of voluntary manslaughter), the streets of SF erupted in what is known as the White Night Riot.

I returned to the march in 1980 with a bagful of film on a mission to document my people in all their activities. (I am still carrying out this mission, though now in digital format and often on an iPhone.) This was NYC's tenth annual celebration of Lesbian and Gay Pride and commemoration of the Stonewall Rebellion, organized by the Christopher Street Liberation Day Committee. The Archives motto "In Memory of the Voice We Have Lost" still resonates, as we worked to bring the stories of our community out of the shadows. Mabel was an inspiration to us all with her generosity, humor and huge staying power. It was a gift to have an elder as a role model, working along with us Mabel through her presence taught us to "keep on keepin' on." It was a very different world in the early years of "Second Wave Feminism," and queers had little visibility, never mind rights in the state or country. We were angry, full of energy, and fighting and organizing on multiple fronts.

Those of us of a certain age look at Trump as just the latest in a long line of horrendous, destructive, lying, inadequate, sneaky, venal, anti-American Presidents we have had to deal with. He may seem the worst in the history of our country, and he may be, but we suffered and struggled through Nixon, Reagan and the Bushes, along with Hoover and others, in lower positions of power. Activists before us dealt with the Cold War and McCarthy. In other words, it is not surprising to find ourselves in busses and cars heading to our nation's capital to demonstrate against the current regime.

In 2017, when I marshaled the Archives contingent at the Women's March in NYC, it reminded me of other marches, where our banner was often one of the few, if not the only clear indication of a lesbian presence. Even if only a handful of us from LHA showed up, once the banner was unrolled others usually joined with us as we moved along the line of march, creating a larger presence and community.

The 1950s lesbian world of Del Martin and Phyllis Lyons (who founded the Daughters of Bilitis) was in so many ways different than today. Then we were seen as "illegal, immoral and sick." It meant we had to change the laws, challenge religious institutions, and fight the medical establishment (especially the APA) to obtain our rights. And it meant we had to come out. In the intervening sixty-five years much of that work has been successful. And as much as Trump and his cronies try to push back on our rights and scare us back into the closet they will not win. One of the biggest changes I have seen over that time is in our families; so many of us have re-united with our birth families, and in that process, we reformed the sense of family in this country in ways the fascists cannot touch.

Bowers v. Hardwick, upheld a Georgia law forbidding oral or anal sex, ruling that the constitutional right to privacy does not extend to homosexual relations.

The Supreme Court's decision was handed down on June 30, 1986. The next night, July 1, about 1,000 protesters blocked traffic with a sit-in at Sheraton Square in Greenwich Village. It took years of protest, organizing, and legal effort, but the Court finally overturned their decision seventeen years later, in 2003. We have had so many examples of how long and how difficult it can be to obtain justice. Despite the setbacks that come with progress, I think in many ways we are better off than at the start of my activist journey. Certainly the citizens of the country have had opportunity to see and know LGBTQ people outside the old stereotypes of "commie, pinko, homo," "child molester," and "predatory lesbian."

The first time the national LGBTQ community organized to march in DC was the "National March on Washington for Lesbian and Gay Rights" on October 14, 1979. The crowd was estimated at 200,000. A second march took place in 1987 with an estimate of 750,000. The weekend included a large display of the AIDS quilt on The Mall. On April 25, 1993, a march for Lesbian, Gay, and Bi Equal Rights had attendance estimated at 1,000,000. It was one of the largest marches ever held in the nation's capital. This was the year the Lesbian Avengers organized a Dyke March the day before and over 20,000 women marched by the White House while Lesbian Avengers ate fire. The Archives was in attendance with the full collection of banners, large face signs and small word signs featuring slang and other languages for "lesbian," with plenty of willing hands to carry them.

Over the years, as our community grew, queer visibility rose in the media and our community was courted by corporate America. The tone of the pride marches changed. The Archives contingent shrank, and we decided to withdraw from the corporate-driven Sunday march. We still took the banner to smaller marches like Brooklyn Pride and many of us participated in the Dyke March every year. Then Trump was elected. It became important to return to the streets, be visible, and help rally our community into action. We took the banner out of its archival gray box and took it to the Women's March in NYC on January 21, 2017. We were welcome by the other marchers and many asked about the banner, being amazed when we told them we had been marching with it for over 40 years.

In 2017 we also attended the first Pride March held in Brighton Beach, Brooklyn, largely focused on immigration issues. And in June 2017 the Lesbian Herstory Archives went full circle and rejoined the NYC Gay Pride March in the lead special activist contingent (driven by Rise and Resist). I was encouraged by this renewed focus on the activism of our community in the face of the Trump regime.

In 1990 the Lesbian Herstory Archives was honored by Heritage of Pride (HOP) be being named one of the "Grand Marshalls" for the March. Pictured is Georgia Brooks (1943–2013), an Archivette, carrying a portrait of Lesbian poet Pat Parker (1944–1989) who had died the year before. I share this image thinking of our motto and how our voices, too, may someday be lost. Trump and his sort would be happy to see us made invisible and be forgotten. But as long as we write our stories, publish our own books and journals, make our own films, write our own blogs, post our photos on Instagram, and create our own art, we will survive in the hands of future generations. The role of the Archives is to preserve as many of our voices as possible, all kinds of lesbian voices. I urge you all to document our resistance, along with the rest of your lives, and someday place those records in a safe place for future generations, perhaps your community archive.

PAT PARKER
1944-1989

FRANKEL ASSOCIATES INC

THE WORLD HAS BEEN REVISED

Stevie Jones

At nearly forty years old, I attended my first gay pride march. I came out at seventeen, left Illinois to attend a women's college, quickly making up for the time I'd lost in the Mid-Nineties, Middle of Nowhere, Midwest . . . made my first lesbian friends, read my first lesbian books, found my first girlfriend, joined my first coven. . . But my twenties were quickly consumed with working late nights, getting a law degree, and, eventually, quitting drinking. After which, I spent most free time as part of a core group of volunteers helping grow and support an animal sanctuary upstate. My little piece toward helping make the world a more just and compassionate place, and LOTS of animals and nature.

In the early years at the sanctuary, I did just about every job at some point. One summer, almost every weekend included leading a tour, helping visiting volunteers, and tabling a booth at an event or street fair. It was a surprising lot of fun, but when there is a choice and plenty of hands for all jobs, I will pretty much always pick something "backstage." Cleaning a barn or helping the staff trim hooves was always more my niche.

When I started volunteering with the Lesbian Herstory Archives, I was often one of the first to sign up to haul books, chairs, and boxes up and down the stairs before and after an event, but also the most likely to be hiding out in the kitchen or busying myself with a task during. It's an introvert thing. Even the best good group energy of people I adore drains my battery fast when there's lots of it all at once.

But last summer I found myself in five marches, ending with the official gay pride march with hundreds of contingents and thousands of people, marching in the 2017 "Resistance Contingent" with the Lesbian Herstory Archives. The need to be counted with this crowd was greater than my desire not to be in one.

The election and its aftermath; what will it mean, this result? Divisive rhetoric that would have seemed impossible years ago casually appearing with your morning news, waking up to an altered reality . . .

***

June 2015
I walk the Manhattan Bridge and loop around Brooklyn Bridge Park, staring across the river at the rainbow-lit Empire State Building and tips of buildings downtown.

The biggest buildings in the city rainbow-lit. It still stuns me.

But so much is surprising these days.

The head of my organization sent a pride-week e-mail applauding the Obergefell Supreme Court ruling. (And, no, marriage wasn't my particular issue, and you can debate what focusing on that one channel means for the community, etc.) But seeing that e-mail in my office inbox meant something.

It is 2015 and my world has been revised.

***

May 2000.
I am twenty-two years old, sitting in a hotel suite in Pennsylvania with my mother, who, several drinks in, comments that she is so glad that I am ok, that I found a job. She is surprised. And so relieved.

It is the most civil conversation we have had on the subject in four years.

I told my mother before I came out to anybody else, and her life had not prepared her for this possibility. For years, she warned me being gay would ruin my life in every way. I was naïve about the world and throwing away our years of hard work and the better life I was supposed to have.

Fuck that. In two days, I will pack my dorm room and start my new life.

Yes, I have a job. I will not be returning to Illinois. I have a paralegal job and a sublet waiting in New York. Thanks, by the way, to another LESBIAN. Who went to the college fifteen years before me and is an investment banker with a miraculously un-ruined life.

But to be safe, I don't discuss my personal life at work for about twenty years.

***

September 2016

The presidential debates have started, and I cannot believe anything that I am seeing. A friend and I text throughout. Mostly punctuation marks.

Focusing on the positive, a woman is on the stage as a final presidential candidate. And she is saying the words "gay" and "lesbian."

This probably shouldn't be so surprising. For a while now, the world has felt so different than the one I grew up with, or even the one I graduated into out of my little women's college bubble in 2000. The country elected Barak Obama. More and more, conversations of privilege and social justice and positive change seem present and possible. LGBTQ issues were on the White House web page just two presidents since Don't Ask Don't Tell. These days it has become politically beneficial for some candidates to acknowledge that gays and lesbians exist. NYC even launched a citywide campaign on bathroom use and gender identity.

Lingering doubts cause friends and me to wonder how deep sexism goes in this country, and the effects of rhetoric, as shocking as alarming, loosed in this election.

Still, there has been so much change. In many ways this new millennium has felt like an altered landscape. Altered by the living and struggling and writing and brave actions of individuals and of groups who refused to be invisible or discounted. This is something to remember as the possibility of the present moment is shadowed by a surge in language of divisiveness, fear, and exclusion.

There has been enormous change. In just a short time, things that would have felt like fanciful hopes have been part of my daily reality. Things I had accepted as facts of how the world was, turned out not to be true or to have stopped being true, or to have stopped being so true.

(The present is a moment.)

***

July 1995.

At seventeen, I am states away from my family for the first time—invited to attend Harvard summer school after the scores came back on my practice SAT.

I'm standing across the street from the theater in Harvard Square looking at the marquis. "The Incredibly True Adventures of Two Girls in Love" is playing, and I have ten dollars. But, even miles and states away from my family, I can't cross the street or buy the ticket. Someone could see me. And tell someone who tells someone in Illinois that I saw a gay movie. And then my life would be ruined. Unlikely, sure, but I am too close to take chances. I'm doing well in my summer classes and slated to be valedictorian of my high school class at home. This fall I apply to college, and when I get in I can get out.

Most nights that summer, the dancer across the hall comes over in the evenings and shares my pillow while we watch another movie or another bit of the six-hour compilations of *Simpsons* episodes my favorite uncle taped for me. The pillow smells like peaches all summer. And I never touch her.

LET'S RAISE THE BAR

Meagan Lyle

Coldness tickled my toes and I felt a nervous shiver run through my body as I prepared for an interview with Freedom for All Massachusetts. This was not my first rodeo. In December of 2017, I had been living at my parents' house for the last month with my partner—too long without having a plan. I had been blessed with many interviews with organizations, but somehow I had fucked them all up. Been too nervous. Wore the wrong lipstick. Felt uncomfortable in my only black dress and cardigan that I bought at the Goodwill. Did not have enough experience. Told them too much about my passion for watercolors, which obviously is not a skill anyone is looking for.

Freedom for All Massachusetts is a campaign that aims to maintain the updated transgender equality law. Here is a little history:

In 2015, the FFAM campaign aimed to "add gender identity as a protected category in the Commonwealth's public accommodations law alongside age, race, creed, color, national origin, sexual orientation, sex, religion, and marital status." This was monumental, and I fully support the hard and necessary work that went into updating the policy. (Hence why I applied to be a field organizer in Worcester, MA.)

In 2016, the law was passed and, on October 1, 2017, the law went into effect. In Massachusetts, trans folk are now protected, by law, from discrimination in all public spaces. Massachusetts is not the first state to pass such legislation, but the eighteenth. Though the law was passed with overwhelming bipartisan support, opponents of the law appealed, requiring a public vote for the law to stay in place in future years. Freedom for All MA launched to a two-year public education campaign to secure these "yes" votes on the 2018 ballot to keep the law in place. The Field

Organizer position I applied for was responsible for rolling out that campaign. I was thrilled by the prospect of talking to folks about this issue, about this positive law, during these otherwise depressing times.

When I heard back about an interview, I immediately started investigating the coalition and mission of Freedom for All.

About ten minutes into my research, I came across their major "funders." I saw names like Google, Dow, and Cisco first on the business page—among several others I did not recognize. Then, I saw Human Rights Campaign on their page for major advocacy organizations.

That damn equal sign has been crawling under my skin for the past couple of years. My excitement turned to critique as I let out a loud sigh. *Here we go.*

My beef with HRC starts with marriage. Yes, anyone who wants to get hitched should be able to. But have we considered the history of violence that the institution of marriage has inflicted on women? On gays? On people of all different cultural and racial backgrounds? What even is marriage anyway?

And then I really got going when I read HRC's *Corporate Equality Index* for 2018, which analyzed and rated large corporations (500 or more employees) on the following criteria:

- Non-discrimination policies across business entities;
- Equitable benefits for LGBTQ workers and their families;
- Internal education and accountability metrics to promote LGBTQ inclusion competency; and
- Public commitment to LGBTQ equality.

Monsanto, a company that profits off of small farmers throughout the world by patenting seeds, made it onto that list. HRC was under *fire* on social media for this move. Monsanto was mentioned frequently because, well, they have depleted the soil, made already poor farmers pay them lots of money for seeds year after year because of their "patent," when farmers have historically (and I mean for CENTURIES) saved seeds from year to year. Monsanto is literally the worst. But all the companies in this fucking report are awful. Amazon. Airbnb. Coca Cola. Home Depot. Home Depot?!?!?!? You mean the same company that funds TRUMP? You mean the same company that banned a woman from wearing a hat that read "America was never great"? How can that possibly be a company that supports equality?

Furthermore, the report assumes that all LGBTQI people are white. Otherwise, they would incorporate racial discrimination into their criteria. But, nah. Let's just assume that LGBTQI discrimination is the only kind that matters and that homophobia is not linked to racism at all.

Clearly, my research into Freedom for All Massachusetts had gone too deep. But I have to ask myself, does this matter? Does it matter if "progressive" campaigns partner with questionable companies? How do these partnerships limit the work?

So I asked in my interview. In a way.

"I noticed you have several large business partnerships on your website. I was wondering how you partner with local organizations that work on connected issues, such as racial justice?" You might be able to tell, I was nervous to ask such a question in a first interview. I might have worded it more clearly if I was given another shot. Maybe, *Is it important to FFAM to partner with other organizations working toward liberation, equity, or justice? What do those partnerships look like? What do you hope they will look like?* I do not know. How do you even ask that without blowing the interview all together? Umm, excuse me, but do you, like HRC, let your funders determine what campaigns you work on, what reports you publish, and who you partner with?

But their answer was most interesting to me.

The answer was something along the lines of: (paraphrase) Yes, we have someone working on local partnerships with organizations. But we have to be careful who we partner with because of our funders.

Careful.

I asked again in the second interview. The answer was: (paraphrase) Yes, we have someone working on developing those partnerships and we have partnered with one of the biggest Black churches in Boston.

Hmm interesting.

The first answer truly was the red flag for me. It made me question everything. What does careful mean? Like you will not partner with more "radical" organizations, like Black Lives Matter, or Black and Pink, or Immigrant Justice and Prison Abolitionist groups because of funders? Are trans people of color not one of the most targeted groups in America? Are prisons and detention centers not the spaces where trans folks encounter extreme harassment and violence?

What is the purpose of this campaign if it only protects certain people and leaves everyone else in the dust? I understand we are fighting an uphill battle and baby steps are necessary, but as an organizer, as a campaign manager, as anyone working on a siloed campaign like this, it is so critical to articulate the larger vision and not compromise that for funding. And yet, FFMA must be *careful*. Careful, instead of collaborative. Careful, instead of compassionate, inclusive, or visionary.

Careful, in that context, so quickly allows the oppressor to win. When we are not able to articulate how one policy, or one vote, fits into a larger vision of equity and justice, we just end up working in separate silos, blindfolded. The mainstream (white) gay rights movement, time and time again, works in its own silo. Which is why Pride Parades are whitewashed and overseen by cops. Why Nellie's sports bar in DC waves a Blue Lives Matter flag. Why HRC speaks up for Marriage Equality, but then comes out with a bullshit Equality Index that encourages queer folks to work at corporations that support an anti-immigrant agenda and racial discrimination.

"Really, we are just focused on passing this one ballot. Then, the Freedom for All MA coalition will no longer be necessary."

Okay, so after this one piece of legislation, this one law, is set in stone. Freedom will be had. By everyone.

That report gave 609 corporations 100% ratings. WHAT. Why would you even make such a report to begin with? Since all these dumb companies value profit over people anyway. Why would you not be telling gay folks to go work at local businesses and companies? Is there not enough of them? Really? Well, tell them to create new ones! Not enough money to do so? I guess it's the fault of those 609 companies.

But where do you draw the line? Where do *I* draw the line? When does my critical eye become a hindrance on the movement that I so deeply believe in. The movement toward creating a world where everyone can authentically belong and feel valued and safe. When should I stop "should-ing" and participate in the process of figuring out how to get to that utopian vision? Am I participating enough? This bill could definitely be a step in the right direction— so who am I to judge? And yet, I am left feeling queasy at the idea of compromising the rights and dignity of others to win a vote. Queasy at the thought of *careful.*

I feel relieved that I never had to decide whether or not I would work for FFMA. I was fortunate to accept work elsewhere, but I'm sure that is not the last time I will encounter this dilemma. It permeates through much organizing and electoral work. We constantly have to ask ourselves where to focus our attention? How to show up for each other? When to listen and when to speak up? In the era of Trump, when everything seems to be tumbling down all at once, where do we turn? I will do the only thing I know how. I will read and practice, listen and learn until I understand where that line falls or if there is a line at all, until I understand the journey and process of liberation, until justice is won. Maybe that is not enough, still.

Photograph by Morgan Gwenwald

Brighton Beach Pride, May 20, 2017

POWER, OR POINT OF ZOO

Red Washburn

In *I Told You So*, Kate Clinton says, "The gender erasure reminds me of something June Jordan once said, there is power and there is point of view, and whoever has power determines the point of view."

I am face down on a filthy table in a Thai massage place in my boxers and socks. I think about my jeans, T-shirt, binder, leather jacket, sneakers, and baseball cap hanging on the door and block out the man's grunts above me. I close my eyes and grind my teeth while a straight cis dude beats the shit of me there. How did I get to a point where stranger's hands are on me – a man's, no less, so that I can feel human again? I instruct him to go deep – that is all that matters to me now. I can feel his elbow in my shoulder blades, his knees on my lower back, his fists pounding my upper back, and his fingers digging into my neck's trigger points. I breathe through a hole encased by a smelly, yellow towel. I feel the bruises. I think about the sound of her voice as she calls me my birth name and reignites my trauma, the refusals to meet with me to do feminist work, the threatening tone of her words at my request to respect my gender identity, and the henchmen who smile at me as they conspire with her to bar me from doing the work I created. I think about commander-in-thief proclaiming "grab them by the pussy," allowing states to choose where gender-conforming people can piss, and banning trans folks from the military rather than banning the military industrial complex itself. I think about the sound of violence as I listen for the echoes of my tears on the floor beneath me, where that same towel should sit before spin. I release the power she and the state have on my body, though I am deeply aware of my white privilege here, for just one hour before I find new tools to build up my inner warrior, because what other choice do we have? As Leslie Feinberg says in "Transgender Liberation: A Movement Whose Times Has Come," "We are the class that does the work of the world, and can revolutionize it. We can win true liberation."

EVERGREEN

Sarah Cavar

I miss the days when it was difficult to open up, challenging to share personal experiences, even with those closest to us. I miss underexposure even though my only memories of that time are surrogate. My images of another time come to me in dreams, my mother's voice a song behind my eyes, narrating some pastoral scene: a small house at the end of a skinny dirt road, carefree-careless people running through green fields, accompanied by nothing and no one, taking on a lush hill without pausing to capture any memory of the event, but rather enjoying it as it unfolds. The dreams are usually felt in a space between sleep and waking, a liminal stage like the gray glow of an untouched device not yet locked. I feel nostalgic for something my mind has most likely created with no attention to reality.

When I wake up from those dreams, the ads never fail to catch me. I open my network and see imitation trees growing smartly by spacious windows of pseudo-glass. A friend and I once went to purchase one of these trees—only after having had a conversation about how we long for the green days we hear about from older folks—to find out it was a hoax. The man selling the trees did not have any trees, but he had several rifles in the back of his home and one small gun that was tucked needly at his hip. Although I might have thought him to be the type with dead animal heads mounted on his wall, there were none. Perhaps he ate his victims whole. In the place of the heads hung some vintage apparel, a red cap turned inside-out caught my eye. Even its insides were red as the blood of a fresh deer or fox; its mess of white embroidery was unreadable from where we stood.

The man had informed us that we were to rate his business with five pixelated stars and share the ad with the technicolor trees and inform our friends without a hint of warning or irony that we had just looked at the best collection of evergreens around, and had only left empty-handed because we were awaiting the shipment which would carry our perfect plant.

Knowing that a positive review meant little and still knowing our lives meant quite a bit, we enthusiastically agreed. "I feel sorry for the guy," I told my friend, us sitting side by side in our rental car. "You saw the way his body shook, right?"

My friend blew out a breath slowly as a whistle. "I found his list of diagnoses pretty quickly after I saw that fake tree page. Couldn't you tell it was a fake?"

I told her I did not really care anymore.

"I guess I still have to care a little about these guys. I'm sure he needs to keep buying that crap that makes him shake, not like there's a decent doctor or anyone around here."

Feeling ill myself, I nodded. Not making eye contact with me, she made a few gestures on her device. I felt a ping against my chest and I knew I had just received a little something in my fundraiser. "Help —— get pain meds! :)" it read. The smile was a generous afterthought, an offering that begged repayment. I had few monthly contributors, but enough that I could scrape a little something together when I needed more medication.

Network pages were something of a middle path when it came to reality: there were few entire hoaxes and there were few absolute realities; most everything the Network featured was a lavish mix of facts and fictions. These were the kinds we never got examples of in school, in courses entitled "Your Network, Your World: Distinguishing Facts from Their Alternatives."[1] On the day it began, both of my mothers sullenly exposed their bare faces to a scanner, greeted in return with the voice that said, "payment successful!" We the children were meant to get training in how to see facts from fiction, but much like the rest of our academic

---

1 Sponsored by a wholly owned subsidiary of The Network, Inc.

subjects, course material was far more logical in the classroom than it is on the outside.

As my friend and I fell into silence, as we often did, our respective devices lit up in front of us. My first advertisement was for a med I had not yet heard of. Its brand name was as unpronounceable as its generic name. It promised to render you "pain free for twenty-four hours with just one Smart Injection®. Do not use —— if you are pregnant, might become pregnant, are breastfeeding; do not give to children under twelve; side effects may include:"

I did not read through them all; no point in torturing myself with something I will not receive until there are six better meds out there already. I ached for the pleasure of heartburn, perhaps nausea; the rest of my body become slack, soft, no longer stretched thin to breaking over my bones.

I do not know why I cared to look at the fake ad for fake trees in the first place. Everyone near to me lived on at least the fifth floor of complexes that cut brutal silhouettes into the clouds that hung overhead. They, the clouds, were occasionally white, more often a dirty white as though someone had peed in the snow. The buildings themselves were a deep gray-brown, with windows that grew larger toward their top floors. Before the buildings came, my parents had told me, there were littler buildings. They called the city this used to be "bohemian," chagrined much like they are when they scroll past one fundraiser and then another on their networks.

"We need to, ah, help you first." They tell me this twelve times a year. "You have pain and you really need it, which isn't to say that—it isn't to say that the good people below don't, it's just that . . ." And then they both go soft, wringing bony hands and mumbling into their chests, "I can't say it anymore. We just need to help our own." Zoë—what I call my mother now that I'm an adult—is always the main speaker; her partner, Leah, mostly stays quiet inside of her shame. I learned in a local history lesson that we are quite far north, but the seemingly impenetrable material that makes our building also made the wall below us.

Built for our protection, this material was designed so as to mitigate the risk of outside invasion. It is hard and cold and unassuming, but can also shock a body unconscious if touched. I only realized just how strong it was when I heard a knock and a scream and a thump outside of our apartment's door. A middle-aged man was laying on the hallway's floor, with a device in his hand. "Help —— get a filter mask!" Read his fundraiser's title in cheerful golden letters. I slipped a pillow under his head and Network messaged him: "i rec a :) or maybe even a <3 i think it helps when ppl think yr v friendly!!"

When I think about trees or gardens, I do not think about luxury; I think about peace. I do not think, for example, that owning a nature factory on top of a high-rise is useful for any reason other than the smug exclusivity that comes with it. I hear the flowers can be beautiful, especially at sunrise, but I doubt in my heart that they compare to the ones you can buy. Scientifically engineered to be your "best and brightest" flowers yet! There was a realness to these violently colored lilies; roses so bright my eyes got sore looking at them. There was a certain ironic authenticity to their unabashed fakery, although even that was called into question when I was woken abruptly in order to give them a Network rating.

When this happened, I was at first confused, not remembering having purchased any. The notification informed me "You recently spent time at the home of ——. Did you enjoy ——'s Flower-Style Decorations?" I resisted the urge to select "no" out of sheer irritation, lest —— find out and approach me with hurt feelings. I selected "yes," then five stars, and rolled over with the flirtatious suggestion, "buy now?"

The president is wearing a mask. Many of us do, as well. His face appears frozen, like hardened clay, liable to crack if one ever knocked into it. I do not believe he has another face underneath the mask; perhaps if I were to rip it off it would reveal plastic and wires and chipping paint, as though I was clenching my muscles and tearing a fake tree in two. Inside the tree isn't green or brown but rather white and gray, the jagged edges of plastic drawing blood. When I am directed toward my news, his elaborately painted face shines under the beating sun. When I click around the Network, lobbing myself down a political rabbit hole different from the one in which I usually burrowed, I was, of course, offered a different set of news. The painted face remained intact.

"Poor Air Quality 'Divine Retribution for Lazy Poor' President —— Says"

"Research Suggests Recent Low O_2 Levels Linked to Tree Death"

We can afford decent-quality filter masks, although sometimes that means forgoing such headlines entirely. Having Basic Network Access is feasible in the short term, if inconvenient. Some, others more than myself, are faced with the challenging choice between death on the inside and death on the outside. Were it up to me, I would often forsake the air.

I have never seen someone drop in the street due to lack of filter masks, but I remember hearing sirens and the rapid falling of feet in some apartment below us, suggesting that it occurred behind closed doors. Someone was dead by an open window. It was hot, and they were breathing in something they shouldn't have been. The headline read "cause of death remains unclear." The dead woman's family could not afford a funeral, but they quietly buried her beneath some crunchy dirt in their designated outdoor box.

Buried in his backyard was the man with the inside-out cap and several guns. The Network keeps a cache of places I have reviewed and one day, with a cheerful ping, informed me of breaking news from the fake business selling fake trees. I thought about his skinny, shriveled trembling body. Old age. I thought about all those bloody and dead things I imagined him swallowing whole after a couple shots fired into the distance and figured he had been a casket for a while. I took the news laying down on my bed, curling my way inside myself and away from my savage joints. My donation request has not received any new views since yesterday, but below the post sat an inquiring ad for a kidney bank. Rubbing absently the side of my stomach, I remembered I only need one.

I have always wondered what a post-apocalyptic world might look like, but then I think, the apocalypse means the world is ending. It no longer exists once the apocalypse is over. Until that happens we are living on but maybe not in a world still living—still possessed by something even though not much grows anymore. I took a pill and refreshed my device.

Life is about choices: choosing which kidney you'd rather live without. Choosing the pain you know or the medical unknown. Taking that chance in the fake tree shop and then choosing to write a review rather than be shot. Rolling over, I watched headlines from my preferred news sources light my device's screen. That news is something I have chosen with care, my friend who wraps me in a tight hug and reminds me I am not alone. When I see ads speaking gently to me before a big newscast begins, I am naked with closed eyes.

HISTORY

Cheryl Clarke

i.

If there was one story I had the power of prerogative to
change—besides the 2016 US Presidential election—Billie
Holiday's is the one. Every time I listen to her sing one of those
droll tunes she made art, I say, "Why'd you have to take yourself
down that narrow drain, baby girl? Your sweet baby voice and cool
precocious passion. Why? You had *everything*." The answers are
not in our stars, baby girl, trying to get a good vein leg atop shabby
dressing room vanity.

ii.

"When an event like the Mike Brown murder occurs, black people
see history: slavery, Reconstruction, Jim Crow, Plessy, Lynch Law,
segregation, Mississippi, *and* police murders. Cops see only the
one event," says a venerable white historian. "

(Cops see history, too—the history of their racist rationalizations
of violence against blacks.)

We both act accordingly.

The cop brings down the
total force of the state upon us—male and female.

And we run like hell.

iii.

President Obama takes to Twitter in twenty-twelve.
Followers tweet:
"WELCOME TO TWITTER, NIGGER."

iv.

While I can casually dismiss having had an affair with a married
woman, I will never forget Louise, with long black hair whipped

back into a ponytail like Billie Holiday in the later '50's and a fabulous, extravagant sense of humor and love of cannabis that sent my inexperienced mind and me into an orbit of nonsense and theater that nearly ended or at least ruined my life. There I was on that fated morning left with husband Billy downstairs shouting up at me: "Tell Louise to come out of that apartment or I'm gonna break the door in." And Billy did, and Louise ran out past him to her Pontiac during his distraction and out of my life, back home, and Billy soon to follow. Police no match for Billy's tall, brown eloquence in gray suit and straight black male desperation to follow Louise with .38 protruding hard against his trouser pocket. I admired his resistance--in spite of myself--for the way the pigs jumped.

"Wait a minute, buddy," they say weakly as they fall back onto their squad car.

"*You* wait, *you* cops. Don't you *buddy* me," says Billy.

The cops later pronounce the "melee . . . a tiff between the boyfriend and the girlfriend." They announced him as "*her* husband" and signified him as "Mr." throughout my request to file a complaint.

v.

I can still recall that desire, though. Walking out onto my street a day before that fated morning to meet her as she left from her Pontiac. We saw each other a block away. Laughter of recognition. Each moseying to the other, heads and hips cocked. On their way to Point Pleasant, friends pass me in their car grunting "Um-hum" at the resonant certainty of our kinesis.

Her fitted linen dress, bare legs, high heel pumps, brief-less.
My boxer shorts, tank top, Converse high-tops, bra-less.

Photograph by Morgan Gwenwald

Maxine Wolfe (r) with other organizers of the 25th Annual NYC Dyke March

BOOK REVIEWS

An Unkindness of Ghosts
by **Rivers Solomon**
Akashic Books, 2017
Paperback, 349 pages, $15.95

Reviewed by Asma (ahs-ma) A. Neblett

A board a *ship* named 'Matilda' is Aster, a member of the lowerdeck, darker-skinned workers that staff the ship. Aster is tasked by Theo, the Surgeon General (a mentor and lover), to care for the oppressive Sovereign who uses social hierarchy to tyrannize and protect specific members of the ship. As the Sovereign falls ill, multiple elements of the ship's world begin to unravel, including order between decks (upper and lower), and the specifics of Aster's legacy as it relates to the ship.

An Unkindness of Ghosts is a striking allegory of the colonial past submerged in a dark future; at times, it's hard to isolate the parallels that link the transatlantic and its aftermath to *An Unkindness of Ghosts.* What sets it apart from other titles of its Afrofuturistic genre is its special queering of diasporic bodies and experiences, which highlight subjectivities and the violence of a time steeped inequity. And by 'queering' or 'queered', I mean to evoke the definitional understanding of these terms (strange, or non-normative) that, in and outside categories of sexuality, gender identity, and racial/appearance.

Queering is most apparent in the language Solomon invents to name Aster's world, identity and legacy as a Tarlander. As a descendent, Aster has masculine and feminine features that speak to her dissimilarity *and* desirability in a refreshing tone – especially as she learns about her heritage from her aromantic Aint Melusine.

Aster also exists in a place where other genders, emotionally-expressive, and physically variant folks are visibilized. She has community and they aren't defined according to what they lack or how they differ from privileged identities aboard the ship. However, this is not to suggest there is consistent comradery among Aster's counterparts, as there are clashes, bullying, and other disruptions that create wedges. Solomon distinguished themselves with character development, as there's something self-determining about the visibility of Aster's counterparts; each character feels tangible because in many ways, Solomon pulls identities from the world we currently inhabit.

There are times, however, where language creates obstacles to understanding Aster's full experiences as a healer, friend, lover, and her trauma. For instance, the medicalized and chemical terminology is informative; it underlines the science and technologies used to surveil and police minoritized persons and highlights the ways Aster manipulates both to heal other people. But it is also heavy throughout the text, which complicated the ways in which the story developed at times . Nonetheless, there is reward in this struggle because Aster also shares a confusion with understanding the poetics her world and experiences – whether it be trauma from the loss of her late mother, or mis/interpreting affection from Theo.

An Unkindness of Ghosts unearths a number of emotions that are not typically attached to futuristic genres, such as anger and agony; or an unshakable fear about the prospect of the future as a dystopic destination. It reminds readers that beyond dismantling structures, there is much emotional work to value and utilize in order to heal for the sake of our futures.

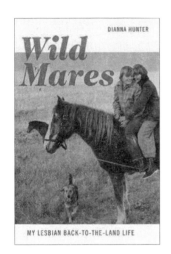

Wild Mares
by **Dianna Hunter**
University of Minnesota Press, 2018
Paperback, 238 pages, $18.95

Reviewed by Sarah Heying

In *Wild Mares: My Lesbian Back-to-the-Land Life,* Dianna Hunter navigates the gap between recollected and recorded life, offering ample proof of memoir's ability to both create and preserve herstory. "The more I age, the more I think about memory," Hunter writes. "This strange mental power of ours can be sketchy and unreliable, but it lets us bring the dead back to life and travel in time through multiple pasts." As someone who both lived and worked collectively for women's liberation and farmers' rights, Hunter frequently compares her stories with those of people who experienced the same moments; rather than smooth out any discrepancies, she hands the reader a magnifying glass to examine every nook and cranny. The view is often less than flattering, but also fiercely vulnerable and self-aware: "We were unsure of ourselves, all under stress. We could be too quick to judge each other sometimes, and also too quick to say anything goes."

Hunter grew up Minot, North Dakota, home to a Strategic Air Command base (a target for nuclear warfare) and felt called to action in the wake of the Vietnam, Cold War, and Civil Rights Movements. "It seemed to me we couldn't separate sexism from the oppressive forces that led to the war," she writes. In college, consciousness raising groups and feminist print culture became

Hunter's way of life, and two women along the way invited her to join them in communal living on their farm. From there, Hunter spent decades learning that "in farming as well as in feminism the political was personal." The wisdom she gained from her many mistakes and successes led her to purchase her own farm--a first for a lesbian woman in her county--and then on to serve as a legal rights advocate for farmers struggling under Reagan's devastating farm policies.

Stylistically, the memoir reflects Hunter's unwavering dedication to political action. As a burgeoning feminist, she was drawn to "The Redstockings Manifesto" for its no nonsense language. Her word choice and sentence structure is likewise blunt and efficient, but this hardly means that she spares any detail, nor that she keeps the reader at arm's length. The memoir often reads like a how-to manual for harvesting crops and milking cows, but also like a journal one might keep under lock and key. She peppers her stories with personal photographs so that reading *Wild Mares* feels like digging through those commonplace, personal archives that are often overlooked, yet are vital to lesbian and feminist herstories.

Beneath the umbrella of inclusive identity politics today, renewed interest in the lesbian land movement may seem a tad out of place. In our nation under Trump, any nostalgia for an idealized, separatist dream is bound to be met with skepticism. Still, it feels vital for many of us to find or create spaces, resources, and languages capable of empowering communal love and liberation and to listen to those who have spent their lives dedicated to similar visions. In lesbian culture, this historical moment even has an updated name--the landyke movement--a portmanteau between our longing for radical sociopolitical change and our respect for the audacious women who already turned said longing into action.

Hunter's recollections, confessions, and meditations offer an important reminder that failure to find these herstories, even in the smallest communities, merely amounts to "a failure of paying attention." Sometimes, paying attention also means honoring imperfect movements for their profound bravery. "Complete liberation, unconditional love, and long-term collective living may have slipped through our fingers," Hunter reflects, "but at least we tried to be ourselves." Sure, these homesteads struggled over personal boundaries and politics, yet "most often it was resources." To "accept that everything we love is destined to transform into something else" does not require forgetting former struggles, successes, and failures in favor of the new. Instead, feminist lesbian politics can flourish by studying the templates these daring women bequeathed to us and by allocating resources to forge more ways to love fully and fight fiercely for our beliefs. Whether or not the landyke movement is dream of the past, Hunter's life story fits right into contemporary conversations of collective love and liberation.

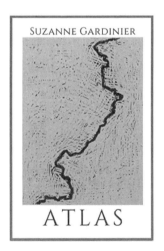

Atlas
by **Suzanne Gardinier**
December, 2017
Paperback, 65 pages, $9.99

Reviewed by Sara Gregory

Suzanne Gardinier latest poetry collection *Atlas,* evokes injustice and geography to explore how colonialism and oppression shape our world. Readers encounter a collection that, like its namesake, offers a collection of maps. *Atlas* charts historical

272 ♀ Sinister Wisdom 110- *Dump Trump: Legacies Of Resistance*

and current breaches of human rights, spanning plantations, *latifundios,* Palestine, the Indies, Tahrir Square, Oyó (present-day Nigeria), Baghdad, and the *Sola* river near Auschwitz. By evoking geography, Gardinier calls on readers to question the authority given to map makers.

Place is the collection's major fascination and with it, Gardinier exposes how power manifests into land and culture. She digs into the topography of colonialism and wonders at how generational loss might carve itself into borders. From underneath *guanabana* trees, rainy cities with curfews and "colonial peripheries", to refugee camps, readers are given enough detail to know where they are without *really* knowing. Gardinier plays with the irony of the violence she seeks to reveal: nowhere is safe and erasure is common. The loss of homeland is universal, memory-breaking, and always under our feet.

With the opening poem "Cain," Gardinier references the biblical story of the damned brothers Cain and Abel. The sons of Adam and Eve, Cain killed his brother Abel after failing to win the favor of God. Cain is punished and forced away from God's lands as a wanderer and fugitive. The poem is less about faith or religion, rather it speaks to the condition of exile, of the spurned. Gardinier muddles the voices of God, men, and hindsight, writing:

> *Scatter them* he said Meaning the people/His gesture like
>   flicking mosquitoes away...
> If we'd had a map of their hell If we'd learned/to breathe
>   there long enough to recover
> The time we lost in astonishment/when we could have
>   Been figuring out what to do (page 15)

While "Cain" is about the consequences of powerful men playing at God, it is not the only way Gardinier manifests a sense of abandonment. Gardinier inscribes vacancy of memory and loss of homeland as a literal loss of text. The poem "Liberty Plaza" tells of the women native to *Mannahatta*, or what the settlers would claim as Massachusetts. She writes:

& took illegal possession of [   ]/& [   ] & [   ] &
   [   ] extinguished...
   History is [   ] now & / [   ] & [   ] here
(page 50).

By omitting names, Gardinier creates space for many stolen lands and its people, while also emphasizing the actual destruction of indigenous lives and cultural memory. Dissonant, simultaneous history— *Mannahatta* vs. Massachusetts— overlap in her poetry, creating "twin soldiers with enemy languages" (15).

Atlas is a challenging read. It forces readers to confront their proximity to violence and their place in complicity. But while much of the poetry is dark, the final poem "Yemayá" transforms the tone of the collection:

Her smell Her taste What she tell you at night

[Your tiny place & she wrap you there]

Every project her tinder / Who know her

[*When you see how it is you'll laugh* she says] [*Laughing*]

[*Sweep of her skirt*]

Gardinier fills up the empty brackets with laughter, sweeping skirts, and women with fire. Other verses threaded throughout the collection offer visions of free worlds, words of solidarity, sweet fruit and joy. These moments spark out of the pages and make *Atlas* not only a testament, but also a map of resistance to the horrors it reminds us of.

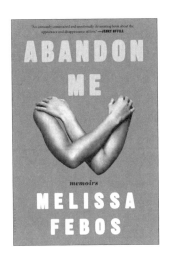

Abandon Me
by **Melissa Febos**
Bloomsbury Press, 2017
Paperback, 304 pages, $17.00

Reviewed by Sara Gregory

*A*bandon *Me* is a powerful essay collection that chronicles author Melissa Febos' struggle towards intimacy, heritage, and love. Her second memoir, *Abandon Me* tells of life after heroin addiction and sex work. Febos uses the formative relationships of her childhood-- including her adoptive father, her half brother Boo who struggles with mental illness, her feminist mother, and biological Native American father -- to explore the feast-or-famine quality of love in her adult relationships.

Abandon Me plays like a tragedy of coming and going. Her adoptive father, whom she considers her true father, was a sea captain and often away for months at a time. Febos spent her childhood years nursing feelings of devotion and abandonment, until finally she hardened against the Captain's returns. Her adult relationships don't fare much better; Febos' twenties are marked by academic success, a hidden heroin addiction, and unstable relationships.

Romantically, Febos writes principally of Amaia, a married lesbian with whom she shares a long distance relationship. At first, Amaia appears loving: she is a hotshot academic, promises Febos her wife is aware of their relationships, and sends lavish gifts. But as the novel progresses, Amaia's presence feels increasingly intrusive as readers, and Febos, begin to understand that Amaia is emotionally abusive. As Amaia's behavior worsens, Febos tethers herself to her lover even more desperately, cancelling plans, neglecting family and friends, and writhing over Amaia's hot-and-cold mood swings. Febos knowingly casts both herself and Amaia in a harsh light, managing a heartbreakingly authentic portrayal of a queer relationship turned sinister. Slowly extrecating herself from the relationship, the essays turn more and more into an exploration of Febos' Indian heritage.

This exploration of biological family not only buoys the end of Febos' relationship with Amaia, but the increasing waves of information, conversation, and interaction between Febos and her alcoholic biological father, her gambling aunt, and blue-eyed half sister offer a story of tentative homecoming. Jon, Febos' biological father was Wampanoag and had a few children in addition to Febos, none of whom he raised. Through her for Jon, Febos delves into all her cultural, blood, and familial ties:

I am Puerto Rican, but not really. Indian, but not really.

Gay, but not really. Adopted, but not really (291).

With this reckoning of self, Febos acknowledges that *Abandon Me* suddenly "seems like a very American story," and releases much of the memoir's tension.

Throughout *Abandon Me*, Febos uses an impressive mix of literary reference, dazzling metaphor, and astute historical observations to interpret herself and translate it to the universal. The memoir feels self-aware as Febos works the peculiarities of her life to create and offer a *wunderkrammer*:

In Renaissance Europe, "cabinets of curiosities" were all the rage of the ruling class. Often they were whole rooms populated with treasures and oddities of the natural world:gems and feathers, fossils and taxidermied animals. They were 'regarded as a microcosm or theater...a memory theatre'...Every curiosity in the cabinet was a totem, pulsing with meaning." (104).

Abandon Me encapsulates a great many totems of Febos' life and her narrative voice often reads like theatre: touching, raw, and sometimes indulgent. She does not place her life on center stage, but rather her emotional relationship *to* and *with* the facts of her life. *Abandon Me* concerns Febos' intimate landscape and landmines. Rather than forcing herself onto the world, Febos wonders how the world and its hostilities found their way inside of her. Febos' dedication to an internal focus makes *Abandon Me* feel feminine, "beautiful and a little gruesome" (104).

Scissors, Paper, Stone
by **Martha K. Davis**
Red Hen Press, 2018
Paperback, 312 pages, $16.95

Reviewed by Roberta Arnold

Scissors, Paper, Stone, by Martha K. Davis, begins with Catherine and her brother, Andy, running away from home as children. Catherine grows up and marries Jonathan; both experience alienation from their families and together arrive at a decision to adopt a Korean child. In their teens during the 1950s, both had listened to radio reports of abandoned, orphaned children made thus by American soldiers during the Korean War. In 1964, they adopt Min who arrives by plane from Korea. Despite an abundance of coveting, Catherine initially finds solace protecting her child against ostracism. Things soon fall apart.

Jonathan and Catherine divorce while Min is in middle school, and Catherine and Min become alienated from each other.

Alienation, identity, and the question of who makes up family are the themes weaving through the book in the narratives of Catherine, Min, and Laura, a classmate of Min's. Catherine's story covers the early 70s: Raising Min as a single parent in a privileged white town, just across the Golden Gate Bridge from San Francisco. Laura's narrative, with parallels to Min's, explores family displacement; Laura's family moved from Vermont to California.

Min's narrative begins in the summer of 1979, when Min and Laura are sophomores in Mt. Tam High School. The two have bonded as outsiders. When a boy in school calls Min a "gook," only Laura empathizes. Catherine grounds Min for throwing her schoolbooks at the boy's back. Min and Laura spend sleepovers together getting in touch with their sexuality, and Min begins experiencing deepening feelings of love for Laura. Throughout high school, their active sexual experiences are with boys, but, by the middle 80s, Min has firmly established her lesbian identity.

Min's lesbian identity emerges in stark contrast to many lesbians of that time in the '70s; lesbians creating shared music, theatre and dance venues, coffeehouses, political actions, bookstores, and small presses. Coming out in the 80s, Min remained outside shared lesbian community. She does not discover it until the summer of 1985, when Min finds the bar Maude's, Judy Grahn's poetry, and a more congruent lesbian identity. Min also re-connects with Catherine again--through bodywork; Min is a masseuse living in San Francisco, and Catherine has become a member of PFLAG. Min still rejects identifying with Asian-Americans, political dykes, and the AIDS movement. In a conversation with a bi-racial African American woman, Natalie, with whom she has established a non-monogamous lover relationship, Min rejects the idea of group identification. "I tend to have a hard time with groups, being the outsider" (159). Instead, Min finds herself through shared sexual prowess on the streets of San Francisco. "I loved walking around the city constantly aware of the women around me, feeling my own appeal to other lesbians. I loved being free to act on my desire every time" (169).

In the fall of 1985, Min is having brunch in her apartment with her mother, her best friend, Laura, and the lesbian ex-lover who has introduced her to Judy Grahn, Margo. The dialogue heats up in a delicious recounting of lesbian life in the 70s. Margo points out to Catherine the joy of being a lesbian: "....I think by being lesbians, we create our own form of freedom" (253). Margo tells Min of the harsh political struggle and work it took to get the gay rights bill passed in California in 1979, and the 1979 March on Washington, where political rallies of over 100,000 gay activists brought gay rights to the forefront of the political sphere. "We were trying to claim our lives" (258). Min counters, saying that things are different now--and different for her in particular. In her head Min is thinking: "All I feel thinking about AIDS is bored. I don't have any interest in working on a hotline or doing educational outreach or buying groceries for men who are bedridden. I am nothing like Margo. I can't imagine a community ready-made, pulling me in to work with them. I can only create my constellation, one by one, each star at some distance from the others, myself in the middle" (259).

At this point, Min is giving Catherine weekly massages, and here mother and daughter connect, at the level of the body. "I now know I am the means of relief, not the cause....And she, for her part, has less need to keep me out. This happens at the level of the body. In our speaking life, we have never been in such accord" (194-5). After a time of division, control, and cutting people out, Catherine finally has a catharsis: seeing *herself* in the abject rejection her brother, Andy, demonstrated when she presented Min to him as family. Taking Min's best friend, Laura, into her arms in a hug, Catherine realizes the self-truth that she is like her brother, and Laura is the daughter she has always wanted. "I'm afraid I will burst apart. I hear a groan, like a tree sawed through starting to fall, and I realize it's me" (265). Catherine has opened a bookstore, is seeing a man who is a friend, not a partner. She now accepts her need for strict boundaries on her heart's expression. "Like the bookstore, where all the titles are labeled, shelved in their proper place. Like what I want my garden to be: something pruned, held back, controlled. Something predictable, something known" (273).

"Scissors, Paper, Stone" is a game called by a variety of names, most commonly, "Rock, Paper, Scissors." Started in China, later picked up by Japan, and then used by Americans, it either settles a dispute between two things, like heads or tails, or is a game for children to play. Each object, scissors, paper, or stone, indicated by a hand and finger configuration, is held behind the player's back while reciting "Scissors, Paper, Stone." Each player's hand then comes out to show the hidden configuration. Best out of three wins. The winner triumphs by one object's power over the other: Scissors cuts paper, paper covers stone, and stone crushes scissors. The three narratives that dominate this book are symbolic of these power-based, decision-making tools. Catherine, the mother, is the scissors, cutting people out of her life and her heart. Laura, the best friend, is paper—the blank canvas; Laura is also adept at smoothing things over. Min, ever intransigent, recalcitrant, and standing alone, is the stone. Told throughout with poetic images and metaphor, the three lives change in relationship to the other--in defiant opposition--until a new kind of relationship is established. Laura and Min live through a conflicting configuration of loving each other in different ways. Min finds the identity she has always been—not Korean, not American, but, a non-monogamous lesbian. Laura goes through a variety of men until she realizes it is Min she wants to be with monogamously. Can Laura smooth over the intractable, hard-headedness of Min in her decision to be non-monogamous? Before they are about to leave each other and go off in two opposite directions, Min and Laura play the game they had played when they first met, "Scissors, Paper, Stone."

Who wins? Or, more accurately, in the new understanding of conjoined relationship, how do they define themselves together now? Well, you really need to read the book.

 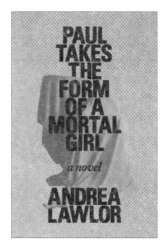

Stray City by **Chelsey Johnson**
HarperCollins, 2018
Hardcover, 416 pages, $24.99

Paul Takes the Form of a Mortal Girl by **Andrea Lawlor**
Rescue Press, 2017
Paperback, 354 pages, $18.00

Reviewed by Sara Gregory

Chelsey Johnson's *Stray City* and Andrea Lawlor's *Paul Takes the Form of a Mortal Girl* are debut novels in a new, electrifying vein of writers fascinated with the 90s. Johnson and Lawlor deal with time in queer ways: the novels are gritty, fast-paced, and frequently bend literary form. They embrace the heyday of lesbian bars, hookups, ACTUP, west coast DIY scenes, Riot Grrl and womyn's music, queer theory and fierce identity politics. *Stray City* and *Paul* are street-smart, bursting with wry cultural references, self-deprecating camp, and sharp intelligence.

Stray City's Andrea Morales is a card-carrying member of Portland's so-called Lesbian Mafia. After being cast out by her religious Midwest family, Andrea's been doing what outcasts like her do in the 90s: survive, watch out for her new queer family, gossip, and deep dive into lesbian feminist punk music. At the novel's opening, Andrea nurses a broken heart after her ex, Flynn, converts to non-monogamy via *The Ethical Slut*, cheats, and then dumps her. It's not a good time for Andrea. Desperate to get away from the speculations of her dyke community, she does the unthinkable: she kisses Ryan, a man, outside a bar. For nearly ten months Andrea leads a double life. Andrea the dyke makes feminist art, works at an antique shop, attends lesbian punk shows, and mourns Flynn. The other Andrea sleeps with Ryan, fixes his guitar, listens to his band's music, and resigns herself to comfortable, if mechanical, sex.

Then Andrea finds out she's pregnant and her split life begins to collide. She decides to keep the baby and out of convenience, Ryan moves in. The two enter a strange quasi-family life that Andrea resists at every turn. Realizing his love will never be reciprocated, Ryan takes a drive one night and never comes back. Relieved, though alone, Andrea prepares for motherhood:

> That night I lie in bed, I lay on my back and rested my hands on my abdomen...
> "You and me," I whispered in the dark. Two selves.
> "Do you think we could do this?" (187).

Ten years later, Andrea lives in a two bedroom in Portland with her daughter, Lucia, and her life partner, Beatriz. The novel's final section is focused on Lucia, a budding musician, and her desire to meet her biological father. It's a strange ending. On some level, Lucia feels she lacks a vital male presence in her life, while Andrea is settled in to almost exactly what she raged against with Ryan. Andrea is a mother, living with her more or less married partner, and concerned with band practice and family, rather than queer revolution. Andrea's story feels real; it's emotionally poignant and believable. But it can be argued that Andrea conformed to the homonormative lifestyle she decried in her youth, and the last part of the novel drags because of it.

In its potential for conformity, *Stray City* sharply contrasts *Paul Takes the Form of a Mortal Girl*. In Paul Polydoris, Lawlor creates an impossibly transgressive character. Paul is a shapeshifter, able to morph his body and gender presentation with his mind. Initially, Paul is motivated primarily by sex, using his abilities to transform into Polly, or other buffer, more beautiful versions of himself.

> His skin shivered all over, belly and back and thighs. He stared down at his skinny chest until it obediently softened, grew, filled out the bra. Not too big...Paul stopped at a 36C. He was going for *regular but hot* (11).

Paul is abrasive, his sex isn't safe, and he doesn't shy away from self-indulgence. Attention motivates most of his sexual adventures. With games, his various forms, and a sharp eye, he's always trying for more:

> Paul tried for a smile, a look back, an eyeful, a number, some illicit hallway kiss, a blowjob, a romance, a massage, a handjob, a finger up an ass, a free show, a licked lip, a passed note, a present, a surprise, something good, something better than the nothing he had (39).

As the novel progresses, Paul (who usually uses a combination of he/him and she/her pronouns) takes to his gender play with more seriousness. Polly goes to MichFest and turns into an "earnest, monogamous lesbian" when he meets Diane, a radical feminist and vegetarian. With this, *Paul* is not only a celebration of the fluidity of gender, but a fascinating take on the camp trans/womyn born womyn divide at MichFest. Diane eventually learns that Polly also takes the form of Paul; the two struggle to work out. Paul knew he was hiding *something* from Diane, but the dissonance doesn't imply his fluid gender performance and identity are inauthentic, or even at the root of his "secret". Trans people negotiate coming out to partners like Diane constantly; Paul's hesitation is amplified by his shapeshifting powers.

With this, Lawlor explores how people navigate the mutability of gender, assigned sex, and sexual attraction. Even the use of "transform" or "taking the form of" is strategic and interrogative, meant to widen readers' understanding of our gendered expectation of queer people and "womanhood". Paul reflects that he "actually feel like I belong [at MichFest] as much as anywhere I've ever been. More even" (99).

Paul and *Stray City* are invested in understanding belonging in lesbian culture and queer community. Paul and Andrea challenge their communities through their bodies, which don't always look how lesbian bodies are "supposed" to. Paul's transformations aren't stable as he subverts the gender binary to better his chances for new, exciting sex. Andrea's body changes as a *consequence of* sex, her stomach swelling with proof of her heterosexual "transgression." Each journey contrasts and compliments the others'; Andrea finds comfort, family, confidence, while Paul embraces ambiguity. Paul is a community of one until he meets another shapeshifter named Robin. Elusive, older, and magnetic, Robin is unsure if he and Paul should be friends, family, or lovers. Paul's story ends unresolved, unlike Andrea's. Taken together, both endings are more satisfying.

Paul Takes the Form of a Mortal Girl and *Stray City* novels are touching bildungsromans set in a vibrant past that informs our present.

CONTRIBUTORS

Donna Aceto is an NYC-based photographer specializing in events and activism. Donna is both Photo Editor and Contributing Photographer to *Gay City News*. She is also a frequent contributor to *Chelsea Now* and *Manhattan Express*.

Blanche McCrary Boyd's latest (and her last, she says) novel, *Tomb of the Unknown Racist*, was published in May by Counterpoint. Her novel *The Revolution of Little Girls* won the Lambda Award for Lesbian Fiction in 1991, and in 1997 *Terminal Velocity* was nominated. Boyd has published widely, or at least she did before she had children. She teaches at Connecticut College.

BITCHES BOOKS & BRUNCH is an intersectional feminist book club and community based in Queens, NYC, committed to furthering feminist education and advancing feminist culture, business owners, and political organizers.

Camila Medina Braz was born in Uruguay and is a twenty-three-year-old Latinx photographer focusing on queer culture, the representation on the female identity in the media and gender construct in our societies.

Sarah Cavar is a full-time student and brain/bodyweird butch lesbian of ambiguous gender. They have been published in the *Mad Scientist Journal*, *Breath & Shadow*, and *Polyester Zine*, and on blogs such as *Epicure & Culture* and genderqueer.me. You can find them at sarahcavar.wordpress.com.

Cheryl Clarke is a longtime black lesbian feminist and the author of five books of poetry, most recently the micro chapbook *Your Own Lovely Bosom* (2015) and the award-winning *By My Precise Haircut*

(The Word Works Press, 2016). She has often been a contributor to *Sinister Wisdom*, dating back to 1982, and in 2018, her article "Are We The Revolution?" appears in *Sinister Wisdom's* special issue *We Are The Revolution: Black Lesbians*. She is one of the co-editors of *Legacies of Resistance, Sinister Wisdom's* "Dump Trump" issue. She thanks her co-editors, Morgan Gwenwald, Stevie Jones, and Red Washburn, for their forbearance.

Alexis Clements is a writer and filmmaker based in Brooklyn, NY. She is currently working on a documentary film focused on the physical spaces where LGBTQ women gather titled *All We've Got*. She guest-edited Volume 101 of *Sinister Wisdom*, titled "Variations." Her writing has appeared in publications such as *The Los Angeles Review of Books*, *The Guardian*, *Bitch Magazine*, *American Theatre*, and *Nature*, among others. She is a regular contributor to *Hyperallergic*. Learn more about her work at www.alexisclements.com.

Denise Conca lives and works in San Francisco.

Kate Conroy is an arts activist. Her Arts Politics master's degree is from New York University's Tisch School of the Arts. She is the founder of the performance series *Venus Biennale* and is the performance art interventionist of *Walking Backwards to Work*, *Clean Drinking Water*, and *Lesbeing*. She directed Babs Davy's play *The Best Medicine* and Ilene Sameth and Barbara Raab's *Bandwidth: The Ups and Downs of a Lesbian Diva* at Dixon Place. She has collaborated with many artist of the "dykeaspora," most recently with Kay Turner on SOHO 20 gallery-based performances. The Pop-Up Museum of Queer History has exhibited Conroy's *Lesbian Cultures* petri dish portraits of lesbian artists and her queer book diorama mash-up *Rubyfruit Jungle with Oranges Are Not The Only Fruit.* Kate is married to Marty Correia, the writer.

286 ♀ Sinister Wisdom 110- *Dump Trump: Legacies Of Resistance*

Marty Correia writes fiction and poetry in the East Village where she has lived with arts activist Kate Conroy since 1996. Marty's work has appeared in several publications including *The Mailer Review, FUSE, Punk Soul Poet, Lady Business*, and *Flock*. She also runs the literary reading series *A Tribe Called Butch* and *Wicked Queer Authors*. A graduate of NYU's creative writing MFA program, Marty recently finished *Bridgeport Con*, a novel rich in dark humor and unexpected histories.

Anne-christine d'Adesky is an Oakland-based writer, journalist, documentary filmmaker, author of four books and parent of three millennial girls. Her 1990s memoir, *The Pox Lover: An Activist's Decade in New York and Paris* (June 2017, University of Wisconsin Press), chronicles the shifting political and social landscape of the 1990s and movement lessons that apply to our frontline political battles today.

Ife da Sylvia is an anarchist/artist/musician multimedia, queer and member of the Anarkoartlab. Lives and works in Lausanne, Switzerland.

Adriana de Luiza is an anarchist/artist/filmmaker/multimedia, queer and is one of the funders of NYC Anarchist art festival (Anarkoartlab) and NYC Anarchist book fair, and lives and works in NYC. See: www.adrianavarella.com.

Alexis De Veaux, PhD, is one of a stellar list of American writers highlighted by LIT CITY, a public art initiative of banners bearing their names and images in downtown Buffalo, New York, in recognition of the city's renowned literary legacy. Co-Founder of The Center for Poetic Healing, a project of Lyrical Democracies (with Kathy Engel), and of the Flamboyant Ladies Theatre Company (with Gwendolen Hardwick), Alexis De Veaux is an activist and writer whose work in multiple genres is nationally and internationally known. Born and raised in Harlem, New York City, Ms. De Veaux is published in five languages: English, Spanish, Dutch, Japanese, and Serbo-Croatian. Her work has appeared in numerous anthologies and publications, and she is the author of *Spirits In The Street* (1973); an award-winning children's book, *Na-ni* (1973); *Don't Explain, A Song of Billie Holiday* (1980); *Blue Heat: A Portfolio of Poems and Drawings* (1985); *Spirit Talk* (1997); *An Enchanted Hair Tale* (1987), a recipient of the 1988 Coretta Scott King Award presented by the American Library Association and the 1991 Lorraine Hansberry Award for Excellence in Children's Literature. Ms. De Veaux's plays include *Circles* (1972), *The Tapestry* (1975), *A Season to Unravel* (1979), *NO* (1980), and *Elbow Rooms* (1986). She also authored *Warrior Poet, A Biography of Audre Lorde* (2004). The first biography of the pioneering lesbian poet, *Warrior Poet* has won several prestigious awards including the Zora Neale Hurston/Richard Wright Foundation Legacy Award, Nonfiction (2005), the Gustavus Meyers Center for the Study of Bigotry and Human Rights Outstanding Book Award (2004), and the Lambda Literary Foundation Award for Biography (2004). In other media, Ms. De Veaux's work appears on several recordings, including the highly acclaimed album, *Sisterfire* (Olivia Records, 1985). As an artist and lecturer she has traveled extensively throughout the United States, the Caribbean, Africa, Japan and Europe; and is recognized for her ongoing contributions to a number of community-based organizations. Dr. De Veaux was a member of the faculty of the University at Buffalo, Buffalo, NY, 1992–2013; teaching, most recently, as an associate professor of women's and gender studies in the Department of Transnational Studies. Recently back in New York City, she completed a novel, *Yabo*, published by Redbone Press (2014) and winner of the 2015 Lambda Literary Award for Lesbian Fiction. She is a member of the US delegation of the "Feminists, Artists, Activists, and Academics: Crossing

Black Geographies" dialogues, co-sponsored by NYU Gallatin School of Individualized Study and the Inkanyiso Collective (South Africa). Further information is available on her author website, alexisdeveaux.com. Follow Ms. De Veaux on Twitter: @AlexisDeVeaux

Morgan Gwenwald is a longtime lesbian activist and photographer living in upstate NY where she works at the Sojourner Truth Library at SUNY New Paltz. She has worked with the Lesbian Herstory Archives since 1979 and is a coordinator. She is currently scanning and organizing her vast archives of queer images for publication, exhibition, and archival purposes.

Jewelle L. Gomez is a writer and activist and the author of the double Lambda Award-winning novel, *The Gilda Stories*, from Firebrand Books. A stage adaptation was performed in thirteen US cities, and the script was published as a Triangle Classic by the Paperback Book Club. Her fiction, essays, criticism, and poetry have appeared in numerous periodicals, including: *The San Francisco Chronicle*, *The New York Times*, *The Village Voice*, *Ms Magazine*, *Essence Magazine*, *The Advocate*, *Callaloo*, and *Black Scholar*. Her work has also appeared in such anthologies as *Home Girls*, *Reading Black Reading Feminist*, *Dark Matter*, and Oxford World Treasury of Love Stories. She is also the author a book of personal and political essays entitled *Forty-Three Septembers* (Firebrand Books, 1993) and a collection of short fiction, *Don't Explain* (Firebrand Books, 1997). She is the recipient of several fellowships, an Individual Artist Commission, and has presented lectures and taught at numerous institutions of higher learning. Some recent projects have included a comic novel about black activists of the 1960s as they face middle age entitled *Televised* and a play, written in collaboration with Harry Waters Jr. is called *Waiting for Giovanni*, a dream play exploring the inner life of author James Baldwin.

Katie Holten is a visual artist based in New York City. She grew up in rural Ireland and represented Ireland at the Venice Biennale in 2003. Her work explores the inextricable relationship between humans and the natural world by challenging the social, cultural, and environmental systems that surround her. Broken Dimanche Press published her book *About Trees* in 2015. She is currently artist in residence with the NYC Urban Field Station, creating the *New York City Tree Alphabet*. See www.katieholten.com.

Teresa Hommel is an emerging writer of short fiction. Her stories have appeared in *Rosebud, SLAB,* and *Santa Fe Literary Review. The New York Daily News* published her op-ed about the need for more poll workers in August 2016. She is also working on a memoir. She grew up in Missouri and now lives in New York City.

Amy Lauren a Mississippi poet and semi-finalist in the Charlotte Mew Chapbook Contest, has published two chapbooks, *Prodigal* (Bottlecap Press) and *God With Us* (Headmistress Press). Her work appears in other publications such as *Cordite Poetry Review, New Orleans Review,* and *Believe Out Loud,* receiving Pushcart and Best of the Net nominations in 2017. Read more at amylauren.com.

Stevie Jones is one of the newer coordinators at the Lesbian Herstory Archives and a co-facilitator of LHA's Lez Create Dyke Arts Workshop. Stevie is also a frequent visitor to Woodstock Farm Sanctuary, where she was a weekly volunteer for years. She belongs to two cats in Brooklyn and several goats upstate.

Dr. Amy Tziporah Karp is Assistant Professor of English and Women's Studies at CUNY Kingsborough. She has published poetry and criticism in publications, such as the *Open Library of Humanities, Gender Forum, Flatbush Review, Shofar, Sophie's Wind,* and *Folio.* Recently, she collaborated in making a short film, *ABC Conjecture,* based on her long poem "Through the

290 ♀ Sinister Wisdom 110- *Dump Trump: Legacies Of Resistance*

Wires," which has been shown in film festivals around the world and looks at liminal ethnic identities within queer communities. She is currently at work on several projects, critical and creative, exploring assimilation, ethnicity, and queer identity.

Ivy Kwan has worked with APICHA (formerly the Asian Pacific Islander Coalition on HIV/AIDS), the People With AIDS: Women's Treatment Group, and the HIV Planning Council of New York since 1990. She is a business owner and mother of two teenagers and can be found protesting on the streets of New York City and sometimes Washington, DC.

Jean Lee is a writer in New York. She works at the Asian American Writers' Workshop. Her poetry has been published in *Canthius* and *No Dear*, among others.

Meagan Lyle is a white queer femme artist, organizer, and educator whose roots lie in the green mountains of Vermont, but she unexpectedly fell in love with a beautiful and vibrant community in Birmingham, AL. Meagan spends free time daydreaming in the forest, mesmerized by the sounds of rushing rivers and swaying pines. And if you stick around for long enough, you're sure to hear her sing along to "White Trash Wedding" by the Dixie Chicks. Meagan just finished a first zine, which combines her love for poetry and watercolor paintings. The zine is a part of a project Meagan started called Beyond Coalescence that aims to build community through sharing art.

Anne Maguire, Dublin native, has been an activist since high school. She worked on civil rights leader, Bernadette Devlin McAliskey's campaigns for a seat in the Republic of Ireland's government in the early 1980s, on Irish Republican women political prisoner rights, and against the misogynist, anti-abortion eight amendment to the Irish constitution (which is now set for a vote to repeal by referendum on May 25, 2018). In 1987 she immigrated to the United States and has lived in New York since then. She was an active member of the Irish Lesbian and Gay Organization, the Lesbian Avengers, and more recently Rise and Resist. She is currently working with Revolting Lesbians, a direct-action group dedicated to following the money, exposing the right-wing agenda, and fighting for justice. She wrote *Rock the Sham! The Irish Lesbian and Gay Organization's Battle to March in New York City's St. Patrick's Day Parade.*

Laura S. Marshall is a writer and editor who lives in New England. She studied linguistics as an undergraduate at Queen's University in Canada and as a grad student at the University of British Columbia. She has studied writing at the Ashbery Home School, the Juniper Summer Writing Institute at UMass Amherst, and the College of Our Lady of the Elms. Her work has appeared in literary publications including *Epigraph Magazine, Junoesq,* and the *Queen's Feminist Review,* as well as newspapers and trade magazines.

Erik McGregor is a New York City-based artist, photographer, and activist. Erik is a member of the People's Puppets of Occupy Wall Street and co-wrote the Occupy Wall Street's Declaration of the Occupation of New York City. As a published photographer, he has documented activist groups actions in NYC since 2011.

Freesia McKee is author of the chapbook *How Distant the City* (Headmistress Press, 2017). Her words have appeared in *cream city review, The Feminist Wire, Painted Bride Quarterly, Gertrude, Huffington Post,* and Sundress Press's anthology *Political Punch: Contemporary Poems on the Politics of Identity.* She has performed poetry in bookstores, prisons, classrooms, summer camps, arts groups, and youth programs. Freesia lives in North Miami.

Grete Miller is a filmmaker, performer, writer, and LGBTQ community advocate based in New York City. Working in media, she serves as a researcher, videographer, and storyteller for The Generations Project. Current programs include the Bridges program with SAGE, and documenting the queer herstory of Provincetown. In June 2017, she directed a LGBTQ storytelling session for Lebanon PA's first ever Pride event, SLAM: An LGBT Colloquium, at Lebanon Valley College. In 2017 her feminist documentary, *Hand Made*, took gold in experimental cinema at that Philadelphia Film Festival and Market. In 2018 she will curate the first Queer series for the Free Library of Philadelphia's Women's History. A coordinator for NYC's Rainbow Book Fair, Grete is committed to making LGBTQ books available to young readers.

Joan Nestle writes: "Shaped by the American 50s and 60s, by my bookkeeper mother, Regina, by my students and colleagues in Queens College SEEK, by every lover who ever touched me, by collective political actions down the decades, I give thanks to all who have written the calls to action, the clear-headed analysis, the cultural activism that are our barricades against the national ugliness that is Trump. Author, archivist, 78 years of life."

H. Ní Aódagaín has been part of the radical feminist-lesbian community for over thirty years. Her fiction, essays, and poetry celebrate lesbians, feminism, aging, spirituality, and land-based living. Her work has appeared in such publications as *Maize*, *Woman of Power*, *Midwifery Today*, *Home Education Magazine*, and the *Oregon Quarterly*. She is seeking publication of her debut novel, *If Not for the Silence*, which explores the silences we live with, and how those silences frame our choices and our destiny. To contact H. Ní Aódagaín, write to hnauthor@gmail.com.

Morgan M. **Page** is a Canadian writer living in the United Kingdom. A 2014 Lambda Literary Fellow, her writing has appeared on

Buzzfeed, The Globe and Mail, GUTS Magazine, Plenitude, and a variety of other magazines and anthologies. She currently hosts the trans history podcast *One From the Vaults.*

Dr. Katia Perea holds a PhD in Sociology from the New School for Social Research. She specializes in Gender and Media Theory, finding the playful transgressions that offer counter-hegemonic potential from within the Culture Industry. Her most recent publications include *Gender and Cartoons from Theaters to Television: Feminist Critique on the Early Years of Cartoons, Girl Cartoons and the Role of Women as Television Executives in the 1990s,* and *The Power Girls before Girl Power: 1980s Toy-Based Cartoons.* She has lectured on gender and cartoons at Amherst College, Vassar College, and SUNY Binghamton, as well as the NYC LGBT Center, Bronycon, and most recently as part of Queer Trekkers at the New York Star Trek Convention.

Jonathan Brooks Platt is an Associate Professor at the National Research University "Higher School of Economics" in St. Petersburg, Russia. He writes on topics including Stalin-era culture, representations of reading in Russian Romanticism, and the actionist tradition in Russian contemporary art. He is a widely published translator of new Russian Left poetry, particularly by the Omsk-born poet Galina Rymbu, and he has collaborated on artistic projects with Chto Delat, the Factory of Found Clothes, and the Texno-Poetry music cooperative. His most recent large-scale project, *The Last Soviet Militant,* engages the controversial legacy of Zoya Kosmodemianskaya, a female partisan who was tortured and executed by German forces in 1941, and who remains an icon of militant devotion in Russia to this day.

Claire Bond Potter is a Professor of History at The New School for Public Engagement, New York, NY. Her specialties are feminism, political history, and cultural criticism. Selections from her

294 ♀ Sinister Wisdom 110- *Dump Trump: Legacies Of Resistance*

scholarly and public writing can be found on her blog: http://www.
chronicle.com/blognetwork/tenuredradical/. You can follow her
@TenuredRadical

Saskia Scheffer has been at the Lesbian Herstory Archives since
1989. She loves the creativity of activism and thinks that any day
that involves some street photography is a good day.

E.F. Schraeder is the author of two poetry collections, most
recently *Chapter Eleven*. Schraeder's work has also appeared in
*Four Chambers, Literary Hatchet, Glitterwolf, Slink Chunk Press,
Lavender Review*, and other journals and anthologies. Schraeder
lives and works in the rustbelt and serves as contributing editor to
an animal advocacy webcomic.

Sarah Schulman is a novelist, nonfiction writer, playwright,
screenwriter, journalist, and AIDS historian. A native New Yorker,
her new novel, a murder mystery called *Maggie Terry*, will be
published in September. Sarah is a Distinguished Professor of
English at the CUNY College of Staten Island.

Pamela Sneed is a New York-based poet, writer, and performer.
She is author of *Imagine Being More Afraid of Freedom Than
Slavery, KONG and Other Works* and a chaplet, *Gift* by Belladonna.
She has been featured in the *New York Times Magazine, The New
Yorker, Time Out, Bomb, VIBE*, and on the cover of *New York
Magazine, Art Forum, The Huffington Post, Hyperallergic*, and in
Nikki Giovanni's *The 100 Best African American Poets*. She is a
Visiting Professor at Columbia University's School of the Arts for
2017–2018, online faculty teaching Human Rights and Writing
Art at Chicago's School of the Art Institute. She has also been
a Visiting Artist at SAIC in the MFA summer low-res program.
Her collage work appeared in Avram Finklestein's *FOUND* at The
Leslie Lohman Museum in 2017. Her latest book, *Sweet Dreams*,
is now available from Belladonna.

Lorrie Sprecher is the author of two novels, *Pissing in a River* (The Feminist Press at the City University of New York, 2014) and *Sister Safety Pin* (Firebrand, 1994). Her work has appeared in numerous anthologies and journals. She lives in Syracuse, New York, with her lovely dog, Kurt. The excerpts appearing in this issue of *Sinister Wisdom* are from her novel *Grab 'Em by the Pussy (Or: How I Became a Feminist Assassin)*.

Oksana Vasyakina is a poet and artist. She was born in 1989 in Ust-Ilimsk, in the Irkutsk region of the Russian Federation. She lives and works in Moscow, and is a graduate of the Gorky Literary Institute. She also studied in the Solyanka Street State Gallery's School of Performance. In 2016 she was a finalist for the Andrey Belyi and Arkady Dragomoshchenko prizes. In 2017 she self-published the collection *Wind of Fury*, dedicated to women who have experienced sexual violence. More than 2,000 copies of the collection have been distributed.

Red Washburn, PhD, is Associate Professor of English and Co-Director of Women's and Gender Studies at Kingsborough Community College (CUNY). They also is Adjunct Associate Professor of Women and Gender Studies at Hunter College (CUNY). Their articles appear in *Journal for the Study of Radicalism*, *Women's Studies: An Interdisciplinary Journal*, and *Journal of Lesbian Studies*. Their poetry collection *Crestview Tree Woman* was published by Finishing Line Press. They co-edited *Sinister Wisdom* issue 103, "Celebrating the Michigan Womyn's Music Festival." Red is a coordinator at the Lesbian Herstory Archives and of the Rainbow Book Fair.

Fran Winant is an award-winning poet and painter. She contributed essays to *Sinister Wisdom* 82 (2011) describing her pioneering 1970s activism. She edited and published the first US anthology of lesbian poetry and art, *We Are All Lesbians*

(1973) @ lesbianpoetryarchive.org/node/110. Her work is widely anthologized and appears in *Poems From the Women's Movement* (2009) and *Lesbian Art in America* (2000). She exhibited in the New Museum's groundbreaking 1982 queer artists' show, *Extended Sensibilities*, and in the 2012 Pop-Up Museum of Gay History at the Leslie-Lohman Museum. Her books of her poetry include: *Looking At Women*, *Dyke Jacket*, and *Goddess of Lesbian Dreams*.

SHARING OUR LESBIAN HERSTORY:
SINISTER WISDOM BACK ISSUES

For the past forty-two years, *Sinister Wisdom* has documented lesbian history in the pages of the journal. Now with over 100 issues in circulation, the journal has an impressive back list and tens of thousands of copies are in circulation. Over the past year and for the next year or two, *Sinister Wisdom* is working to ensure that all of our back issues find homes with appreciative lesbian readers. We would love for you to help us in this work.

In December 2016, *Sinister Wisdom* editor and publisher moved the over 9,000 copies of back issues from a storage facility in Berkeley, California to her home office in Dover, Florida. While that seemed like a monumental task, the real work began when the issues arrived: distributing them throughout the world to people interested in reading and cherishing lesbians's words. The goal is to have all 9,000 copies of these issues out of the Dover offices by the end of 2018. Will you join us and help distribute the journal's back issues?

Here is our plan for distribution:

- Individual copies are available for purchase. The *Sinister Wisdom* website is complete up-to-date and people can order back issues online. The first fifty-seven issues are also available as PDF downloads to anyone interested.
- *Sinister Wisdom* is free on request to women in prisons and psychiatric institutions. Back issues can also be requested by women and shipped to these locations. *Sinister Wisdom*'s goal is to communicate to these women that they are not alone and are a part of a larger community that supports them.

- <u>All available back issues are available for only the cost of shipping ($20)</u> to LGBT centers, women's resource centers, and other community centers that provide support and resources for lesbian communities. A set of all available back issues of *Sinister Wisdom* is free upon request to community centers who wish to provide *Sinister Wisdom* as a resource.

- <u>Teach *Sinister Wisdom*</u>! Teaching guides are available for these issues of *Sinister Wisdom*: *Sinister Wisdom* 32: *Special Issue on Death, Healing, Mourning, and Illness* (Summer 1987), *Sinister Wisdom* 36: *Surviving Psychiatric Assault & Creating Emotional Well-Being in Our Communities* (Winter 1988/89), *Sinister Wisdom* 43/44: *The 15th Anniversary Retrospective* (Summer 1991), *Sinister Wisdom* 47: *Tellin' It Like It Tis'* (Summer/Fall 1992), *Sinister Wisdom* 48: *Lesbian Resistance* (Winter 1992/93), *Sinister Wisdom* 49: *The Lesbian Body* (Spring/Summer 1993), *Sinister Wisdom* 50: *The Ethics Issue... Not!* (Summer/Fall 1993), *Sinister Wisdom* 51 (Winter 1993/94), *Sinister Wisdom* 54: *Lesbians and Religion: Questions of Faith and Community* (Winter 1994/95), and *Sinister Wisdom* 58: *Open Issue* (Winter/Spring 1998).

- Instructors who adopt any of these issues can receive for only the cost of shipping enough copies of the journal for each and every student in the class. (The Women's Movement is generous and wants young people to have books of their own!)

- *Sinister Wisdom* documents lesbian historical issues often missed in history books. *Sinister Wisdom's* back issues come with full teaching guides that contain the historical background, key concepts, discussion questions, teaching activities, and a breakdown of what is in the issue. A full teaching set of an issue is free upon request to professors and universities interested in teaching an issue(s) of the journal.

- Read *Sinister Wisdom* with your book group! Back issues, paired with discussion/teaching guides, are perfect for reading groups that want to explore lesbian literature and art that chronicle lesbian history over the past forty-one years. Issues of *Sinister Wisdom* stand alone, but they can also be used as introductions to readings of the notable contributors whose work have been published in *Sinister Wisdom* such as Adrienne Rich, Audre Lorde, tatiana de la tierra, Minnie Bruce Pratt, Pat Parker, Elana Dykewomon, and others. Select copies are available free for book groups interested in reading them. Check out the Sinister Wisdom website for more information: www.sinisterwisdom.org/bookgroups
- *Sinister Wisdom* actively places collections of the journals with institutional archives and community archives. If you know of a local archive without a run of *Sinister Wisdom*, put us in touch so that we can preserve the journal for people to read and enjoy.
- *Sinister Wisdom* would also be delighted to send back issues of the journal to any other spaces that celebrate lesbian art and culture. Reach out to us; we are happy to ship back issues.

For interested groups or individuals, contact Julie R. Enszer, editor of *Sinister Wisdom*, at julie@sinisterwisdom.org. Find a list of back issues at sinisterwisdom.org/issues.

If you have back issues of the journal that you no longer want, first look to see if there is a local organization or archive that would like to have an maintain copies. If you cannot find a great home close to you, please feel free to send copies to us and we redistribute them. Send them to us at 2333 McIntosh Rd. Dover, FL 33527.

CALL FOR SUBMISSIONS:
THE LESBIAN HERSTORY ARCHIVES
45TH ANNIVERSARY

This special issue of *Sinister Wisdom* is dedicated to commemorating the forty-fifth anniversary of the Lesbian Herstory Archives (LHA). It celebrates LHA, an institution committed to collecting, preserving, and honoring lesbian identities, herstories, and lives across generations. The issue will be curated by a collective of LHA volunteer coordinators.

We will curate a diversity of lesbian voices, values, traditions, and experiences at LHA. We will document our past and present, imagine a future, and we will honor the power of this important space. We are particularly interested in works that reflect the personal impact of the Archives--the collections, the organization and the space--on lesbian lives and self understanding, on our research, work, and politics.

Contributors may wish to explore topics such as:
- intergenerational respect and collaboration
- consensus and radical organization and praxis
- archival documentation and herstorical repositioning
- art and culture as resistance
- difference and coalitional work
- LHA's events and at-homes
- issues of access and power
- the Archives' influence on your/group activism
- the recollection of being in LHA, a space dedicated to Lesbian herstory
- memories of events experienced, friendships made, love found or lost at LHA
- learning and teaching at LHA
- staffing and volunteering at LHA

- stack by stack: the herstory of the LHA building
- origins of LHA in 13A, the apartment of LHA founders, and the feeling of home still maintained at LHA
- reminiscences of being transported by a box of diaries, letters, an album of photographs, the voice of someone reading their work
- excitement and/or anxiety of donating to the LHA collection
- grief and resolution-the commemoration of the life of a loved one through donating to the collections
- your transformative experience at LHA
- intergenerational respect and collaboration
- consensus and radical organization and praxis
- archival documentation and herstorical repositioning
- art and culture as resistance
- difference and coalitional work
- LHA's events and at-homes
- issues of access and power
- the Archives' influence on your/group activism
- the recollection of being in LHA, a space dedicated to Lesbian herstory
- memories of events experienced, friendships made, love found or lost at LHA
- learning and teaching at LHA
- staffing and volunteering at LHA
- stack by stack: the herstory of the LHA building
- origins of LHA in 13A, the apartment of LHA founders, and the feeling of home still maintained at LHA
- reminiscences of being transported by a box of diaries, letters, an album of photographs, the voice of someone reading their work
- excitement and/or anxiety of donating to the LHA collection
- grief and resolution-the commemoration of the life of a loved one through donating to the collections
- your transformative experience at LHA

We are seeking submissions from those who feel themselves to be intimately connected to LHA as well as visitors, and those whose works have been touched by the existence of LHA, including researchers, coordinators, interns, volunteers, educators, donors, speakers, guests, writers, artists, organizers and activists. We welcome submissions of poems, personal essays, short stories, oral histories, interviews, plays, zines, comics, mixed-genre or experimental pieces, and other original writing of no more than 3,000 words. Shorter works or excerpts are welcome. Visual artists can send up to five paintings, drawings, photos, or other original artwork in black and white. All writing submissions should be in docx, or in any format to lhasinisterwisdom@gmail.com and for art, please use .jpg or .tif (300dpi). The deadline for submissions is December 31, 2018; however, early submissions are encouraged and appreciated. Please submit electronically at www.sinisterwisdom.org/submit. We encourage lesbians and queers from all races, ethnicities, ages, abilities, religions, and gender identities to submit.

Deborah Edel, Morgan Gwenwald, Stevie Jones, Joan Nestle, Flavia Rando, Shawn(ta) Smith-Cruz, Red Washburn, and Maxine Wolfe are the guest editors of this special issue of *Sinister Wisdom.*

Sinister Wisdom 2019 Calendar
Order Yours Today!

Sinister Wisdom is proud to release our first-ever calendar.
As part of our year-end fundraiser, the 2019 *Sinister Wisdom*
calendar celebrates the best of lesbian-feminist herstory and
features the best of *Sinister Wisdom*'s art and poetry
over the last forty-two years.

The *Sinister Wisdom* 2019 calendar is a limited edition,
get your copy today!

$12 for one or 5 for $50 (includes shipping and handling)

Order online at **www.SinisterWisdom.org/calendar**

Or mail a check to
Sinister Wisdom, **2333 McIntosh Rd., Dover, FL 33527-5980**

Sinister Wisdom **Back Issues Available**

109 Hot Spots: Creating Lesbian Space
    in the South ($14)
108 For The Hard Ones.
    Para las duras ($18.95)
Sister Love: The Letters of Audre Lorde
    and Pat Parker ($14.95)
107 Black Lesbians—
    We Are the Revolution! ($14)
104 Lesbianima Rising: Lesbian-Feminist
    Arts in the South, 1974–96 ($12)
103 Celebrating the Michigan Womyn's
    Music Festival ($12)
102 The Complete Works of Pat Parker ($22.95)
98 Landykes of the South ($12)
96 What Can I Ask ($18.95)
93 Southern Lesbian-Feminist
    Herstory 1968–94 ($12)
91 Living as a Lesbian ($17.95)
88 Crime Against Nature ($17.95)
84 Time/Space
83 Identity and Desire
82 In Amerika They Call Us
    Dykes: Lesbian Lives in the 70s
81 Lesbian Poetry – When? And Now!
80 Willing Up and Keeling Over
78/79 Old Lesbians/Dykes II
77 Environmental Issues Lesbian
    Concerns
76 Open Issue
75 Lesbian Theories/Lesbian Controversies
73 The Art Issue
71 Open Issue
70 30th Anniversary Celebration
67 Lesbians and Work
65 Lesbian Mothers & Grandmothers
63 Lesbians and Nature
62 Lesbian Writers on Reading and Writing *
58 Open Issue
57 Healing
54 Lesbians & Religion
53 Old Dykes/Lesbians – Guest
    Edited by Lesbians Over 60
52 Allies Issue

51 New Lesbian Writing
50 Not the Ethics Issue
49 The Lesbian Body
48 Lesbian Resistance Including
    work by Dykes in Prison
47 Lesbians of Color: Tellin' It
    Like It 'Tis
46 Dyke Lives
45 Lesbians & Class (the first issue of a
    lesbian journal edited entirely by
    poverty and working class dykes)
43/44 15th Anniversary double-size
    (368 pgs) retrospective
39 Disability
36 Surviving Psychiatric Assault/
    Creating emotional well being
34 Sci-Fi, Fantasy & Lesbian Visions
33 Wisdom
32 Open Issue

Issues 1-58 are available online for free as
    downloadable PDFs.

Some recent issues are available as ebooks,
    visit www.SinisterWisdom.org for more
    information.

Back issues are $6.00
unless noted plus $3.00
Shipping & Handling
for 1st issue; $1.00 for each
additional issue.
Order online at
www.sinisterwisdom.org

Or mail check or money
order to:
Sinister Wisdom
2333 McIntosh Road
Dover, FL 33527-5980